REA: THE TEST PREP AP® TEACHERS RECOMMEND

AP® U.S. GOVERNMENT AND POLITICS
ALL ACCESS®

Michael Zanfardino, M.S.
AP U.S. Government/AP U.S. History Teacher
Bayside High School
Bayside, New York

James Lutz, Ph.D.
Professor of Political Science
Indiana University-Purdue University
Fort Wayne, Indiana

Thomas D. Berve, M.S.
AP U.S. Government & Politics Teacher
Papillion LaVista High School
Papillion, Nebraska

G. Pearson Cross, Ph.D.
Chairperson, Department of Political Science
University of Louisiana at Lafayette
Lafayette, Louisiana

Katherine Wares Newman, M.A.
AP U.S. Government & Politics Teacher
Arlington High School
Arlington, Washington

Katherine Anne Ellerbrock, M.A.
Teacher, American Government/American History
Lakeview High School
St. Clair Shores, Michigan

Research & Education Association
Visit our website: www.rea.com

Research & Education Association

61 Ethel Road West

Piscataway, New Jersey 08854

E-mail: info@rea.com

AP® U.S. GOVERNMENT & POLITICS ALL ACCESS®

Published 2015

Copyright © 2012 by Research & Education Association, Inc.
All rights reserved. No part of this book may be reproduced in
any form without permission of the publisher.

Printed in the United States of America

Library of Congress Control Number 2011943738

ISBN-13: 978-0-7386-1024-5
ISBN-10: 0-7386-1024-0

Contents

Chapter 5: Political Parties, Interest Groups, and Mass Media 69

Chapter 6: Institutions of National Government: the Congress, the Presidency, the Bureaucracy, and the Federal Courts 99

Chapter 7: Public Policy 167

Chapter 8: Civil Rights and Civil Liberties — 191

Practice Exam (also available online at *www.rea.com/studycenter*) — 217

Glossary — 251

Index — 267

About Our Authors

Michael Zanfardino, M.S., is a teacher at Bayside High School in Bayside, New York, where he has taught for the past nine years. He studied at Hofstra University for both his undergraduate degree in history and his master's degree in social studies education. Most recently he attended Stony Brook University for an Advanced Certificate in Educational Leadership. At Bayside High School he teaches AP U.S. History and in the past has taught Global History, American History, Economics, and Participation in Government. He has worked in conjunction with the Gilder Lehrman Institute of American History through the Teach American History group. He has also authored *Cliffs Test Prep Regents U.S. History and Government Workbook*.

James M. Lutz, Ph.D., is a professor of political science at Indiana University-Purdue University at Fort Wayne, Indiana. Dr. Lutz has taught a variety of courses in American Government, International Relations, and Comparative Politics. He has published widely on terrorism and international trade. He has co-authored (all with Brenda J. Lutz) *Global Terrorism* (1st and 2nd editions), *Terrorism in America*, and *Terrorism: Origins and Evolution*. He has also authored or co-authored numerous articles and book chapters. He received his Ph.D. from the University of Texas at Austin.

Thomas D. Berve, M.S., currently teaches AP U.S. Government & Politics and Comparative Government, AP European History and non-honors American Government. Mr. Berve has been teaching for 34 years at the high school level after receiving degrees in International Affairs from the University of Colorado at Boulder and spending a year studying in France at the Université de Bordeaux. Mr. Berve has been an AP Reader for both the U.S. Government and Comparative Government exams for six years.

G. Pearson Cross, Ph.D., is head of the Political Science Department at the University of Louisiana at Lafayette. Dr. Cross's principal areas of teaching are state and local politics, Southern politics, and Louisiana politics. He is a regular commentator on Louisiana politics on national, local, and statewide media.

Katherine Wares Newman, M.A., teaches U.S. History, AP U.S. Government & Politics, Contemporary World Issues at Arlington High School in Arlington, Washington. Ms. Newman is in her sixth year teaching at Arlington High School.

Katherine Anne Ellerbrock, M.A., is a teacher at Lakeview High School, St. Clair Shores, Michigan. Ms. Ellerbrock has been teaching endorsements in History, Political Science, and Social Studies. She recently completed her Master of Arts in History at Oakland University. She began her teaching career at Utica High School in Utica, Michigan, where she taught 10th grade American History and 11th grade American Government. In Troy, Michigan, she worked for the Troy School District's summer school program for two consecutive years, where she taught advanced World History and advanced U.S. History. She specializes in American Government and American History.

About Research & Education Association

Founded in 1959, Research & Education Association is dedicated to publishing the finest and most effective educational materials—including software, study guides, and test preps—for students in middle school, high school, college, graduate school, and beyond.

Today, REA's wide-ranging catalog is a leading resource for teachers, students, and professionals. Visit *www.rea.com* to see a complete listing of all our titles.

Acknowledgments

In addition to our authors, we would like to thank our technical reviewer, Nina Therese Kasniunas, Ph.D. Dr. Kasniunas's research focuses on interest groups in the legislative process and the pedagogy of political science. She has several published chapters on interest groups in elections; religion and the courts during the Bush presidency; gay rights; and re-enactment theatre in the classroom. She also co-published a book, *Campaign Rules,* with Dan Shea. She is currently an Assistant Professor of Political Science at Goucher College.

We would also like to thank Larry B. Kling, Vice President, Editorial, for supervising development; Pam Weston, Publisher, for setting the quality standards for production integrity and managing the publication to completion; John Paul Cording, Vice President, Technology, for coordinating the design and testing development of the online REA Study Center; Diane Goldschmidt and Michael Reynolds, Managing Editors, for coordinating development of this edition; S4Carlisle Publishing Services for typesetting; and Christine Saul for cover design.

Welcome to REA's All Access for AP U.S. Government and Politics

A new, more effective way to prepare for your AP exam

There are many different ways to prepare for an AP exam. What's best for you depends on how much time you have to study and how comfortable you are with the subject matter. To score your highest, you need a system that can be customized to fit you: your schedule, your learning style, and your current level of knowledge.

This book, and the free online tools that come with it, will help you personalize your AP prep by testing your understanding, pinpointing your weaknesses, and delivering flashcard study materials unique to you.

Let's get started and see how this system works.

How to Use REA's AP All Access

The REA AP All Access system allows you to create a personalized study plan through three simple steps: targeted review of exam content, assessment of your knowledge, and focused study in the topics where you need the most help.

Here's how it works:

Review the Book	Study the topics tested on the AP exam and learn proven strategies that will help you tackle any question you may see on test day.
Test Yourself & Get Feedback	As you review the book, test yourself. Score reports from your free online tests and quizzes give you a fast way to pinpoint what you really know and what you should spend more time studying.
Improve Your Score	Armed with your score reports, you can personalize your study plan. Review the parts of the book where you are weakest, and use the REA Study Center to create your own unique e-flashcards, adding to the 100 free cards included with this book.

Finding Your Strengths and Weaknesses: The REA Study Center

The best way to personalize your study plan and truly focus on the topics where you need the most help is to get frequent feedback on what you know and what you don't. At the online REA Study Center, you can access three types of assessment: topic-level quizzes, mini-tests, and a full-length practice test. Each of these tools provides true-to-format questions and delivers a detailed score report that follows the topics set by the College Board.

Topic-Level Quizzes

Short online quizzes are available throughout the review and are designed to test your immediate grasp of the topics just covered.

Mini-Tests

Two online mini-tests cover what you've studied in each half of the book. These tests are like the actual AP exam, only shorter, and will help you evaluate your overall understanding of the subject.

Full-Length Practice Test

After you've finished reviewing the book, take our full-length exam to practice under test-day conditions. Available both in this book and online, this test gives you the most complete picture of your strengths and weaknesses. We strongly recommend that you take the online version of the exam for the added benefits of timed testing, automatic scoring, and a detailed score report.

Improving Your Score: e-Flashcards

With your score reports from our online quizzes and practice test, you'll be able to see exactly which topics you need to review. Use this information to create your own flashcards for the areas where you are weak. And, because you will create these flashcards through the REA Study Center, you'll be able to access them from any computer or smartphone.

Not quite sure what to put on your flashcards? Start with the 100 free cards included when you buy this book.

After the Full-Length Practice Test: *Crash Course*

After finishing this book and taking our full-length practice exam, pick up REA's *Crash Course for AP U.S. Government and Politics*. Use your most recent score reports to identify any areas where you still need additional review, and turn to the *Crash Course* for a rapid review presented in a concise outline style.

REA's Suggested 8-Week AP Study Plan

Depending on how much time you have until test day, you can expand or condense our eight-week study plan as you see fit.

To score your highest, use our suggested study plan and customize it to fit your schedule, targeting the areas where you need the most review.

	Review 1-2 hours	Quiz 15 minutes	e-Flashcards Anytime, anywhere	Mini-Test 25 minutes	Full-Length Practice Test 2 hours, 25 minutes
Week 1	Chapters 1-3	Quiz 1	Access your e-flashcards from your computer or smartphone whenever you have a few extra minutes to study. Start with the 100 free cards included when you buy this book. Personalize your prep by creating your own cards for topics where you need extra study.		
Week 2	Chapter 4	Quiz 2			
Week 3	Chapter 5	Quiz 3		Mini-Test 1 (The Mid-Term)	
Week 4	Chapter 6	Quiz 4			
Week 5	Chapter 7	Quiz 5			
Week 6	Chapter 8	Quiz 6		Mini-Test 2 (The Final)	
Weeks 7–8	Review Chapter 2 Strategies				Full-Length Practice Exam (Just like test day)

Need even more review? Pick up a copy of REA's *Crash Course for AP U.S. Government and Politics*, a rapid review presented in a concise outline style. Get more information about the *Crash Course* series at *www.rea.com*.

Test-Day Checklist

✓	Get a good night's sleep. You perform better when you're not tired.
✓	Wake up early.
✓	Dress comfortably. You'll be testing for hours, so wear something casual and layered.
✓	Eat a good breakfast.
✓	Bring these items to the test center: • Several sharpened No. 2 pencils • Admission ticket • Two pieces of ID (one with a recent photo and your signature) • A noiseless wristwatch to help pace yourself
✓	Arrive at the test center early. You will not be allowed in after the test has begun.
✓	Relax and compose your thoughts before the test begins.

Remember: eating, drinking, smoking, cellphones, dictionaries, textbooks, notebooks, briefcases, and packages are all prohibited in the test center.

Strategies for the Exam

What Will I See on the AP U.S. Government and Politics Exam?

One May morning, you stroll confidently into the school library where you're scheduled to take the AP U.S. Government and Politics exam. You know your stuff: you paid attention in class, followed your textbook, took plenty of notes, and reviewed your coursework by reading a special test prep guide. You can identify the main beliefs of political parties, explain the lawmaking process, and describe the effects of various landmark Supreme Court decisions on the nation's government. So, how will you show your knowledge on the test?

The Multiple-Choice Section

First off, you'll complete a lengthy multiple-choice section that tests your ability to not just remember facts about the various fields of government and politics, but also to apply that knowledge to interpret and analyze political information. This section will require you to answer 60 multiple-choice questions in just 45 minutes. Here are the major fields of inquiry covered on the AP U.S. Government and Politics exam:

- Constitution and federalism

- Political beliefs and behaviors

- Political parties, interest groups, and mass media

- National government institutions

- Public policy

- Civil rights and civil liberties

So, being able to name which state first ratified the Constitution (Delaware, but you know that, right?) will not do you much good unless you can also explain how the process of constitutional ratification shaped the country's enduring political institutions and overall governmental system. It sounds like a lot, but by *working quickly and methodically* you'll have plenty of time to address this section effectively. We'll look at this in greater depth later in this chapter.

The Free-Response Section

After time is called on the multiple-choice section, you'll get a short break before diving into the free-response, or essay, section. This section requires you to produce four written responses in 100 minutes. Like the multiple-choice section, the free-response portion of the exam expects you be able to *apply your own knowledge to discuss and analyze political information* in addition to being able to provide essential facts and definitions.

What's the Score?

Although the scoring process for the AP exam may seem quite complex, it boils down to two simple components: your multiple-choice score plus your free-response scores. The multiple-choice section accounts for one-half of your overall score, and is generated by awarding one point toward your "raw score" for each question you answer correctly. The free-response section accounts for the remaining one-half of your total score. Within the free-response section, each question counts equally toward your final score. Trained graders read students' written responses and assign points according to grading rubrics. The number of points you accrue out of the total possible will form your score on the free-response section.

The College Board reports AP scores on a scale of 1 to 5. Although individual colleges and universities determine what credit or advanced placement, if any, is awarded to students at each score level, these are the assessments typically associated with each numeric score:

5 Extremely well qualified

4 Well qualified

3 Qualified

2 Possibly qualified

1 No recommendation

Section I: Strategies for the Multiple-Choice Section of the Exam

Because the AP exam is a standardized test, each version of the test from year to year must share many similarities in order to be fair. That means that you can always expect certain things to be true about your AP U.S. Government and Politics exam.

Which of the following phrases accurately describes a multiple-choice question on the AP U.S. Government and Politics exam?

(A) always has five choices

(B) may cover ideas, events, and people from the past up to the present day

(C) may ask you to find a wrong idea or group related concepts

(D) more likely to test big ideas than names, dates, and figures

(E) all of the above*

> Did you pick "all of the above?" Good job!

What does this mean for your study plan? You should focus more on the application and interpretation of the various fields of U.S. government than on nuts-and-bolts details about, for example, specific beliefs of various interest groups or the dates when laws were passed. Keep in mind, too, that many political concepts intertwine. This means that you should consider the connections among ideas and concepts as you study. This will help you prepare for more difficult interpretation questions, and give you a head start on questions that ask you to think about the relationships between ideas. Let's examine a typical question that might require you to do just this:

---

*Of course, on the actual AP U.S. Government and Politics exam, you won't see any choices featuring "all of the above" or "none of the above." Do, however, watch for "except" questions. We'll cover this kind of item a bit later in this section.

Republican Party activists tend to be more _____ than the general public, while Democratic Party activists tend to be more _____ than the general public.

(A) liberal, conservative

(B) conservative, liberal

(C) active, passive

(D) passive, active

(E) elderly, youthful

> Answering a "fill-in-the-blank" question is easy if you literally fill in the blank with what you assume to be the correct answer. Seeing your answer in the question will help you decide if it is the right one. Don't try to do it all in your head if you have any doubt at all. Try each of the choices out. Which choice correctly compares the relationship between each group of activists and the general public? Choice (B) gives the best answer. Choice (A) reverses the correct order. Choices (C), (D), and (E) are not relevant.

Types of Questions

You've already seen a list of the general content areas that you'll encounter on the AP U.S. Government and Politics exam. But how do those different areas translate into questions?

Content Area	Sample Question Stems
Constitutional Underpinnings of United States Government	*The Constitution establishes a federal form of government. Which of the following best illustrates this governmental form?*
Political Beliefs and Behaviors	*The most common form of political participation in the United States listed below is . . .*
Political Parties, Interest Groups, and Mass Media	*Which of the following innovations has had the greatest role in weakening the role of parties in U.S. politics?*
Institutions of National Government: The Congress, the Presidency, the Bureaucracy, and the Federal Courts	*Which statement best explains the evolution of the powers of the presidency over time?*
Public Policy	*Which of the following constitutes the largest single non-defense item in the 2011–2012 federal budget?*
Civil Rights and Civil Liberties	*The Supreme Court has interpreted the Equal Protection Clause of the Fourteenth Amendment to require that . . .*

Throughout this book, you will find tips on the features and strategies you can use to answer different types of questions.

Achieving Multiple-Choice Success

It's true that you don't have a lot of time to finish this section of the AP exam. But it's also true that you don't need to get every question right to get a great score. Answering just two-thirds of the questions correctly—along with a good showing on the free-response section—can earn you a score of a 4 or 5. That means that not only do you not have to answer every question right, but also that you don't even need to answer every question at all. By *working quickly and methodically*, however, you'll have all the time you'll need. Plan to spend about 45 seconds on each multiple-choice question. You may find it helpful to use a timer or stopwatch for a few questions to help you get a handle on how long 45 seconds feels in a testing situation. If timing is hard for you, set a timer for ten minutes each time you take one of the 15-question online quizzes that accompany this book to help you practice working at speed. Let's look at some other strategies for answering multiple-choice items.

Process of Elimination

You've probably used the process-of-elimination strategy, intentionally or unintentionally, throughout your entire test-taking career. The process of elimination requires you to read each answer choice and consider whether it is the best response to the question given. Because the AP exam typically asks you to find the *best* answer rather than the *only* answer, it's almost always advantageous to read each answer choice. More than one choice may have some grain of truth to it, but one—the right answer—will be the most correct. Let's examine a multiple-choice question and use the process-of-elimination approach:

Which of the following is outside the American political tradition?

(A) Equality before the law

(B) Equality of political participation

(C) Equality of economic outcomes

(D) The freedom to practice your religion

(E) The freedom to speak your mind

To use the process of elimination, consider each option. Eliminate ideas that are clearly part of the U.S. political tradition, such as those covered by the First Amendment. Cross out each choice as you eliminate it. Then consider the remaining choices. If you're unsure, you can return to the question later or just guess. You've got a one-third chance of being right.

Students often find the most difficult question types on the AP exam to be those that ask you to find a statement that is *not* true or to identify an *exception* to a general rule. To answer these questions correctly, you must be sure to carefully read and consider each answer choice, keeping in mind that four of them will be correct and just one wrong. Sometimes, you can find the right answer by picking out the one that just does not fit with the other choices. If four answer choices relate to the powers of Congress, for example, the correct answer choice may well be the one that relates to a power of the executive branch. Let's take a look at a multiple-choice question of this type.

The Constitution and its amendments expressly forbid all of the following EXCEPT:

(A) private trials.

(B) self-incrimination.

(C) excessive fines.

(D) trials without juries.

(E) early voting.

> To answer a NOT or EXCEPT question correctly, test each option by asking yourself: *Is this choice true? Does this correctly tell about the contents of the Constitution?* The Fifth, Sixth, and Seventh Amendments contain the provisions stated in choices (A), (B), (C), and (D). It doesn't matter if you don't remember that *early voting* is not mentioned in the Constitution. It only matters that you remember that the other four choices are specifically prohibited.

Predicting

Although using the process of elimination certainly helps you consider each answer choice thoroughly, testing each and every answer can be a slow process. To help answer the most questions in the limited time given, you may find it helpful to try to predict the right answer *before* you read the answer choices. For example, you know that the answer to the math problem two-plus-two will always be four. If you saw this multiple-choice item on a math test, you wouldn't need to systematically test each response, but could go straight to the right answer. You can apply a similar technique to even complex items on the AP exam. Brainstorm your own answer to the question before reading the answer choices. Then, pick the answer choice closest to the one you brainstormed. Let's look at how this technique could work on a question on the AP U.S. Government and Politics exam.

Which of the following constitutes the largest single non-defense item in the 2011–2012 federal budget?

> Read the question. Think about what you know about the federal budget. What areas require high spending? What costs have grown most quickly in recent years? Answer these questions for yourself before you read the answer choices.

(A) Medicare

(B) Medicaid

(C) Social security

(D) Foreign aid

(E) Welfare

> In which area of government did you predict the answer would be? Hopefully you remembered that Medicare makes up the largest component of non-defense spending. If so, you could immediately go to choice (A) as the correct answer.

What should you do if you don't see your prediction among the answer choices? Your prediction should have helped you narrow down the choices. You may wish to apply the process of elimination to the remaining options to further home in on the right answer. Then, you can use your knowledge of government and politics to make a good guess.

Learning to predict takes some practice. You're probably used to immediately reading all of the answer choices for a question, but in order to predict well, you usually need to avoid doing this. Remember, the test maker doesn't want to make the right answers too obvious, so the wrong answers are intended to sound like appealing choices. You may find it helpful to cover the answer choices to a question as you practice predicting. This will help make sure that you don't sneak a peek at the choices too soon.

Sometimes, though, you need to have a rough idea of the answer choices in order to make a solid prediction, especially when there are lots of possible ways to interpret a question. Let's apply this strategy as we work our way through the next example:

The Supreme Court has interpreted the Equal Protection Clause of the Fourteenth Amendment to require that

The Equal Protection Clause has been tested in many Supreme Court cases, so your prediction here could be quite broad. Quickly skim the answer choices to see that you need to think about the clause in terms of both gender and race. How has the Supreme Court generally ruled in cases on these issues? Has it generally interpreted the clause broadly or narrowly? Remember, questions like this one test your knowledge of overall trends and patterns but also require you to acknowledge when exceptions occur. What prediction can you make?

(A) government must protect ethnic and gender minorities more than it protects ethnic and gender majorities.

(B) government can treat ethnic groups and genders differently by law, but only if there is a very strong justification for doing so.

(C) government can treat ethnic groups and genders differently by law, as long as it can offer a rational reason for doing so.

(D) private individuals and businesses must treat different ethnic groups and genders completely the same.

(E) government cannot intervene in matters or gender or ethnicity.

You should have predicted something along these lines: *The Supreme Court usually— but not always—interprets the clause to protect these groups' rights to equal treatment.* This prediction would allow you to narrow down your choices to just (B) and (C). Then consider cases in which the court has allowed different treatment. Have these taken place for any reason or for overwhelmingly strong ones only?

Avoiding Common Errors

Remember, answering questions correctly is always more important than answering every question. Take care to work at a pace that allows you to avoid these common mistakes:

- Missing key words that change the meaning of a question, such as *not, except,* or *least.* You might want to circle these words in your test booklet so you're tuned into them when answering the question.

- Overthinking an item and spending too much time agonizing over the correct response.

- Changing your answer but incompletely erasing your first choice.

Some More Advice

Let's quickly review what you've learned about answering multiple-choice questions effectively on the AP exam. Using these techniques on practice tests will help you become comfortable with them before diving into the real exam, so be sure to apply these ideas as you work through this book.

- Big ideas are more important than minutiae. Focus on learning important concepts, themes, and patterns in government and politics instead of memorizing names and dates.

- You have just 45 seconds to complete each multiple-choice question. Pacing yourself during practice tests and exercises can help you get used to these time constraints.

- Because there is no guessing penalty, remember that making an educated guess is to your benefit. Remember to use the process of elimination to narrow your choices. You might just guess the correct answer and get another point!

- Instead of spending valuable time pondering narrow distinctions or questioning your first answer, trust yourself to make good guesses most of the time.

- Read the question and think of what your answer would be before reading the answer choices.

- Expect the unexpected. You will see questions that ask you to apply information in various ways, such as picking the wrong idea or interpreting a map, chart, or even a photograph.

Section II: Strategies for the Free-Response Section of the Exam

The AP U.S. Government and Politics exam always contains four free-response questions in its second section. This section allows you 100 minutes to respond to all four of these questions. Typically, each question has a series of layered parts. The first part may ask you to define a particular concept; later ask you to apply your knowledge of politics and government to that concept in increasingly sophisticated ways. Thus, questions usually build in difficulty within themselves. You receive points for the sections for which you give a correct response but do not lose points for wrong information. This means that you should at least attempt to answer each free-response question, even if you don't necessarily know a lot about the content involved. Students with a deeper understanding on the content tested in the free-response questions will normally receive higher scores on these items than students with a superficial knowledge of the content.

Although it's tempting to think of the free-response section as the essay section, that's not exactly correct. Unlike many other AP exams, such as those on History or English, you don't need to write a formal essay with an introduction and conclusion to answer the free-response questions on the AP U.S. Government and Politics exam unless you receive a rare question that specifically requests one. However, that doesn't mean that you should expect to just make a bulleted list of facts as your written answer to a free-response question. Instead, you'll need to write complete sentences that provide specific information requested in the various parts of a free-response question. Let's examine a sample free-response question.

Demographics of Voters Polled vs. Overall District

	Polled Voters	Overall District
Race	African American: 35% White: 65%	African American: 25% White: 75%
Sex	Men: 40% Women: 60%	Men: 50% Women: 50%
Political Affiliation	Democratic or lean Democratic: 65% Republican or lean Republican: 35%	Democratic or lean Democratic: 55% Republican or lean Republican: 45%

Free-response questions may provide a table, graph, or other visual stimulus. Study and interpret this information as you construct your response.

A text stimulus will precede the actual questions you must answer. This may provide additional information helpful in answering the questions.

In preparation for his reelection bid, a Democratic congressman decided to authorize a poll to indicate his chances for reelection and also to plan his media strategy. The poll was conducted by a Democratic Party supporter over a five-day period in August, three months prior to the election. The pollster interviewed 450 likely voters, with a $+/-$ error rate of 4.5%. Based on his poll, the pollster told the congressman that his support for reelection was at 52%, his opponent was at 40%, and 8% were undecided.

(a) How reliable is the information that the pollster provided the congressman? Discuss in the context of:

- the population,
- the sample, and
- the sampling error.

> Question parts will build in difficulty throughout the free-response item. Be sure to number or letter the parts of your written response to help essay scorers follow your thinking.

(b) How confident can the congressman be of victory based on your understanding of what the poll showed?

(c) What steps would have to be taken to make the poll more accurate and the congressman more confident that he was receiving useful information?

Achieving Free-Response Success

The single most important thing you can do to score well on the free-response section is *answer the questions you are asked.* Seems silly to point that out, doesn't it? But if you've ever written an essay or even a research paper and received a mediocre grade because you didn't fully answer the question asked, or because you wrote about an almost-but-not-quite-right topic, you know how easy it can be to stray off topic or neglect to include all the facts needed in a written response. By answering each of the four free-response questions completely, you'll be well on your way to a great score on the AP exam. Let's look at some strategies to help you do just that.

Organizing Your Time

Although you have 100 minutes to write all four free-response items, you may choose to spend as long as you like on each individual question. The test maker suggests that you plan to spend 25 minutes on each question, but you may find that you need more or less time for any given item. Before you begin, take a few minutes to make a plan to address the section. Read each question and consider whether any of them seem especially difficult or easy to you. You can then plan to spend more time addressing the harder items, leaving less time for the simpler ones.

Remember that you may also answer the questions in any order you wish. You may find it tempting to answer the simplest question first to get it out of the way. However, answering the hardest question first is usually a better use of your time. Why? Answering that item first will make you feel less pressed for time, and getting it out of the way will be a relief. You'll be freshest on your first answer, so dealing with easier items when you're tiring out toward the end of the free-response section will be more manageable. Budgeting your time can come in handy here, too. If you think one question will take you longer to answer, you can plan to spend less time addressing the easier questions. Knowing the material to a given item especially well will probably make it take less time for you to write your response. Don't be concerned that you're not spending enough time on a given question if you know that you've written a good, thorough answer. You're being scored on content, not effort!

Prewriting and Outlining

Yes, you have only 25 minutes for each of the four free-response questions on the AP U.S. Government and Politics exam. Yes, that seems like very little time—too little time to waste even a second. Your best strategy is just to jump in and start writing, right? Wrong.

Spending four to six minutes on prewriting will make your written response clearer, more complete, more likely to fully answer the (right) question, and even quicker and easier for you to actually write. That's because creating a simple outline will allow you to organize your thoughts, brainstorm good examples, and reject ideas that don't really work once you think about them. You can use the structure of the free-response question to help build a quick outline. Let's look at another free-response question:

There is a close relationship between the American political culture and tradition and the organization of the U.S. government. What are the fundamental principles of American culture, and how are they reflected in U.S. institutions?

(a) Describe two fundamental principles of American political culture.

(b) Show how these two principles are reflected in U.S. government institutions or practices.

(c) Describe one situation in which a fundamental principle of American political culture and the operation of an institution may conflict.

(d) Do any of the fundamental principles underlying American political culture conflict with one another? Explain why or why not.

Divide your outline into the same parts as the question stem. Then write phrases that directly answer each section of the question. For the first part, select two fundamental principles, for example, and then write a brief definition that describes each. You could then draw arrows or another visual reminder to connect those principles to specific institutions or practices. Continue writing short notes to yourself as you brainstorm ideas to complete your outline. Be sure to label which ideas go with which question part. Remember, you don't need to write a formal outline or even one that would make sense if you returned to it the next day. You just need to capture your ideas to make a quick plan.

Stick to the Topic

Once you've written a good outline, stick to it! As you write your response, you'll find that most of the hard work is already done, and you can focus on *expressing your ideas clearly, concisely, and completely.* Don't include your own opinions about the subject, and don't include extra information that doesn't help you fully answer the question asked and *only* the question asked. Essay scorers will not award you extra points for adding lots of irrelevant information or giving personal anecdotes.

Remember, too, that the essay scorers know what information has been provided in the stimulus. If a free-response question contains a chart or table, don't waste time and effort describing the contents of the chart or table unless you are adding your own interpretation. In the question above, for example, writing, *The table shows that there are both men and women in the district* will not help your score any. If a question tells you that James Madison wrote a particular essay in the *Federalist*, you do not need to restate Madison's biography in your response or tell why you personally think Madison's essay was important—unless, of course, the question asks you to assess the impact of Madison's ideas on modern U.S. government. Make your outline short, to the point, and complete, and by following it, your response will naturally have the same qualities.

Make It Easy on the Scorers

As you're writing your responses, keep in mind what the AP Readers will see when they sit down to consider your answers weeks from now. Expressing your ideas clearly and succinctly will help them best understand your point and ensure that you get the best possible score. Using your clearest handwriting will also do wonders for your overall score; free-response graders are used to reading poor handwriting, but that doesn't mean they can decipher every scribble you might make. Printing your answers instead of writing them in cursive will make them easier to read, as will leaving a space between lines.

Another good way to point out your answers to scorers is to literally point them out with arrows and labels. Adding labels to each part of your response will help the AP Readers follow your response through the multiple parts of a free-response question, and it can only help your score.

Revision in Three Minutes or Less

Even the best writers make mistakes, especially when writing quickly: skipping or repeating words, misspelling names of people or places, neglecting to include an important point from an outline are all common errors when you're rushed. Reserving a few minutes at the end of your writing period will allow you to quickly review your responses and make necessary corrections. Adding skipped words or including forgotten information are the two most important edits you can make to your writing, because these will clarify your ideas and so help your score.

Remember that essay graders are not mind readers, so they will only grade what's on the page, not what you thought you were writing. At the same time, remember too that essay graders do not deduct points for wrong information, so you don't need to spend time erasing errors. Just write a sentence at the end of your essay or, if you've skipped lines, on the line below that corrects your mistake.

A Sample Response

After you read, considered, outlined, planned, written, and revised, what do you have? A thoughtful free-response written answer likely to earn you a good score, that's what. Remember that free-response graders must grade consistently in order for the test to be fair. That means that all AP Readers look for the same ideas in each answer to the same question using a rubric. Let's examine a sample response to one of the questions above.

There is a close relationship between the American political culture and tradition and the organization of the U.S. government. What are the fundamental principles of American culture, and how are they reflected in U.S. institutions?

(a) Describe two fundamental principles of American political culture.

(b) Show how these two principles are reflected in U.S. government institutions or practices.

(c) Describe one situation in which a fundamental principle of American political culture and the operation of an institution may conflict.

(d) Do any of the fundamental principles underlying American political culture conflict with one another? Explain why or why not.

Part A: Two important principles of American political culture are popular

sovereignty and majority rule. Popular sovereignty means "the people rule." This

principle suggests that the ultimate source of all political authority is the people.

A second example is majority rule. Under this idea, political decisions come from

the will of the overall majority. This means that they reflect the will of the greater

part of the people.

Part B: The principle of popular sovereignty is reflected in the many

elections that Americans hold for nearly every elected position. Americans

assume that legitimacy can only be determined by support of the people. Hence,

U.S. leaders are elected by the people and their power comes—initially, at

least—from this procedure. In nearly every instance, the majority of people, or

the majority in an institution of government (e.g., Congress), votes to determine

questions of policy. In the vast majority of cases, the person receiving the most

votes or the bill receiving the most support wins.

Part C: The interaction of the court system and legislation shows an example of when a fundamental principle and an institution may conflict. Legislatures embody the will of the people and are evidence of majority rule in action, but on occasion, their laws are overturned by courts through the operation of judicial review. Thus, courts are not necessarily in favor of the majority, and this conflicts with the idea of majority rule.

Part D: Fundamental principles can and do sometimes conflict with one another, as in the conflict between majority rule and minority rights. As the Constitution makes quite clear, minority rights (speech, religion, expression) trump the ability of the majority to rule, hence two components of American political culture exist in uneasy tension with one another. People may voice even extremely unpopular ideas that are not part of most Americans' political beliefs, but people must tolerate those expressions. For example, fringe political groups such as the Nazi Party are allowed to hold public marches even though the majority of people disagree with their ideals.

Some More Advice

What have you learned about the free-response section? Keep these ideas in mind as you prepare for the AP U.S. Government and Politics exam. Becoming comfortable with these techniques will make you feel confident and prepared when you sit down to take the exam in May.

- You don't have to spend the suggested 25 minutes on each question. One question may be very straightforward and you may not need 25 minutes to answer it. If you know it, write your response and move on.

- Consider previewing all the free-response questions before starting to write. You can choose to answer the hardest question first and leave the easiest for last when you're tired.

- Make a clear and concise outline before you begin writing. This will help you organize your thoughts and speed up the actual writing process.

- Stay on topic and answer the question! Addressing the question fully is the single most important way to earn points on this section.

- Handwriting is important and must be legible! If the AP Reader can't read your writing, you'll get no points, even if your response is correct.

- Be sure to label the parts of your responses. Make it easy for the AP Reader to award you points by being able to easily navigate your response. If you make it clear and easy for them, you'll earn the reward!

- Leave a few minutes to quickly review and revise your answers. You don't need to check the spelling of every single word, but you do need to make sure that all of your ideas made it onto the page. Leaving space between lines while you write will provide room for you to add important words and ideas, and make it easier for the scorer to read your handwriting.

Two Final Words: Don't Panic!

The free-response questions can and probably will ask you to connect specific political concepts and examples that may not seem to have a lot to do with one another—the role of public policy in reshaping a political institution? The influence of the media on what the public believes about the intent of various portions of the Constitution? The possibilities are practically endless. Remember that all free-response questions seek to test your knowledge of important political theories and concepts, not highly specific facts. Applying what you know to unfamiliar scenarios will help you get a great score, even if you've never thought much about the particular scenario described in the question.

Constitutional Underpinnings of United States Government

The formation of the United States was greatly influenced by the freedom of the colonists to govern themselves and to develop a sense of self-reliance. The colonists' first experience with a national government occurred with the Articles of Confederation, which became the first government of the country during the American Revolution. The inadeqacies of the Articles of Confederation resulted in the development of a new constitution, which in the process raised numerous issues, including the role of the central government versus state governments, the rights of citizens, and questions about what type of democracy would be present. The creation of the new Constitution (the second government of the United States) was a key event in the evolution of the political system. It provided for a new governmental structure that would create a stronger national government for the thirteen states.

Considerations that Influenced the Formulation and Adoption of the Constitution

Colonial Times

The creation of the English colonies in North America initially ran into major difficulties. The early settlers faced an uncertain future due to lack of knowledge of the land, Indians who were hostile at times (usually in response to the efforts of settlers to claim more and more land and resources), and threats from other European countries. The Indian threat was reduced when the settler population increased. The English displaced the Dutch from North America early on, but Spain and France remained as threats. One characteristic of the early colonies as they developed was that they had a great deal of freedom. Their distance from England and slow communications between the two locations meant that the colonies often had to fend for themselves. Local autonomy was a necessity, and the king and Parliament tolerated the autonomy because it required fewer resources from the English government. In fact, as the colonies developed, the settlers frequently had many more freedoms than their counterparts in England. Under royal charters granted by the king and Parliament and other charters, the colonies established representative institutions and had a great deal of discretion in terms of running their own affairs. Colonial legislatures levied taxes and funded activities based on local need and initiative. The colonies in turn provided useful natural resources for England and a market for English goods. England was essential for the colonies as well since France and Spain constituted a continuing threat that led to a stronger bond between the colonies and England.

French and Indian War

England frequently found itself at war with France during the colonial period. While alliances often shifted among the European countries, Spain often was allied with France in these struggles. The colonists found themselves threatened by the presence of these enemies in North America. For many of the colonists, the danger of French or Spanish occupation was heightened due to religious differences. Most of the settlers in the English colonies were Protestant. They were suspicious of Catholicism because of domestic problems in England when there were attempts to re-establish Catholicism and in Scotland when Spain or France supported dissident outbreaks among the Catholics there. Spain and France, as Catholic countries, were seen as especially dangerous since they were considered to be tools of the Pope's efforts to force Catholicism upon Englishmen everywhere.

The struggles between France and England and their respective allies spanned the globe and led to conflict not only in Europe, but in India, the Caribbean, and North America, as well. While the struggles in the New World were an extension of European conflicts, they had their own issues and sources of conflict between French and English colonies. Prior to the French and Indian War, the English had managed some small gains in North America at the expense of the French. However, the French remained entrenched in Canada, and the English were restricted to the Atlantic coastline and areas around Hudson's Bay.

The outbreak of the Seven Years' War, as it was called in Europe, affected the English colonies. They found themselves in conflict with the French in Canada and the Spanish to the south. In North America, this conflict was known as the French and Indian War. The conflict reflected the colonists' fears of a French takeover and activities from France's Indian allies. The first fighting in the war actually occurred in North America between British and French forces. Although the conflict involved major issues among countries in Europe, it was to have profound consequences for the English colonies. After several failed campaigns directed against the French in Canada, English troops were able to capture Quebec and Montreal in Canada and to end the French presence in North America. In the peace treaty that ended the war in 1763, England kept control of Canada at the expense of France, and Florida was taken from Spain. England now had complete control of the Atlantic seaboard. Louisiana, in the interior of North America, was transferred from France to Spain in compensation for Spanish territorial losses elsewhere (although France later regained control of Louisiana in time to sell it to the United States). The elimination of France from its position in Canada removed a major threat to the English colonies. Spain by itself was seen as less threatening than France had been, in part because the centers of Spanish power were further removed from the frontiers of English America, and because Spain was obviously a major power in decline while France has been gaining more power. One unexpected and unanticipated consequence of the English victory was that the colonies were now less dependent on the military forces of England to defend them from external enemies. The Indians could still be a problem in frontier areas, but by themselves they did not constitute a major threat to the more settled areas. In fact, the English victories in this war would lead to a series of circumstances and events that weakened England rather than strengthening it.

Road to Revolution

The English victory in the French and Indian war had been costly. The country had gone into debt to finance the war. The king and Parliament rather naturally felt that it was quite appropriate for the colonies to help to pay for the cost of the war. The campaigns against the French in Canada had been expensive, and other resources had gone directly to defend the colonies. Passing some of the costs along to the colonies also made sense, since the colonies had benefited so greatly from the peace settlement and were now more secure.

In order to help pay down the war debt, Parliament passed the Stamp Act and other acts that levied taxes on the colonies. The Stamp Act required everyone to pay a fee for an official stamp for all contracts, other official documents, and even newspapers. While the colonists agreed in theory that they should help pay the war debts, they also argued that they should be consulted and have the right to approve any taxes that they would have to pay. So, the colonists refused to pay these taxes. Popular reaction was so negative that the taxes could not be collected. Individuals appointed to collect the taxes were assaulted, and their property was destroyed. Colonial assemblies even passed laws giving legal recognition to documents that did not bear the stamps required by the

Stamp Act. Leaders in various colonies also established committees of correspondence to coordinate activities in opposition to the implementation of the taxes. Bowing to the inevitable, Parliament withdrew the taxes but maintained the principle that it still had the right to levy taxes on the colonists without their approval.

TEST TIP

Let's face it: cramming doesn't work. A 2008 study by University of California-San Diego psychologists found that if you review material relatively close to when you first learned it, you will remember it better. According to the study, the best time is after a wait of 10 percent of the time between when you first learned the material and when you'll need to know it for the test. So if you have a government lesson on Monday and a quiz on the following Monday, the best time to study for the quiz would be Wednesday.

The disappearance of the threat from the French in Canada had the unanticipated effect of reducing colonial dependence on England. The colonists no longer needed the English navy or army for protection; therefore, the colonial leaders and population were less willing to compromise as a matter of political principle or to agree to the levels of taxation. The opposition to the Stamp Act also demonstrated to the colonists that successful opposition to English authority was possible. Perhaps even more importantly, it taught the settlers in the different colonies that they could effectively cooperate with each other.

A few years after Parliament withdrew the Stamp Act, it attempted to reassert its authority and authorized new taxes in the colonies, including one on tea. These new taxes generated new opposition among the colonies because the colonial legislatures were again not consulted. The colonists adopted many of the same tactics they had used to defeat the implementation of the Stamp Act. The Boston Tea Party came to be a defining moment of this opposition. The English authorities now felt they had to respond to the dissident activity or else lose all control over the colonies. When Parliament closed the port of Boston and sent troops to Boston, the stage was set for the American Revolution. The other colonies rallied to the support of Massachusetts and sent assistance to Boston and Massachusetts, in general. Continued conflict in the colony finally led to military action, including the skirmish at Lexington and the battle at Concord. All thirteen colonies mobilized militia forces in opposition to England. As fighting between the British and the Americans escalated, the Continental Congress adopted the Declaration of Independence, separating the colonies from England. American victories during the war made it clear that military action would not bring the colonies back to their original allegiance, and eventually, peace was negotiated providing for the independence of the thirteen colonies.

The Articles of Confederation

After the Declaration of Independence, the leaders of the individual colonies were faced with the issue of how to organize the new country and how to form a government to fight the war with England. The Articles of Confederation was the first constitution of the United States of America, drafted by the Second Continental Congress to create a permanent governmental framework for the thirteen states. The articles were in many ways a "league of friendship" among the states that left most of the power in the hands of the individual states.

In many respects, the Articles of Confederation were a reflection of the limited degree of unity that existed among the states at that time. At the time the Declaration of Independence was approved, the thirteen colonies were only a voluntary union without any official affiliation or allegiance to a central authority. The state leaders were determined to make sure that the new government would not threaten individual freedoms or the freedoms of the states. The issue of the balance of power between the states and national government was decidedly weighted in favor of the individual states (see chart below). This fear of an over-powerful, potentially dictatorial central government, of course, reflected the recent experiences of the colonies in their dealings with the king and Parliament in England.

The Articles of Confederation: Accomplishments and Limitations
Highlights of the Articles of Confederation
Created the union of the states into the United States of America
Granted Congress the power to authorize the Revolutionary War
Limitations of the Articles of Confederation
Weak Central Government
No executive or central executive agencies
No central judiciary
Nine of thirteen states' approval required for normal legislation

(continued)

The Articles of Confederation: Accomplishments and Limitations *(continued)*
Required unanimous consent of all thirteen states for some actions
No central tax base
States controlled the monetary supplies
Inability to render judgment when conflict arose between States
Amendments to the articles required the unanimous consent of all thirteen states

The Articles of Confederation proved to be a weak government for the new country. The fear that a central government would become a threat to the liberties of individual citizens and the states led the leaders of the United States to create a structure that permitted the national government do very little. Exceptional majorities (nine of the thirteen states) were required to pass even the simplest of legislation. Legislation that was considered to be especially important required the approval of all thirteen states. The central government had no independent tax base. The government had to request that each state provide its share of the contributions to the national budget that had been requested. As it turned out, state governments often were facing significant financial difficulties on their own, and they were naturally more concerned with paying their own expenses than meeting their obligations to the national government. The new government did have some funds that came from the sale of lands in the western part of the country, but that source of revenue was limited. The government of the new country also found it difficult to enforce some of the provisions of the peace treaty with England over control of western lands. The English, when faced with a weak central government, refused to implement some provisions of the treaty and also entered into intrigues with individual state governments about the future of the region.

The weakness of the new government was also obvious in the area of trade. Each state had the power to negotiate treaties of commerce with foreign countries. They were free to tax imports and exports from international trade. They were also free to tax trade between the states and to impose barriers to trade in other ways. The limitations on commerce resulted in economic difficulties in many of the states and made it difficult for the new country to build an economic base that could contribute to general prosperity. The Articles of Confederation became less a league of friendship among the states and more a league of competing states. Individual states sought to gain economic advantages at the expense of their neighbors, and there was no incentive for foreign countries to even attempt to negotiate with the Continental Congress or its representatives on commercial issues.

The weaknesses of the articles became apparent when discontent exploded in western Massachusetts in 1786 in what came to be known as Shays's Rebellion. Hard economic times in the state meant that farmers were losing their land. The farmers mobilized to protest their economic circumstances and the state policies that were hurting them. They used many of the same techniques used against the British to protest policies before the outbreak of the American Revolution. Local authorities could not control the situation, particularly when the protestors armed themselves and pushed Daniel Shays, a former officer in the Continental Army, into a position of leadership. The government of Massachusetts was initially unable to deal with the protestors, and the central government could offer no support since it had no money or troops to offer. The protest was finally controlled when troops were hired from funds collected from private individuals to put down the rebellion. There were only a handful of casualties in the conflict, but the threat placed the states on notice that they could lose control of their own territory. As a consequence, several delegates decided that a meeting needed to be held to discuss the problems of the central government and propose modifications to the structure of government. The delegates understood there could be resistance to this idea, so they hid their intent by calling for a meeting in Annapolis in Maryland to discuss trading issues. Representatives of only five states (New York, New Jersey, Pennsylvania, Delaware, and Virginia) attended, but the meeting did have one noteworthy accomplishment: the group petitioned Congress to call a meeting of all states for the following year. The meeting was to be held in May 1787 in Philadelphia, and it came to be known as the Constitutional Convention.

The Constitutional Convention

The delegates who were in attendance in Philadelphia were charged with fixing the inadequacies present in the Articles of Confederation. As the first delegates arrived, they quickly realized that it would be an impossible task to just correct the deficiencies of the articles. The requirements of equal representation for each state and the need for unanimity for any amendments to the articles suggested that any meaningful changes would never be approved, because any major changes to the articles would

> **DIDYOUKNOW?**
>
> Roger Sherman from Connecticut was involved in creating the Great Compromise at the Constitutional Convention. He is also the only delegate present for the signing of the Declaration of Independence, the signing of the Articles of Confederation, and the signing of the Constitution.

create sufficient disadvantages for at least one state. While there was general agreement that changes were necessary, there was much less agreement on what the changes would be or how to resolve the differences among the states and different groups in the country.

The Constitutional Convention attracted many of the best and the brightest of the American political scene. While the final version of the Constitution was a joint effort, James Madison had more input than any other single individual who was present. He prepared the Virginia Plan and was involved in the discussions that led to the final document. Other notable founding father contributors both formally and informally were John Dickinson, Gouverneur Morris, Alexander Hamilton, Charles Pinckney, Edmund Randolph, James Madison, Benjamin Franklin, Roger Sherman, James Wilson, and George Wythe. Of the notable founding fathers absent from the convention were Thomas Jefferson, John Adams, and Patrick Henry, as they were serving as ambassadors abroad or were serving in elected positions at the state level.

A Document of Compromises

The delegates in Philadelphia quickly discovered that there were significant disagreements on many issues. One of the major issues involved whether there would be a unicameral legislature, as had been the case with the articles, in which each state had one vote, or some other form of legislature in which states with larger populations would have more seats – the smaller states naturally favored equal representation. The southern states were concerned about protecting slavery from the northern states where slavery was not present and not popular. The delegates were also concerned about financing the central government. The larger states wanted to avoid supporting the smaller states, and the richer states were afraid that they would be taxed to support the poorer states. The southern states were also concerned about a central government that would enforce economic policies that favored the industrial interests of New England at the expense of southern agricultural interests.

A number of delegates came prepared with plans for what the new central government should look like. James Madison prepared the Virginia Plan that favored more populous states such as Virginia and New York, since the national legislature would have representation based on population. There was also the New Jersey Plan, prepared by Thomas Patterson, that favored the smaller states by granting each state equal power (one vote) in the national legislature. This issue of representation was one of the most difficult to resolve at the convention since the interests of the small states and the large states were so different.

House/Senate Population ↱ Equal

The Connecticut Plan, supported by Benjamin Franklin and Roger Sherman, tried to bridge the differences between the small states and the large states. The Great Compromise (the Connecticut Plan), resolved the differing opinions on representation. Seats in the House of Representatives would be distributed among the states based on population. Each of the states would have equal representation in the Senate, with two

Plans Prepared for the Constitutional Convention

Virginia Plan

Three Branches—legislative, executive, and judicial. The legislature was the most powerful branch since it would choose the people to serve in the executive and judicial branches.

Legislature—would consist of two houses (bicameral). The House of Representatives would be elected by the people, and the Senate would be elected by the state legislatures. Seats in both houses would be proportional to state population.

Other Powers—the legislature would be able to regulate interstate trade, strike down laws deemed unconstitutional, and use armed forces to enforce laws.

New Jersey Plan

Three Branches—legislative, executive, and judicial. The legislature would appoint people to serve in the executive branch, and the executive branch would select the justices of the Supreme Court.

Legislature—would consist of one house (unicameral). States would be represented equally, giving all states the same power regardless of population.

Other Powers—the national government could levy taxes and import duties, regulate trade, and state laws would be subordinate to national laws.

Connecticut Plan

This plan attempted to reconcile the differences between the Virginia Plan and the New Jersey Plan.

This plan used parts of both the Virginia Plan and the New Jersey Plan. It resolved the differences between representation based on population and equal representation regardless of size or population.

Congress consist of two houses: Senate and House of Representatives.

Seats in the House of Representatives would be distributed on the basis of population. The House would have the power to initially propose all bills/laws for taxation.

The Senate would provide equal representation for each state.

VP + NJP = CP

James Madison, "Architect of the Constitution"

Before becoming the nation's fourth President, James Madison was instrumental in shaping both the Constitution and the Bill of Rights. Many of his ideas, including separation of powers, checks and balances, and limits on the majority were included in the final version of the Constitution. While other delegates at the Philadelphia convention were important in developing the ideas for the new government, he was the single most important individual. After the convention, he was one of the leaders in the fight to get the document ratified. To win support of the ratification of the Constitution, Madison, Alexander Hamilton (first Secretary of the Treasury), and John Jay (first Chief Justice of the Supreme Court) authored 87 articles under the pen name PUBLIUS that came to be known as the Federalist Papers. These articles helped to sway public opinion in favor of the Constitution in key states such as New York and Virginia.

senators. Both chambers would have equal power in terms of legislation. Any law would have to pass both houses. The different basis of representation in the two parts of Congress created a situation in which legislation might be difficult. This possibility was one that was acceptable to the delegates at the convention since it balanced the inter-

DID YOU KNOW?

The Founding Fathers were worried about an aristocracy, yet John Quincy Adams was John Adams' son; Benjamin Harrison was William Henry Harrison's grandson; Franklin Roosevelt and Theodore Roosevelt were cousins; and George W. Bush is George H. W. Bush's son.

ests of the more populous states with those of the smaller states that were afraid that their interests would be overwhelmed in a legislative chamber that was based solely on population.

Slavery presented another major issue that was dealt with at the convention. The southern states were determined to protect the institution that they felt was essential for the continued agricultural productivity of the region. The northern states were less interested in maintaining slavery as there were few large farms where slaves could be used, and slaves never appeared to be a good idea as workers in factories. The continuation of slavery was never in much doubt at the convention. Even delegates who were personally opposed to slavery recognized that the southern states would never ratify the Constitution if it banned slavery. Slaves were also an issue in terms of counting population for determining how may seats in the House of Representatives each state would have and for taxation purposes. The southern states wanted slaves counted for purposes of determining seats, but conveniently did not want them counted for purposes of any taxes that would be based on population. The northern states wanted slaves counted for

People realized that w/out slavery South would never ratify

3/5 comp.
3 out of every 5 slaves would be counted for representation

purposes of taxation but not for purposes of representation. The delegates compromised on these positions by agreeing to count each slave as three-fifths of a person for purposes of representation and for taxation. The Constitution also provided that Congress could not provide any interference in the importation of slaves for twenty years. A number of the delegates were uncomfortable with some aspects of this compromise, but they accepted it in order to gain southern support for the final document.

Only taxes originally in place were tariffs

Financial support for the central government was a concern in 1788, as it is today. Under the articles, the Continental Congress could only request contributions from the states, and these contributions often were not forthcoming. In order to deal with the concerns of the richer states that feared being taxed to support programs in the poorer states, the national government was only permitted to directly tax individuals based on a simple population count (with the appropriate adjustment for slaves). Other indirect taxes, such as those on imports from abroad, did not have to be adjusted for population. This restriction on direct taxing only on the basis of population is why the Sixteenth Amendment was necessary to permit the national government to levy a federal income tax. Even with restrictions the Constitution placed on direct taxes, it was an improvement over the articles since it permitted Congress to levy direct taxes on individuals and on economic activity. It also provided the means for Congress to provide mechanisms whereby the national government could borrow and tax, regulate foreign and interstate commerce, and coin money and establish currency.

States can no longer tax each other

Trade proved to be another area in which states took differing views. Under the Articles, the individual states taxed exports and imports to and from foreign countries and even each other. These taxes and other regulations seriously limited trade within the country and hindered foreign trade, as well. As a consequence of the past problems, the Constitution prohibited any state interference in both domestic and foreign trade. Only the national government could place restrictions or create regulations that affected foreign trade or trade among the various states. A related financial issue involved trade. The southern states were afraid that the new national government would tax exports. Such an export tax would be easy to administer and could raise a significant amount of money. The funds that were raised could be used to support a number of government programs, including the possibility of assisting new manufacturing industries in the northern states. As a consequence, the Constitution contained another adjustment to regional concerns by prohibiting the new government from levying taxes on exports. The new government was able to place taxes on imports as a means of raising revenue since such taxes would affect all states relatively equally. The requirement that the Senate had to approve treaties by a two-thirds vote was also linked to these concerns. The most important international agreements that the new country was likely to negotiate were treaties of trade and commerce. The requirement for a supermajority meant that the South and New England as regions were in a position to protect their important economic interests.

There were a number of other important issues that the delegates had to deal with at the convention. There was some discussion about who should be allowed to vote. States had different views on voting—and different standards. Some permitted a relatively higher percentage to vote, and some were less open to public input. A number of states had two voting rolls. The more open voting roll let individuals vote for members of the lower house of the state legislature. The more restrictive roll had a more limited number of voters who could elect people to the more "aristocratic" upper house. The Constitution left decisions about voting to the states, with one exception. The Constitution did specify that for elections to the House of Representatives, *if* a state had two such electoral rolls, it would use the less restrictive one. It was still left to the states to determine just how restrictive the more open electoral roll would be if they had two.

The Constitution initially said very little about individual rights or personal freedoms, even though questions of personal rights were at the core of the disputes that led to the American Revolution. The framers were mindful that explicitly defined rights would override any states' rights on the issue and could cause a rift between northern and southern states. They were also sensitive to the fact that states would jealously guard their rights. Many of the Founding Fathers also feared that it would be a powerful central government that would be the greatest threat. They saw the individual states as protectors of these rights. The vagueness of the Constitution on personal rights would cause many problems in the coming years, but in the interests of increasing the chances of ratification, the issue was purposely left to others to decide. What the Constitution does explicitly include reflects the attitudes of those who felt oppressed by British Parliament. The Constitution provided some basic guarantees by prohibiting the suspension of habeas corpus (no one can be detained without being charged with a specific crime), prohibiting bills of attainder (legislative judgments of guilt), and prohibiting ex post facto laws (punishing people for actions before a law was enacted). The Constitution also indirectly addressed religious issues by preventing any religious qualifications (adherence to a particular church) for holding national office. While religious qualifications were not required for holding national office, a number of states still had religious restrictions on who could vote or hold office at the state level. In particular, many states had prohibitions on Catholics holding office or being allowed to vote, reflecting the recent past and the concerns about foreign invasions from Catholic powers such as France or Spain. It is interesting to note that while most of the Founding Fathers believed in a Supreme Being, they made the decision not to include any direct or indirect reference to God in the Constitution itself.

TEST TIP

Taking the mini-tests and practice test provided with this book is a great way to prepare for the AP exam. You can also review free-response questions from several past AP U.S. Government and Politics exams at *www.collegeboard.org*.

The bill of rights included to guarantee individual freedoms

Some important issues on individual rights were quickly addressed when the decision to add a Bill of Rights to the Constitution gained widespread support. Such individual rights had great importance for the Founding Fathers. Most of them believed that individual citizens had natural rights. These natural rights were God-given, and it was not up to any government to allow or disallow them. The Founding Fathers drew upon current writings of the political philosophies of their time in defining these rights. The ideas of these natural rights were very obvious in the Declaration of Independence (a document designed to mobilize public opinion and support a war effort, not to create government institutions), but they were recognized as important by the delegates in Philadelphia. The designers of the Constitution agreed with writers like John Locke and Jean-Jacques Rousseau that government embodied a social contract between the people and their leaders. Locke was particularly important in terms of the ideas that he laid out about the contractual nature of government. His ideas on the political contract clearly indicated that governments should only continue while they were upholding their portion of the contract. There was no such thing as the Divine Right of Kings. Government should only survive while it adhered to the basic principles of that social contract.

Locke Rousseau were very influential in the Constitution

Separation of Powers

The Constitution had to provide compromises between different groups that would make it workable as the blueprint for a new government. The Constitution also had to provide for the basic institutions of the government that would make decisions for the future. One of the key elements in the document was the separation of powers among three branches of government. These ideas were derived from French philosopher Baron de Montesquieu, who described a system of government in which power was divided among three different entities. This view drew heavily from the British constitutional system in which powers were separated among the monarch, Parliament, and the courts of law. The system devised in Philadelphia was a system that carried these ideas further and in which power of the government was divided into three branches of government: legislative, executive, and the judiciary.

Three separate Branches
Congress / Supreme Court / President

The new Constitution developed a complex system of checks and balances for the three branches of government that were created. The writers wanted to be sure that no one branch became too powerful at the expense of the other two or at the expense of the indi-

DIDYOU**KNOW?**

John Jay was the first Chief Justice of the Supreme Court. He also negotiated a treaty with England in 1794, while still Chief Justice, that resolved some outstanding issues between the United States and Britain.

vidual states. The basic fear of a too-powerful government that led to the weak Articles of Confederation also led to efforts to prevent a too powerful national government

Highlights of Separation of Powers (Checks and Balances)

Legislative Branch

Checks on the Executive

- May override presidential vetoes by two-thirds vote of both houses
- Power to declare war
- Power to enact taxes and allocate funds
- Senatorial approval of treaties required with two-thirds vote
- House has the power to impeach members of the executive branch, including the president.
- Senate has the power to deal with impeachment charges and remove persons from office by a two-thirds vote.
- Congress would select the president (House) and vice president (Senate) in the case of no candidate receiving a majority of electoral votes.
- Senate approves appointment of cabinet officials and ambassadors.
- The Constitution requires that the president must, from time-to-time, deliver a State of the Union address.
- The Twenty-fifth Amendment approved in 1963 adds an additional check by requiring that a majority of the House and a majority of the Senate approve a presidential nominee to fill a vacancy in the vice-presidency.

Checks on the Judiciary

- Senate approves federal judges
- House has the power to impeach federal judges.
- Senate has the power to deal with impeachment charges and remove judges from office by a two-thirds vote.

Highlights of Separation of Powers
(Checks and Balances) *(continued)*

- Power to initiate constitutional amendments
- Power to establish lower courts below the Supreme Court
- Power to set jurisdiction of courts
- Power to alter the size of the Supreme Court

Internal Checks

- Bills must be passed by both houses of Congress.
- Neither house may adjourn for more than three days without the consent of the other house.
- All journals with information on debates and legislation are to be published.

Executive Branch

Checks on the Legislature

- Veto power
- Vice president is President of the Senate (but only votes to break a tie).
- Recess appointments can be made without senatorial approval if Congress is not in session
- Emergency power to call one or both houses of Congress into session
- May force adjournment when both houses cannot agree on adjournment.
- Compensation cannot be diminished

Checks on the Judiciary

- Power to nominate judges
- Pardon power

Judicial Branch

Checks on the Executive

- Judicial review of actions of president or other executive officials
- Judicial review of treaties
- Chief Justice presides over Senate during presidential impeachment (but has little power).

Checks on the Legislature

- Judicial review of congressional laws
- Judicial review of treaties
- Judges continue in office on good behavior and can only be removed by impeachment.
- Compensation of sitting judges cannot be diminished.

The founder's fear of powerful government reflected in their check/balances system.

No ONE branch should ever have too much power.

Because of previous experience w/ Britain (King/Parliament) checks and balances were necessary

under the new document. The Constitution placed limits on each branch of the new government from the other two branches. The Constitution provides the greatest detail on the new Congress. The writers understood legislatures, and they also realized that the British Parliament, not just the British king, had been responsible for many of the issues that drove the colonies to rebellion. The table above details the most important checks and balances incorporated into the document. Since the state legislatures initially elected senators and were involved in the choice of electors, they had some indirect involvement in the checks that these institutions relied on.

Federalism

The Founding Fathers devised a system whereby power was split between the national government and the state governments. This division was another indication of the fear that many of the delegates had of a strong national government that could potentially usurp the powers of the states and deny the citizens their liberties. The federal system that was devised was in many ways an experiment on the part of the delegates in Philadelphia. They realized they did not want a centralized system with a strong national government, such as existed in England or other European countries. They had experienced the dangers that came with concentrated power. They understood that a confederation was too weak from their own experience with the articles and from the experience of other confederations that went back to the days of ancient Greece. There was no in-between example that they could copy; therefore, they devised a system that was somewhere between the strong centralized political systems of Europe and the weak confederation represented by the Articles of Confederation. States retained the power to determine who could vote. The states determined how Senators would be chosen (they all were initially elected by state legislatures to represent the interests of the states as component units in the federal system). States also retained the right to institute their own taxes. The Second Amendment of the Bill of Rights also guaranteed to each state the right to maintain a militia. Each state had control over its own system of government subject to the single provision that state governments had to be organized on a republican basis (no hereditary titles were possible, and it was necessary for the people to elect state leaders).

While the writers were quite clear that they wanted to divide power between the national and state levels, they were unsure of exactly how the power would be divided. This uncertainty was due in part to the lack of examples elsewhere, and it resulted in many later debates on the rights of states relative to the national government. The division of political power between the states and the national

The lack of examples contributed to the vagueness of the constitution.

government also had an element of military power attached to it; in 1787, state militias had military capabilities on a par with whatever national army might be formed. The delegates were afraid of large standing armies. They had seen how standing armies had been negatively influenced by political systems in Europe by providing emperors, kings, and dukes with the means to control their populations. This fear of a large standing army led to the constitutional requirement that appropriations for the military could only be approved for two years at a time. This requirement meant that each new House of Representatives would have to approve defense spending.

Limits on Majorities and Minorities

Different parts of government have different terms.

The Founding Fathers had a fear of intemperate majorities passing laws or trampling on the rights of the political minority. The Constitution, as a consequence, provided for safeguards against such events. The separation of the national government into three branches with checks upon each other meant that any majority would need to control all three branches in order to be able to act. Officials in the different branches served different terms of office—the president for four years, representatives for two years, and senators for six years with one-third elected every two years, and members of the judiciary served during time of good behavior (life). Thus, it would take a number of election cycles for the majority to prevail and to implement unwise changes. In addition, only representatives were directly elected. Senators were elected by state legislatures, and it was electors in the Electoral College who elected the president (although the Electoral College quickly came to reflect popular vote). These indirect elections added another obstacle to quick change. Federalism also meant that the majority would need to control not only the national government but many of the state governments, as well. These provisions were not designed to prevent changes by the majority but to make sure that the majority views had staying power. While the Founding Fathers made it possible for the Constitution to be amended, it was difficult to do so, meaning that these limits on the majority were protected from change.

Everything is changeable but its hard.

While the Founding Fathers, including James Madison, feared intemperate majorities, they were also concerned about minorities as well. Madison wrote about his fear of the negative effect of factions that represented only parts of the population could have on the political system. Madison feared that such factions, which he had observed in the English Parliament, would be more interested in their own economic interests and would ignore what would be in the national interest. These factions included the forerunners of political parties in England and other powerful groups (interest groups). The system of checks and balances with three branches, different terms of office, federalism, the size of the republic, and the amendment process, however, also provided protection against any faction or minority group gaining control of the government to impose its will on the majority. The competition of factions might make it difficult for government to operate, but it would prevent minority rule.

Amending the Constitution

The Founding Fathers were never convinced that they had developed a perfect document. They were not even sure that the Constitution would last any longer than the Articles of Confederation. They realized that changes would be necessary and that some mechanism for amending the document should be available. They created a number of ways in which the Constitution could be amended, but regardless of which paths were followed, it would be a difficult process. Amendments could be proposed two ways. The most common way is for two-thirds of the House and two-thirds of the Senate to propose an amendment. Since the houses had different bases of representation (population and equality), the supermajority could be even more difficult to achieve. A second way is for two-thirds of the states to call a convention to consider proposing an amendment. Although this process has never been used, it was important for the passage of the Seventeenth Amendment, which required the direct election of Senators. The proposed amendment had been blocked by Senators who were appointed by state legislatures, but once nearly two-thirds of the states had approved the proposal of such an amendment, it was passed through the Senate by the individuals who had previously been obstructing the process.

Amendments can be ratified by the states in two ways. The most frequently used method has been that three-fourths of the state legislatures approve the amendment in question. The ratification can be even more complicated since some state constitutions require a supermajority in their legislatures to pass an amendment to the U.S. Constitution. A second way is to require the approval of three-fourths of state conventions specially chosen to review the amendment. The system is similar to the way in which the Constitution was ratified by state conventions. This ratification process has been used once to deal with the Twenty-first Amendment that repealed prohibition.

Given the supermajorities required for ratification, it is not surprising that amendments of the Constitution have been frequently proposed but seldom passed. There have only been twenty-seven amendments that have passed to date, and the Bill of Rights (the first ten) was virtually guaranteed of passage. Changes to the document are indeed possible. Some of the amendments that have passed have been quite important, such as the ones permitting an income tax, providing for the direct election of Senators, and the one outlawing slavery (necessary since the Constitution implicitly recognized slavery). The Constitution has withstood the test of time better than the Founding Fathers thought would be the case given the limited number of amendments that have been successfully ratified.

Although amendments are included at the end of the Constitution in most conventional printings, they are not trivial additions nor are they less important than the articles of the Constitution. In fact, the amendments are in many ways more important than the original document because they frequently change provisions of the original Constitution. Thus, it does not matter in some cases what the Founding Fathers originally intended, since the amendments have substituted the intent of later politicians for the original intent. The Founding Fathers, for example, clearly intended to recognize the existence of slavery, but the Thirteenth Amendment clearly outlaws such practices. The delegates in Philadelphia protected the right of individual states to appoint Senators, but that has changed. The Fourteenth Amendment mandated equal treatment of all U.S. citizens, including former slaves, a provision that was not intended by the delegates. As such, these amendments take precedence over the original words of the Constitution.

Ratifying the Constitution

Writing the Constitution was just the first step. The document had to be ratified in order to become the new document for governing the United States. The ratification process required that nine of the thirteen states had to ratify it. Opposition to the new Constitution had appeared. The supporters of the new Constitution became known as the Federalists, while the opponents were known as the Anti-Federalists. The Anti-Federalists included those who feared a stronger central government and wanted power to remain in the hands of the states. There was even a limited amount of opposition from some religious groups that were offended by the absence of any reference to God in the document. By June 21, 1788, nine

Procedure for Amending the Constitution

Amendment proposed by 2/3
vote of House and Senate

Amendment ratified by 3/4 vote
of state legislatures

Amendment ratified by 3/4 vote
of state conventions called to
consider amendment

states had ratified the Constitution. The vote was close in Massachusetts but was obviously never in much doubt in the other eight states. Even though nine states had ratified, and technically the document had been passed, the key states of New York and Virginia had still not decided. It was essential that these large and populous states in the center of the country support the ratification. The vote in both of these states was going to be close.

TEST TIP

Beginning in May 2011, the AP exam stopped penalizing test-takers for incorrect responses to multiple-choice questions. Entering a response for every question—even a wild guess—may help improve your score.

The strength of the opposition to the new Constitution led to a number of moves by the Federalists. One move was their agreement to support the addition of a Bill of Rights to the new document. At the convention, some delegates wanted a Bill of Rights to protect individual citizens from an overzealous national government. They felt that a listing of rights was essential. Other delegates also believed in individual rights, but they felt that a listing of rights would turn out to be a limitation since it would permit some to assume that only the listed rights would be protected; this view carried the day at the convention, but during debates on ratification, it became obvious that the public was very much in favor of a listed Bill of Rights. As a consequence, those who had previously opposed a Bill of Rights agreed to support the proposal of a set of amendments by Congress to list these rights and to support ratification by the states. The Federalists did indeed honor this commitment in the first Congress when the Bill of Rights was proposed and sent to the states. The Ninth Amendment was designed to deal with the concerns of those who felt that a listing of rights would be limiting. This amendment specifies that the listing of certain rights in the Constitution (which includes the first eight amendments) does not preclude there being additional (unlisted) rights that are protected under the Constitution.

Highlights of Federalist 10 and 51

Federalist 10
Daily Advertiser—Thursday, November 22, 1787

Madison warns against the dangers that would come if factions gained too much control and ignored what was good for the country.

Federalist 51
Independent Journal—Wednesday, February 6, 1788

Madison covered various topics including the problems that factions presented, especially in applying political pressures to secure appointments to government offices. He discussed the system of checks and balances as part of the division of power between the three branches. The individual branches needed to operate autonomously so that a concentration of power was avoided. He argued that for the sake of liberty, it was necessary for judges to be free of elections so that they could maintain their objectivity.

The Federalists and the Anti-Federalists also engaged in a public debate in newspapers over the wisdom of ratifying the Constitution. James Madison, Alexander Hamilton, and John Jay wrote a series of articles that came to be known as the Federalist Papers. Hamilton had begun the Federalists papers and penned fifty-one of the eighty-seven, but Madison is responsible for two of the most influential essays. Federalist 10 and 51 both warn about factions and argue that by the creation of a system of checks and balances, a faction would have a difficult time overriding the will of the people. Many of the Federalist Papers were written as part of the major efforts to convince voters in New York and Virginia to select delegates to their state conventions who would support ratification. The votes in New York and Virginia by these conventions, as it turned out, were in favor of ratification. There was significant opposition in Virginia led by Patrick Henry, who feared the power of the national government as laid out in the Constitution. The vote, however, was especially close in the New York convention. If two delegates changed their vote, it would not have passed. It would appear that the arguments that were presented in the Federalist Papers had been helpful in mobilizing those who were in favor of the new Constitution. After ratification by Virginia, North Carolina ratified the Constitution by a substantial majority. The vote was timely in that North Carolina was able to send representatives and senators to the first Congress. Rhode Island held out until 1790 and then ratified the Constitution by only the slimmest of margins. Rhode Island had refused to send delegates to the convention in Philadelphia because it rightly felt that such a convention would make too many changes in the Articles of Confederation.

The intransigence of Rhode Island was also one reason why the Founding Fathers knew that unanimous approval for the document was a practical impossibility.

Ratification of the Constitution				
Votes	State	Date	Yes	No
1.	Delaware	December 7, 1787	30	0
2.	Pennsylvania	December 11, 1787	46	23
3.	New Jersey	December 18, 1787	38	0
4.	Georgia	January 2, 1788	26	0
5.	Connecticut	January 9, 1788	228	40
6.	Massachusetts	January 9, 1788	187	168
7.	Maryland	April 26, 1788	63	11
8.	South Carolina	May 23, 1788	149	73
9.	New Hampshire	June 21, 1788	57	47
10.	Virginia	June 25, 1788	89	79
11.	New York	July 26, 1788	30	27
12.	North Carolina	November 21, 1789	194	77
13.	Rhode Island	May 29, 1790	34	32

Constitution was "officially" ratified, but the passage in New York and Virginia was essential for actually putting the new document into practice.

The New System

The constitution that resulted from the Constitutional Convention was a document that was full of political compromises. No one group or state got everything it wanted, but the final product provided something valuable to virtually all groups in the new country. The necessity of compromising on many issues meant that at the conclusion of the convention, not all of the delegates agreed to sign the Constitution as written. They disagreed with some of the compromises or because of the vagueness in some areas or even issues that were not addressed during the convention. The ambiguity intentionally left in some areas left some fearful that when these issues were addressed at a later time, decisions would be made on the basis of what was best for those involved rather than for the country in general. The New York delegation did not sign the document. Alexander Hamilton, who was obviously a strong supporter of the new Constitution, was thus not one of the signers. Some of the compromises in the document probably played a role in the ratification efforts. It would not always be clear whether the particular compromises were a positive factor or a negative factor since the votes were so close in some states. Since the Constitution was indeed ratified by all thirteen states, the compromises ultimately would have to be considered to have worked in achieving their purposes.

It is very important to note that the new Constitution was designed to provide a framework for a government that would then make decisions and pass laws for the country. The Founding Fathers saw themselves as providing a set of institutions that would then make the necessary political decisions that would decide the future of the new country. While there is no doubt that many of the individuals present in Philadelphia felt strongly about laws that the new Congress should pass, it was not part of their job to write laws but to create legislative, executive, and judicial bodies that would make laws, carry them into practice, and to make judgments about them. Many of the delegates did indeed go on to serve in the executive, legislative, and judicial branches, and thus they did influence the future of the country. In this way their intent about what policies that government should follow had a hearing.

The Constitution, complete with compromises, did in fact support the view of many of the delegates that it might not last. While the Constitution has proven to be an effective document, it only papered over some of the underlying conflicts present in the country. It ultimately required the Civil War to resolve the basic questions involving slavery. The Civil War also dealt with some questions about the relative balance of power between the national government and state governments, with the advantage going to the central government. The Civil War represented a clear failure of the political institutions created in Philadelphia to deal with issues. It is likely that there was no set of democratic institutions that could have dealt with these issues, but the particular framework set up in Philadelphia did not work to resolve all the important issues that faced the country in its first seventy years.

The new constitution also attempted to create a relatively democratic system for the new country. There are many definitions of democracy that can be used, but many definitions frequently include the idea of competitive elections, opportunities for input in the political process beyond the simple act of voting, and protection of the rights of political minorities (those who have lost the previous election). Elections had long been competitive in the individual colonies and states, and they often continued to be in the new system. There were opportunities for input beyond Election Day, and the new country was very open to political debate in many areas. The campaign of competing newspaper articles between the Federalists and the Anti-Federalists is a prime example of political input that was present in the new country. While opportunities for the open and unfettered expression of different opinions were not always honored in practice in the decades to come, the principles were expressed in the Constitution. The idea of the need for protection of the rights of the political minority was explicit in the concerns of Madison and others about the dangers of majority tyranny. Majority rule is a simplistic definition of democracy and not an adequate one since it would permit violation of the basic natural rights that the Founding Fathers believed that individuals held. The Bill of Rights by its very nature limited the scope of majority rule by guaranteeing individual rights that those in the political minority would have and that the government could not abridge.

By necessity, the democracy that was established was a representative democracy rather than direct democracy. Direct democracy could be practiced by the pilgrims in their colony or at the township level in New England where everyone eligible to vote could participate and vote on outcomes. Such direct democracy had become impossible at the state level by 1787 and was obviously impossible for a national government. The people would have to elect representatives to look after their interests. The Founding Fathers made the elections for the members of the House of Representatives very frequent ones with the two-year terms to force members of the chamber to respond to their voters. The indirect election of senators and the president for longer terms was designed to provide protection against popular movements that could reflect a lack of thoughtful consideration of issues, but the House of Representatives could also serve as a check on the Senate and president if these institutions sought to undertake actions that were not acceptable to the people. The representative democracy that was established was designed to be balanced between the desires of the general public and protection of political minorities.

While there were clear limits on the level of democracy that was present under the new constitution, as it was recognized that states would have different levels of participation, the national system was relatively democratic for its time, especially when compared with other political systems in existence in Europe. While the system discriminated against slaves and freed blacks and disenfranchised all but a handful of women, these shortcomings were present at the state level rather than the national level. Slaves and women had a similar lack of power elsewhere in the world. It would be many generations before these problems were rectified, but the level of democracy present in the system has to be judged by the standards of 1790, not 1890 or 1990. Leaving the voting decisions in the hands of the states was actually seen as one way of avoiding a national government that would be undemocratic. The value of the Constitution can be better seen in the fact that it was eventually possible to make the political system much more democratic over the course of time. The flexibility of the document and amendments meant that improvement was possible and did in fact occur.

Time for a quiz
- Review strategies in Chapter 2
- Take Quiz 1 at the REA Study Center
  (www.rea.com/studycenter)

Political Beliefs and Behaviors

Founding the Republic

The Founding Fathers clearly looked to the past to determine the future of the new country. It is important to remember that all of the political ideologies that were incorporated or referred to at the Constitutional Convention were concerned with how to control the power of individuals within their own spheres of influence. Elections and voting were important aspects of the political process. The delegates in Philadelphia were unable to reach a compromise on voter eligibility, so they left the matter mostly in the hands of the states. The Constitution allows, but does not require, Congress to alter any state regulations regarding congressional elections. The only provision explicitly explained was that a popular election was necessary to choose members of the House of Representatives.

Beliefs That Citizens Hold About Their Government and Its Leaders

Political Culture

Political culture is a distinctive and patterned way of thinking about how political and economic life ought to be carried out. A political culture consists of fundamental assumptions about how the political process should operate. For example, Americans assume that when an election is lost, the loser will accept the results and not hinder the winner from taking office. Political culture is not to be confused with political ideology, which is a consistent set of individual beliefs that people have concerning the policies government should pursue or should avoid interfering in. Even though individual exceptions abound, Americans share a number of basic beliefs about the system. Americans are fiercely protective of their rights and personal liberties. They believe they are granted the rights to do as they see fit, with some exceptions, as long as they do not hurt other people. They also generally support the idea of a free-enterprise system within certain boundaries. Most Americans believe everyone must have an equal vote and an equal chance to participate and succeed in the political system and to attempt to bring about political changes. They are more willing to tolerate economic inequality than political inequality; they believe in maintaining "equality of opportunity" but not "equality of results." Most Americans will support education and training programs to help disadvantaged people but are opposed to anything that looks like preferential treatment. Most Americans think government officials should be accountable to the people and that people should take community affairs seriously and contribute when they can. Most Americans also believe that individuals are responsible for their own actions and well-being. Most will support individuals who are truly in need, but are skeptical of assistance given to those who can take care of themselves.

The ongoing balance between liberty, social, and religious control has created an adversarial electorate dominated by partisan politics. Americans' mistrust of authority and power led to a Constitution designed to curb and control the threats that come with the limitations of human nature and the tendency to usurp power in times of great duress. Political parties have grown in size, scope, and influence over the course of time. An important early event in partisan politics occurred when John Adams had to give up his presidential seat to Thomas Jefferson, a political opponent, in what was the nations' first great test of peaceful transfer of power. Jefferson took the presidency, and the role of a loyal opposition party became legitimate and a part of American political culture—even though, to this day, there are times when disagreement with the government is considered to be close to treason.

While the Constitution protects religious freedom, any attempt to introduce greater religious tones has been met with concern. American traditions initially were based in Puritanism and later the Protestant religion, although these influences have waned. One important tradition that has persisted through time stems from the Puritan work ethic. It stresses an individual's obligation to work, save money, and obey secular law. Another tradition that evolved was the centrality of the family in socialization. This extends to the political realm, where an individual is socialized in political matters, including party affiliation.

Americans have learned from early on in school the ideal that every person has rights, such as life and liberty, that deserve protection. Class consciousness has been low to non-existent in the United States. In part, this is due to how we were colonized; it was people in lower lots in life who were willing to take on the challenges and risks of starting anew in America. The absence of an aristocracy by birth in the colonies

reduced class differences. As a consequence, class was less important as a
basis for political parties. As national
identity developed, parties developed
along the basis of fundamental beliefs
about the role, purpose, and size of
government. These differences persist

today, but voters now also choose a party affiliation based on their own personal reaction to different topics. In recent times, controversies involving abortion, gay rights, school prayer, pornography, and taxes have become central. The disputes that arise along with these concerns can leave little room for compromise and result in very emotional politics. In previous years, taxes would not be included in this list, but with the rise of the Tea Party and the multiple protests of Wall Street, taxes have become an emotional issue.

Since the late 1950s, the nation has seen a decline in the level of trust that Americans have in the government. There have been brief times where the people have "rallied around the flag," such as during the assassination of JFK in 1963 and most recently in 2001 after the terrorist attacks. During these periods, the American people have trusted the government to act on the behalf of the safety of the American people. Outside of "rallying around the flag" effects, many Americans have had an increasing mistrust of government and its officials. The anti-war demonstrations of the 1960s contributed to this mistrust. The discovery that the FBI and CIA routinely spied on antiwar groups and civil rights organizations also contributed to the mistrust, as did the Watergate scandal during the Nixon administration. Watergate was followed by the discovery that the United States was, in effect, transferring arms to Iran and using the profits to fund violent insurgents in Nicaragua in covert operations that skirted the law. The mistrust escalated with the personal scandals surrounding President Clinton as well as other politicians who have been forced to resign for unethical behavior in the recent past. Of course, scandals have always been present in government, but Americans tend to forget the earlier history in this regard. Officials close to President Harding and President Grant were involved in major corruption scandals, and in the latter part of the nineteenth century, a common witticism was that the United States had "the best Congress money could buy," reflecting the high level of bribery and corruption that was present.

With the rise of bureaucracy, red tape, political scandals, and the media, a citizen's capacity to understand and influence political events has waned. A citizen's understanding of his or her capacity to influence political events is called **political efficacy**. It indicates a citizen's belief that he or she can understand and influence political affairs.

It is commonly measured by surveys and used as an indicator for the broader health of civil society. There are two types of political efficacy: internal efficacy (the belief that one can understand politics and therefore participate in politics) and external efficacy (the belief that one is *effective* when participating in politics—for example, that the government will respond to one's demands). Declining efficacy is in part a reflection of an increasingly complex society, but the complexity of society reinforces the decline in feelings of efficacy.

Democratic politics depends on individuals listening to and defending the rights, opinions, and actions of others, even if they personally disapprove. Democracy does not require tolerance, but citizens must allow the free discussion of ideas to allow society to grow without oppressing others. Most Americans are willing to let many people with whom they disagree politically have great latitude in expressing their views. However, unpopular groups have been persecuted in the past. There was a distrust of Catholics when the country was formed. Irish immigrants were looked down upon, as were later groups of immigrants. Black Americans were second-class citizens after the end of slavery. Mormons were persecuted in the first half of the nineteenth century, and today, some people view Muslims with suspicion and a lack of tolerance. The government has had to become actively involved at various times in order to permit these groups and others to actively participate in American society and politics. Recent surveys have found that the level of civility in political arguments has declined, and people holding differing political views are treated with suspicion and less respect.

Political Socialization

Our political choices are based on a combination of several factors and are the result of a complex process known as **political socialization**. Families are one factor. Families define more than just DNA-related bonds; they also contribute to party identification. The majority of young people identify with their parents' political party because that is what they have predominantly been exposed to at home. The exposure may be subtle rather than the result of any attempt at indoctrination. As individuals age, their experiences are broader and they are exposed to additional ideas, and they can independently determine their political outlook. Still, for the most part, children will define their party allegiance along the same lines as their parents.

Religion can also be a powerful agent of political socialization. All religions implant a set of values in the young that will influence their view on politics and the policies that they believe governments should follow. Different religious environments, or the lack of any religious environment, can influence attitudes toward other religions, other ethnic or racial groups, and/or other kinds of minorities. It has generally been found in the United States and in other democracies that those citizens who are more religious tend to favor more conservative policies and parties.

Educational systems are another powerful source of political socialization. Many Americans initially have a positive view of the government because they learn about the system in a positive way at an early age. High school civics classes or the equivalent often form the basis of knowledge of the political system, building on earlier courses in American history. As students advance through the education system, they may be exposed to more competing ideas and, as a result, change their views. Studies have found that college students tend to be liberal when compared to the rest of the voting population. Conservatives believe that students are indoctrinated by liberal professors while liberals would argue that the liberalism of college students is a consequence of education. Another explanation, of course, would be that college students encounter a broader range of people, ideas, and experiences that serve to make them more liberal than they were before they entered college. Both Republican and Democratic students experience the liberalizing effect of college.

The media and peer groups also influence political attitudes. In today's world, the media is not overwhelmingly conservative or liberal, and individuals can easily find media outlets that reinforce their own existing political attitudes. The wide variety of outlets, however, can expose people to additional viewpoints. Peer groups and the workplace can also influence political attitudes. In some cases, the workplace is overwhelmingly Democratic or Republican, and the particular viewpoint is constantly reinforced. Studies have found that people living in homogenous neighborhoods who originally have different political attitudes tend to adopt the community attitudes over time.

There are obviously a variety of influential sources of political socialization. At a very basic level, most Americans support the idea of a democratic system, even if they may have somewhat different views as to how that democratic system should operate. The average American also accepts the general outlines of the system. They value a two-party system and cannot understand why other countries have so many parties. They also value a separation between the president and Congress, especially in times of divided government, when one of those institutions (controlled by their own party) is a check on the other institution (controlled by the opposition party).

TEST TIP

Remember that you need to sign up for the AP exam at least several weeks before the test date, so be sure to talk to your AP teacher or your school's AP coordinator about taking the exam well before the scheduled exam time. If you are home schooled or if your school does not offer AP programs, you can still take the exam. However, you will need to contact AP Services directly to learn how to register. Usually, you need to do this by the beginning of March to take the exam in mid-May.

Public Opinion

Variations in Public Opinion

Common social and economic factors contribute to a varied forum of public opinion, beliefs, and behaviors. Despite these differences, Americans share a common political culture based on democracy. Today, public opinion can be a powerful tool, especially during elections or for use in creating political action and legislation. Increasingly, politicians, pundits, and even voters are paying close attention to what polls tell them is the public's opinion. Public opinion is the sum of individual attitudes or beliefs held by the adult (over age 18) population. There are many complex methods that can be used to determine the public's views and opinions, which makes public opinion quite difficult to assess. The average person is most often uninformed about the daily accomplishments of the government, and further still, the belief of many people today is that the government does too little while taking too long to enact meaningful legislation. This opinion can change based on the fickle nature of the public and its perceptions, which can be influenced by how the media reports what the government is accomplishing.

Still more troubling is how public opinion is formulated and how accurate it is. Most opinion reporting is based on polling, and public-opinion polling techniques pose a problem in and of themselves. How a pollster words a question can dramatically affect the answer received. For instance, rates of agreement or disagreement with a one-sided statement can differ when two balanced statements on the same issue are offered. The order in which possible responses are listed can also have an effect on the poll. Accurate polling requires a random sample of diverse people free of any bias or manipulation to meet a predetermined outcome. Major polls such as Gallup, Harris, etc., conduct fair and unbiased polls, and they have large enough sample sizes so that the results have a high level of validity. Many organizations that commission polls, however, have a political agenda and will often attempt to generate results to further that agenda rather than to report a true picture of public views.

Public opinion polls have other potential dangers. There is some concern that politicians pay too much attention to the polls. At some level it is expected that the leaders of the country should lead rather than simply follow public opinion. Public opinion polls could become a mechanism for majority tyranny. The views and opinions, and even the rights, of political minorities could be ignored. Public opinion polls can only provide general guidelines at best. They are not a substitute for the study of policies, discussions among those involved in deciding on policy (presidents, members of congress, party leaders, leaders of groups, etc.), and the forging of compromises that are an essential part of the political process. The Constitutional Convention in Philadelphia is a classic demonstration of how discussion, debate, compromise, and reworking can lead to a positive, even if imperfect, outcome.

A cleavage in public opinion means that the public is divided in their opinions on various topics. Most common cleavages are based on social class, race, ethnicity, and religion. There are other factors that interweave and overlap, helping individuals determine their political identity, which party they identify with, and whether they participate or abstain from politics. Social class and socioeconomic differences no doubt play a role in politics, but political ideologies are now being framed around specific policy issues such as gun control, abortion rights, prayer in public institutions, and race relations. The race of an individual often has determined his or her party affiliation. For example, black Americans are more likely to be Democrats and white Americans are more likely to be Republican. This may be a result of the roles each party played in the 1960s in civil rights legislation. Region has also played a role in political identification, with the South often being aligned with the Republican Party (with the exception of black southerners). Rural Americans are also more likely to support the Republican Party, whereas those who live in urban areas identify with the Democratic Party. There is also an important gender gap in the United States. Beginning with the 1980 election, women began to support the Democratic Party more than the Republican Party, perhaps because the Democratic Party was more active in supporting the movement for women's equality and supports issues of importance to women such as social welfare and increased education spending.

Elections and Voting Behavior

Elections are the processes through which power in government changes hands. Elections allow voters a voice in policymaking because people choose the candidate who is most likely to act in their own personal interests or are inline with their own political beliefs. For this process to work, candidates must represent constituents' views on the issues. There are three kinds of elections in the United States: primary elections, general elections, and elections on specific policy issues, which take place at the state and local level through referenda (state-level method of direct legislation) and initiative petition (voter-proposed changes in a state's constitution or laws). Suffrage (the right to vote) has been steadily expanded throughout American history. Although the Constitution left the issue up to the states, initially only white, male property-owners or those who paid a particular amount of taxes had the right to vote. Today, almost all Americans over the age of 18 can vote in elections.

The Founding Fathers clearly believed that elections and voting were important aspects of the political process. (Remember, the delegates in Philadelphia were unable to reach a compromise on voter eligibility, so they left the matter mostly in the hands of the states.) However, over the course of time, control of the voting process evolved and gradually has shifted from state to federal control. Early elections varied greatly. Some states picked their representatives at large rather than by district. Others had elections in odd-numbered years. Through law and constitutional amendment, Congress has required that all members of the House be elected by district and that all federal elections be held in even-numbered years on the first Tuesday following the first Monday in November. There have been three additional major changes on the voting population via constitutional amendments.

The Fifteenth Amendment states that the right to vote cannot be denied to anyone "on account of race, color, or previous condition of servitude." Though straightforward, several states passed laws that denied suffrage to African Americans and emboldened their constituents. Literacy tests and poll taxes were used to disqualify poor illiterate blacks, but an unintended consequence was that these rules also limited poor, illiterate white voters. To counteract the effect on poor, illiterate white voters, a **grandfather clause** was created that would allow a person to vote if his ancestors had voted before 1867. If these limiting rules were not enough to deter African Americans from visiting the polls, they were overtly intimidated, harassed, and threatened by government officials, law enforcement, and racist vigilantes. When challenged, these rules were overturned at the federal level. The grandfather clause was declared unconstitutional in 1915, and later, literacy tests were overturned by the Voting Rights Act of 1965. While it took nearly a century, African Americans were ultimately freed of the state and local barriers that stood in the way of their right to vote under the Fifteenth Amendment.

The Nineteenth Amendment (1920) guaranteed women the right to vote in elections. Many states had individually already given women the right to vote, but the only way to make sure that all states permitted women to vote was through a constitutional amendment. The Twenty-sixth Amendment (1971) provided eighteen-year-olds the right to vote. The impetus for this change was related to the military draft. It was argued that if eighteen year olds were old enough to be drafted and sent into combat, they should be allowed to vote for the politicians that decided whether or not military troops were going to be placed in harm's way. Immediately after the ratification of the Twenty-sixth amendment, candidates courted the youth vote, which has since become less of a priority, as voter turnout in this demographic group has been consistently much lower than that of other groups.

TEST TIP

Don't worry about including everything you ever learned about a particular topic in your essays. Scorers look for a strong thesis supported by a clear, logical argument and relevant evidence, not a laundry list of names, dates, and facts.

The Constitution requires that a **census** be taken every ten years. The data is used to identify population trends in the United States. This data is used to ensure that funding is distributed for federal and state programs in proper proportion to population density, to assign seats in the House to each state, to determine each state's number of electors in the Electoral College, and to redraw state and federal congressional districts. Recently, the census has become a source of political controversy. The census is required to count "persons" in the United States. It does not distinguish between voters and non-voters, citizens and non-citizens, legal residents and illegal residents. All free persons were to be counted with the exception of Indians "who were not taxed." Certain groups of individuals are more difficult to count accurately. The homeless are obviously more difficult to count, and illegal residents will avoid any government official. Even legal residents may fear government officials because of experiences in their home countries when the only time they would see census takers was when the government needed to know who to tax and who to draft into military service.

An inaccurate census count has political repercussions. The undercount inevitably occurs in urban areas that are more likely to be Democratic; counts in suburban areas, which are more likely to be Republican, are much more accurate. Democrats suggested making statistical adjustments to the census count for purposes of assigning seats in the House of Representatives. The resulting numbers would be more accurate than the actual count. Republicans favored using the actual count. If a more accurate, statistically adjusted count were used, some states would gain seats and others would lose seats, and the gains would likely benefit the Democrats. Even if a state kept the same number of representatives, the district boundaries would have to be drawn differently since there is a requirement for general equality in terms of population. Such a count could change the distribution of seats in the House of Representatives and in state legislatures.

Participation

In recent years, the number of voters who participate during elections has generally dwindled, although turnout was noticeably higher in 2004 and 2008. This increasing voter apathy has permitted political elites to have greater influence. Voting is the most common form of political participation that most Americans practice. Traditionally, the highest turnouts are for presidential elections, and trends show that the electorate votes less during midterm elections. Voter turnout is low due to a number of structural reasons, including the need to register early to vote; the fact that election day is a work day, making it more difficult for some to get to the polls (and some who do may lose wages); shorter poll hours; and other requirements that vary from state to state. In addition, some voters do not have any competitive elections in their district or state. Turnout in the United States is lower than almost every other industrialized democracy.

Political participation can take many forms beyond voting. About twenty percent of Americans are **inactive participants**. They do not vote for a variety of reasons, with the most cited reason being voter apathy. This group often does not discuss politics and they tend to have lower levels of education. Young voters tend to be included in this group as they are a highly mobile group and are less engaged in their communities than older Americans. At the other end of the spectrum are those who could be termed **specialists**. They vote because they have a right to do so and feel it is their civic duty, but they do not participate beyond election day. There are **communalist** voters. They are outspoken on local problems and are active in contacting local officials to help alleviate their concerns. This group of people could evolve into an interest group. A fourth group are **campaigners**. They tend to be focused on their particular political party and will take strong positions to sway undecided voters toward their causes. Another group would be **parochial participants**. They avoid election activity, but they are often active at the local level, and they are likely to contact local politicians about specific, often personal, problems.

There are some other trends in terms of participation. Studies show that college students/graduates tend to participate more often in politics than those with less education. Traditionally, older voters vote more than younger voters. Churchgoers tend to participate more than non-churchgoers if all other factors are equal. Men and women vote at about the same rate. Members of most ethnic or racial groups vote less than whites. Union members are more likely to vote, as are those who are married. Those who could be considered members of elite groups are the most likely to vote. In general, voting is higher among those people with greater feelings of political efficacy or for those who have a larger, direct stake in government activities, such as the level of taxes imposed or the types of services provided. About ten percent of the population are political activists involved in political activities beyond voting.

DIDYOU**KNOW?**

During the height of the Cold War, about 10% of the population of the Soviet Union were active, involved members of the Communist Party of the Soviet Union. Approximately 10% of the population of the United States were considered active participants in the Democratic, Republican, or third parties.

Levels of American Political Involvement

Civic and Political Involvement in America	
Proportion of adults who did each of the following in the last 12 months	
Sign a petition	32%
Contact a national, state, or local government official about an issue	30%
Work with fellow citizens to solve a community problem	28%
Attend a political meeting on local, town, or school affairs	24%
Contribute money to a political candidate or party or any other political organization or cause	18%
Be an active member of a group that tries to influence public policy or government	15%
Attend a political rally or speech	12%
Send a letter to the editor of a newspaper or magazine	10%
Work or volunteer for a political party or candidate	8%
Make a speech about a community or local issue	7%
Attend an organized protest	4%
Any of these	63%

Studies reveal that if voter turnout increased among groups with low rates of participation, Democratic candidates would receive more votes. This was the case with the 2008 election of President Obama, as traditionally low-voter-turnout groups unified and voted. The general rule is that when turnout is high, Democrats do better, and when turnout is lower Republicans do better, although there can be variations among the states in this regard. Since turnout does affect outcome, it means that some political groups have an incentive to increase general turnout while other groups have an incentive to decrease turnout. Of course, both major parties and other groups always have an incentive to get those groups that identify with their views out to the polls.

Americans cast their votes on the basis of a number of criteria. They often vote on the basis of party affiliation because the candidate from their party is assumed to share their political beliefs. For a period of time, parties were seen as providing less useful labels for the voters because party members did not always vote together. Since the 2000 election, however, Republicans and Democrats have more frequently voted along party lines on major issues. Voters evaluate what is published about those running for office, and they can learn about the candidates' personalities. A candidate's physical appearance may play an unconscious role in voter decision-making. Viewers' decisions about who won the John F. Kennedy vs. Richard Nixon debates were based more on the visual imagery on television than on the substance of the answers. Listeners who heard the debate on the radio as opposed to watching it on television felt that Nixon did much better in the debates. People also value integrity, competence, and humility in a candidate and are unlikely to value overbearing arrogance and manifest incompetence. Many voters also have firm policy convictions. These views vary and are formed through a variety of mechanisms, including a familiarity with each candidate's policy preferences. Voters may have more difficulty making a choice when candidates have similar stances on key issues. It is also possible that policy preferences may lead voters to avoid candidates who do not take a clear stand on a controversial issue they are passionate about.

Why Low Turnout?

Political scientists debate why the trend of low voter turnout has occurred while the population has steadily increased. Some theorize that the rise of partisan politics and the weakening of the competitiveness between the two major parties have left voters with fewer options and have bred voter apathy. History shows that the elections of the late nineteenth century were bitterly contested and had great sway over the electorate. The parties worked harder to motivate their constituents to become active and become involved with their respective parties. Interest began to wane in the early twentieth century when the Republican Party dominated national elections resulting in many elections where there was not much doubt about whom the winner would ultimately be.

There are other views on why voter turnout has declined. Corruption within politics is often cited when little is changed with each successive election. The voters, in this view, regard the lack of change as a sign of a corrupt political system. Of course, the lack of change results at times from the system of checks and balances and in other times because it is really only a minority that wants change. It is the perceptions of the voters that influence turnout, not the actual level of corruption that exists in the system. There are many historical examples of voting fraud during the late nineteenth century. "Vote early and often" was not meant as humor but as a fact, as political parties controlled the counting of votes. It is easy today to compare census data versus votes in this time period and find that the number of votes counted was often larger than the number cast, and the number cast was often larger than the number of individuals eligible to vote. To safeguard against the fraud of the late nineteenth century, strict voter-registration procedures were developed. As is the case when decisions are made, the unintended consequence of the new strict voter-registration procedures led to difficulty for some groups of voters to register, and the political machines that existed in some areas also used these new procedures to dissuade eager voters from registering, which severely restricted those that could vote in the first place.

Today, registering to vote in this country falls entirely on individual voters. As a result, young registrants must learn how, when, and where to register. They must have some intrinsic motivation to go through the registration process and even further motivation if they relocate to a new town or state. Younger voters are more likely to be more mobile, on average, which would be one reason why they have one of the lowest turnout rates. The 1993 Motor-Voter law required states to allow people to register to vote or re-register within a voting precinct when applying for driver's licenses or changing their address. States that allow same-day registration—voters can register on the day of the election—make it easier for more people to vote.

Political Ideologies

For the most part Americans consider themselves conservative, moderate, or liberal. In the early 2000's, many identified themselves as conservatives; however that tide seems to have switched to the liberal side with the large voter turnout for President

Obama in 2008. It is sometimes hard to define liberal and conservative since they mean different things to different people, but there are some basic characteristics that are noted in the table below. Generally, Republicans are more conservative in their ideology while Democrats are more liberal. A strong defined ideology will create consistency over time in patterns of how individuals within that group vote and the stances they will take on issues. While fluctuations exist, studies show that moderates are the largest group among American voters, conservatives the second largest, and liberals the smallest.

Political Ideologies Defined

Conservatives favor a limited-government approach and freedoms for the private economic sector. They believe in militarism and support military spending, free markets, prayer in school, and reduced taxes, and tend to oppose abortion, affirmative action, and government spending on social programs. They are more likely to support legislation that prohibits "unacceptable" social or moral behavior.

Liberals favor a larger government with social and economic responsibilities, more equal distribution of wealth, government spending, additional and restrictive regulation of big business, and women's rights. They oppose increases in defense spending and military actions, prayer in school, and tax breaks for the wealthy.

Women and minorities tend to be more liberal as a result of the oppression they endured and their long fight to attain more equal rights (and who see the need for a continuing struggle to reduce the differences that still exist). Women, who gained suffrage much later than men, have developed a gender gap that predicts the likelihood women will vote for a Democratic candidate.

The definitions of *liberal* and *conservative* have changed over time. Traditionally, a liberal was a person who favored personal and economic liberty that was free from the controls and powers of the government, and the term conservative was first applied to those who opposed the excesses of the French Revolution. The rise of the more recent definition of the term liberal in the United States coincides with Franklin Roosevelt's New Deal, and it was used to describe a supporter who desired an active government who would intervene on behalf of the people to provide economic relief from the Great Depression. Conservatives evolved from rugged individualism and desired a free market with little to no government intrusions at all. This is based on the belief that individuals have the ability to achieve the goals they need to survive.

Basic Differences between Liberals and Conservatives		
	Liberal	**Conservative**
Economy	Regulate	Hands Off
Social Welfare	More benefits for the poor	Less benefits for the poor
Moral Concerns	Differing life styles	Traditional Family values
Civil Rights	Affirmative action	No group rights
National Security	Prudent defense	Protect at all costs
U.S. Role in the World	Mutual engagement	Isolationist
Purpose of Government	Help the people	Very limited intrusion
Private or Public Solutions	Government solutions	Private charity causes
Federalism Questions	National solutions	State solutions

Those who define themselves as moderates fall somewhere between the typical liberal and the typical conservative in their views. Others may find themselves unsure of their general attitudes. For example, a classic liberal would oppose a government role in either the economy or in the area of moral concerns and would find himself or herself at odds with either party. The Libertarian Party in the United States tends to better reflect this set of beliefs. There are undoubtedly more "**libertarians**" in the country than the number of members of the party. Others might favor a more active government role to support those in need and the poor while still favoring an emphasis on traditional moral values, including active governmental programs to bring out these values or to enforce them. These individuals frequently are linked to a **populist** strain in the American political culture. The Populist Party of the late nineteenth century epitomized this particular combination of views. Other voters will simply defy labels. There are individuals who are social liberals (in favor of affirmative action, alternative lifestyles as a matter best left to the individual, etc.) but fiscally conservative (less spending, not only on defense but to some extent social programs as well). The diversity of opinions is one of the factors that have made for a population of voters (and non-voters) who are as likely to differ on their opinions as they are to share them.

DIDYOU**KNOW?**

Libertarians in the United States combine aspects of both the conservative Republican ideology and liberal Democratic ideology. They opposed government involvement in the economy and government involvement in matters of personal choice (marriage, life style, etc.).

Detailed Policy Differences of Liberals and Conservatives in the United States		
	Liberal	**Conservative**
National Security	Adequate	Strong
	Internationalism	Isolationism
	Multilateralism	Unilateralism
Economic	Keynesian theory	Economic liberalism
	Government regulation	Free markets
	Deficits	Balanced budget
	Progressive taxes	Low taxes
	Strong government	Limited government
	Private oligopoly	Relationship with corporations
	Government spending	Tax cuts
Social	Social safety net	Individual responsibility
	Public welfare	Private charity
	Extended Social Security	Privatize Social Security
	National healthcare	Private health coverage
	Government run prescriptions	Private prescription drug coverage
	Insurance medication plans	Insurance plan
Family Values	Various Types of Families	Traditional family
	Various Lifestyles	Marriage
	Tolerant of Many Religions	Judeo-Christian
	Freedom of Choice	Opposed to abortion

Political Elites

Political elites are those who hold higher positions or have more status than the average citizen. The political elite is made up of those who have a disproportionate amount of money or influence or power in policymaking or all of these characteristics. Not everyone with money would be considered part of the political elite. At some level the political elite have to be involved in the political system and attempt to influence what occurs. Individuals who are not personally wealthy can be members of the political elite, as well. Perhaps the most obvious examples in the United States are religious leaders who can, at least on some issues, carry a great deal of political weight. In the United States the political elites tend to be outspoken activists. The political elites are likely to espouse a purely liberal or purely conservative ideology. Elites tend to work for campaigns or newspapers, be actively involved in interest groups or social movements, or try to influence a wide audience by speaking out on both local and national public concerns. As stated previously, the more active people are, the more likely that they will show ideological consistency and take a hard-line position and at times can be more extreme in their liberalism or conservatism.

Elites and citizens view the political landscape differently. These differences are important because the elites have more access to the media, which creates the power to raise and define political issues from their perspective. A study found that elite views shape mass views by influencing both which particular issues capture the public's attention and how those issues are debated, viewed, disseminated, and decided. Elites also have the ability and clout to determine the range of acceptable and unacceptable policy options of an issue. This ability creates pressure that their opponents are hard pressed to overcome. While elites do not have unlimited influence on or in the American government, they can, by emphasizing—or not emphasizing—the problem, frame policy options and promote them as the best options for the populous at large. The elite can attempt to influence the public through their elected positions or through traditional media outlets in the hopes that the average person will have limited access to conflicting information that would lead to different opinions. There are currently many sources of information that are not elite-directed that can provide information or alternative views to the general public.

Political elites and political activists are important for promoting ideologies because they generally are more conservative or liberal than members of the Democratic or Republican Parties. Elites and activists help to influence the nature and tone of political debate, and activists are more likely to run for office—and therefore to be elected. Even though they need the support of the average voter, they may not reflect their own supporters in terms of the intensity of their views. While a large number of voters occupy the middle ground between liberal and conservative, there are a relatively smaller number of elected officials who do.

Changing Political Beliefs

Average Americans do not usually alter their political beliefs or ideologies once they have been established. The government, on the other hand, is swayed by public opinion as well as the party that is in control of the executive or legislative branch, or both. This movement, of course, is what democracy is all about. A political system that does not respond to changes in the leadership or public opinion would not normally qualify as very democratic. Trends in political attitudes and changes develop somewhat slowly over time. For instance, from 2000 until 2004, Republicans controlled both the executive branch and the legislative branch, which meant that the country's political beliefs tended to be conservative in approach. During the 2004 election, the executive branch remained under Republican control, and the Republicans remained in control of Congress. In 2006, however, the Democrats regained control of both houses of Congress. This trend continued in 2008, when both the executive branch and the legislative branch were decidedly Democrat controlled. This control, however, ended in 2010 at the midterm elections when the Republicans were elected to a controlling majority in half of the legislative branch. This has led to a stalemate on many issues due to the political ideological differences between conservatives and liberals. Also noteworthy is the rise of a conservative political movement known as the Tea (Taxed Enough Already) Party. This movement, which is an offshoot of the Republican Party, has a decidedly stricter interpretation of the term *conservative*. The 2010 election demonstrates how quickly political beliefs can change to meet the desires of the American public. This volatility is somewhat unusual. Underlying the situation are not necessarily large shifts in the attitudes of American voters. The Republican surge that began in 1994 was fueled to a major extent by the appearance of new, relatively young voters who favored the Republican Party. There now appears to be a shift to where the new young voters are more favorably inclined to the Democratic Party. Because Americans often stay loyal to their initial voting attitudes, winning over a young cohort of new voters can be very important for the future of a political party.

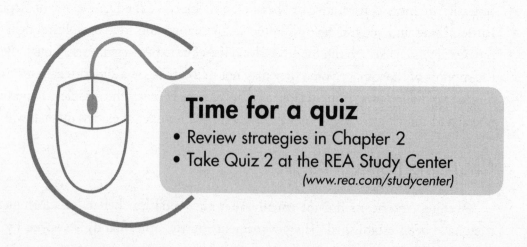

Time for a quiz
- Review strategies in Chapter 2
- Take Quiz 2 at the REA Study Center
  (www.rea.com/studycenter)

Political Parties, Interest Groups, and Mass Media

Political Parties and Elections

Political factions, or parties, have existed for as long as the United States has. Beginning with the battle between the Federalists and Anti-Federalists over the ratification of the Constitution (as discussed in Chapter 3), factions have played a vital role in the nation's politics. It is significant that in his farewell address, George Washington, who is routinely placed as the top president in opinion polls ranking the top ten presidents in U.S. history, warned the nation about the dangers he felt were posed by political parties. Washington warned, "I have already intimated to you the danger of parties in the state, with particular reference to the founding of them on geographical discriminations. Let me now take a more comprehensive view, and warn you in the most solemn manner against the baneful effects of the spirit of party, generally."

It would be quite interesting to know what Washington's opinion would be of today's government, dominated by the Republicans and the Democrats. The actuality of political parties, of course, is more complex, as there are also smaller parties that can play a role in politics. For example, the **Tea Party**, which, ahead of the 2012 presidential election is more of a movement than a party but has nonetheless gained influence. Other smaller parties routinely support one of the big two parties' candidates to gain concessions, although the smaller party candidates occasionally win offices.

Functions of Parties

Political parties perform a number of functions in the political system and have become an essential element of democratic processes. Some of the functions include political recruitment, running campaigns, providing political identity, organizing the government, implementing policies, political education, and agenda setting. Political parties have taken control of nominating candidates and running campaigns. Parties provide a basic mechanism for recruiting individuals to serve in the government. Many officials

work their way up through the ranks by first serving in the state legislature and then in Congress. Many presidents have been former governors. Even candidates with a great deal of personal appeal and popularity would find it difficult to get elected without first winning the endorsement of either the Republican Party or the Democratic Party in a primary election. While independents or third party candidates do occasionally win office, most of the time the viable candidates are Democrats or Republicans. Once candidates have been chosen, parties—including smaller parties—provide a means of campaigning for public office. The campaign itself helps connect constituents with politicians to help bring the concerns of the people to the political arena.

Parties also help to organize the government. Being the majority party in the House of Representatives and/or the Senate is important for controlling and organizing both bodies. Presidents use their party affiliation when organizing the executive branch and putting together programs that they will attempt to pass. Although many think that politicians are only interested in winning and enjoying the power and prerogatives of being in office, many candidates for office clearly want to implement particular policies, usually in line with the president's political affiliation. It makes a difference whether Democrats or Republicans win elections. There may not be major disagreements about the basic structures of the American political system between the parties, but there are clear differences about what policies should be implemented, how they should be paid for, and who should pay for them.

Political parties also provide for agenda setting by raising issues for discussion and suggesting how government should deal with the issues. Many issues never manage to get on the agenda, but those endorsed by political parties will be discussed, even if they do not get enacted into law. Parties also provide for a means of political education, even if unintentionally. Because the two major parties exist, they provide an alternative to the party in power and provide an alternative point of view on many key issues. The average voter undoubtedly knows more about what is going on in government because the parties exist. Parties may educate as a by-product of their efforts to win office and control the government, but they do provide information to the voters. Further, when the parties select candidates, run campaigns, and try to implement policies, they provide political identity to voters. These actions unite groups of politicians and the electorate and offer an ideological framework for voters. This ideological framework helps to give them a political identity.

Recent Events

Two competing trends have been developing for the last decade. One trend has been increased bipartisanship in which members of one political party work with members of the opposing political party to create legislation. This process is not an especially new phenomenon. In the 1960s, observers talked about the **Conservative Coalition** in Congress, which joined most Republicans and conservative Democrats (from the South) in a group that would cooperate in certain areas of legislative activity. The Conservative Coalition faded, in part, because conservative Democrats from the South were replaced by Republicans in many cases. During the Cold War, members of both the Democratic and Republican parties cooperated on foreign policy topics. More recently, cooperation across party lines has been on the decline, as conflict between the parties has become more contentious and both sides have seen that benefits at election time could come with uncompromising stands on some issues. This situation, for the moment, has led to a divided party government in which the president may be of a different party than the majority party in Congress. Lack of bipartisan cooperation can cause slowdowns in government and prevent any new legislation from being enacted. It is instructive to note, however, that divided government alone does not explain the lack of legislation. When President Bill Clinton was first in office, he had majorities in both the House and the Senate, and he was still unable to push through a healthcare reform package. The system of checks and balances was designed to create tensions between branches independent of party affiliation, and has been successful in that regard. As we've seen in recent years, however, when bipartisanship is on the wane, divided government does create more problems.

Organization

Of the two main political parties, Democrats tend to be more liberal than Republicans. However, both parties often tend toward moderate views in order to achieve a majority. Both parties face challenges from groups within their ranks that are more ideologically motivated and want the Republican Party to be more conservative or the Democratic Party to be more liberal. These purists are not exactly willing to give up the chance of winning by taking uncompromising ideological positions; rather, they actually believe that a true ideological commitment will result in victory. Unfortunately for those that hold this point of view, when either party nominates candidates who are distant from the moderate middle ground, those candidates tend to lose.

The two major parties are in some respects national parties in name only. They are decentralized to the state or even local level. The national parties have a convention every four years and rely on national committees to define party positions between these conventions. However, there is not much activity at the national level; most of the action is at the state level. Candidates, after all, are elected at the district or state level. Help from the local party organization may be essential in a successful election campaign. The national party has limited resources by comparison. When district boundaries for the House of Representatives are redrawn every ten years, it is local legislative leaders and party leaders who determine whether the Representative's district makes him or her more electable or less so. Members of the House, as a consequence, have to be sensitive to the opinions of local party leaders. The majority leader or minority leader in the House can do relatively little to help them. Members of the House, and even the Senate, may be more attuned to the interests of local political leaders than national ones, and it is probably appropriate that they pay some attention to the voters who elected them.

The parties have two basic selection processes for candidates. The one used most often is a direct **primary** in which candidates within each party run for their party's nomination. Variations of the primary are also used to select delegates to the national conventions that nominate the presidential candidates. The delegates that are chosen in this fashion are obligated to vote for their candidate for at least the first ballot (how long the obligation exists varies from state to state), unless their candidate withdraws from the race and releases them to vote for someone else. The second selection process is the **caucus system** in which party members meet at a precinct level to send delegates to the county meeting. At the county meeting, delegates are selected to go to a district level, and at the district level, delegates are selected for the state convention. At each level, the delegates nominate individuals for county offices, district offices, and the state-level offices.

Very few states use the caucus system to select candidates. Most rely on some form of primary election. More states use a caucus system to choose delegates to the national conventions. It is state rules and regulations that determine the system that is used. Many states require the major parties to use a direct primary. Other states have permissive legislation that lets the party decide whether to use a primary or caucus system, especially when choosing delegates to the national conventions. In states with permissive legislation, the Democrats may use a primary system for choosing delegates while the Republicans use a caucus system.

The caucus system tends to attract party regulars who are committed to their particular parties. Primaries also attract more committed party members, but a larger group of individuals is involved in the primary nomination process or in the selection of delegates. The nomination process, whether primary or caucus, does favor those more involved in the party, which does have implications for political recruitment. People involved in primaries and caucuses are typically either more conservative or more liberal than the typical voters. These voters are the "**party in the electorate**" for the major parties. This situation results in the Republicans tending to nominate candidates who are more conservative than the average Republican voter, while Democratic candidates are more liberal than the average Democratic voter. This situation is evident at the national level, as well. Just as party members are more liberal or conservative, delegates to the national conventions also tend to be more liberal or conservative than the general voting population or even the more involved party members.

Differences between party members and voters can have consequences in the voting booth. One consequence is that voters often have to choose between a Republican candidate who is too conservative for their tastes and a Democrat who is too liberal for their tastes. Another consequence of this nomination process is that individual voters engage in ticket-splitting—voting for Democrats for some offices and Republicans for others. While independents are the most likely voters to engage in such ticket-splitting, even people who normally might vote for candidates of one of the major parties will split their votes, as well—perhaps to balance too conservative Republicans with too liberal Democrats.

DID YOU KNOW?

New York has a Conservative Party and a Liberal Party in addition to the Democrats and Republicans. Sometimes candidates from these parties win, especially if they are recognized Democrats or Republicans who failed to win their party's nomination.

The relationship between parties and voters has also changed over time. At the beginning, the party system often relied on patronage, as party machine bosses offered jobs and other incentives for voter loyalty. The advent of a secret ballot reduced the control of parties and party leaders. In addition, over time, government jobs became merit based; government workers at all levels kept their jobs regardless of which party won an election. They no longer received their jobs as **patronage** appointments by presidents, governors, or other officials of their parties. The creation of government social services also weakened loyalty to parties since the parties used to help their voters in very tangible ways—with food, clothing, and other assistance. The advent of television campaigns has further weakened parties, as candidates with sufficient funds can mount expensive campaigns without having to rely on party workers to help mobilize voters.

Why Are Political Parties Important?

Political parties are the lifeblood of a democracy, and they are essential for a democratic system to flourish. Although some of the Founding Fathers feared political factions, these parties help ensure that the state does not gain unlimited authority to regulate every aspect of public and private life. The competition among parties, complete with the accompanying political education, prevents the accumulation of too much power in too few hands. There are, however, critics of the two-party system.

One major concern of critics is that a two-party system provides little choice for the electorate. Critics contend that parties will strive to keep the largest group of voters appeased with their political stances, keeping certain parties in power because they do not venture very far from the conventional ideas and practices of the political system for fear of losing important offices. This also means that there is less opportunity for political change, and the party system is so decentralized that it fails to translate campaign promises into policy because politicians do not have to vote with the party line. Of course, the fact that the parties must stay toward the middle ground in order to win elections suggests that the general wishes of the voters are being respected. Major changes in policy do not normally occur because the large moderate group of voters does not want major changes. True liberals and true conservatives are dissatisfied with the system because it is not liberal or conservative enough, but really, when you boil it down, they are dissatisfied because voters are not liberal (or conservative) enough for them.

Critics of the two-party system will often cite **rational choice** as the reason for the failures of party politics. The voters do not have the necessary choices placed before them to effectively choose a government that would follow distinct policies. These critics often cite and propose a new system based upon the responsible party platform, a situation in which parties must have clear policy platforms and offer distinct choices to voters. Members of each party must actively work to enact their party's platform. In addition, the system requires the electorate to be aware of the differences between the parties and vote based on party platforms. Of course, this proposed system seems ideal to the critics of the existing system, but it currently does not really appear to be the type of system that the voters want.

The American political party system as currently constituted is set up for a winner-take-all system, a system that rewards parties that are strong across the country and can concentrate votes. It awards the first-place winner victory regardless of the total number of votes received or the number of candidates. So as we see, the system favors the two current large parties, making it unlikely that the status quo will be challenged by a third party that has a new agenda. This is true in presidential elections, as the candidate who receives the most popular votes also receives all of the electoral votes regardless of how close the popular vote was. The same is true for congressional elections since individuals are elected from districts where the person with the most votes wins the seat. While an occasional third-party candidate or independent candidate may win a House or Senate seat or offices at the state level, the system clearly favors the two major parties. Given that the Democrats and Republicans benefit from the current system, they have very little incentive to change it.

Political Party Systems

Since the creation of the Constitution, there have been opposing sides on many of the key questions facing the country. The parties have had conflicting ideologies. While it took years for political parties as the driving force of our national identity to come to the fore of political consciousness, there have always been organizations for citizens who had divergent opinions about the course of government. These actions have given rise to parties that supported the decisions of the government and other parties that opposed both the existing parties and the prevailing decisions of the government. The Founding Fathers represented the full spectrum of views on the balance of power that needed to be achieved between centralized and decentralized governance. There were those in favor of a stronger national government as well as those who were opposed to it—resulting in the Constitution, a document that is full of compromises. So, what began as a Federalist and Anti-Federalist Party system has evolved into a Republican and Democratic Party System.

TEST TIP

Nothing will hurt your essay score more than failing to directly answer the free-response question. Be sure to clearly state your thesis at both the beginning and the end of your essay, to ensure that your writing adequately conveys that you have responded to the question asked.

The United States has frequently had a two-party system, although there have been significant third parties present in many periods of U.S. history. When George

Washington was elected, political parties had not yet appeared. The Federalists and Anti-Federalists were more ad hoc groups of, respectively, supporters and opponents of the Constitution. During Washington's two terms of office, the Federalist Party, led by Alexander Hamilton, was created in support of the idea of maintaining a strong national government. Hamilton, as Secretary of the Treasury, was instrumental in creating a national bank as part of his efforts to establish a strong national government. Thomas Jefferson took the lead in creating the **Democratic Republican Party**, which was in many ways the successor of the Anti-Federalists. This party was opposed to efforts at strengthening the national government and saw the states as the bulwark of democracy.

In the presidential election of 1796, John Adams, a Federalist, defeated Democratic Republican Thomas Jefferson. However, in the 1800 election, the Democratic Republicans triumphed, and Jefferson became president. The Democratic Republicans came to so dominate the national political scene that by 1820, James Monroe ran virtually unopposed for his second term. This unity under a one-party system did not last, and in the 1824 election, there were four Democratic Republican candidates vying for the presidency. John Quincy Adams won the election, and the **National Republican Party** formed around him while the Democrats formed around Andrew Jackson. Then, in 1828, the **Democratic Party** gained control of government, and the National Republicans faded from the scene.

The Democratic Party continued, and the **Whig Party** appeared as the major opposition. The Whigs were at times successful as a party, and on two occasions, a Whig candidate won the presidency (William Henry Harrison and Zachary Taylor). Unfortunately for the Whigs, both of their victors died in office and were succeeded by vice-presidents who lacked the stature and popularity of the presidents they replaced.

In the period before the Civil War, both the Whigs and the Democrats suffered from splits between the northern and southern branches on the issue of slavery. The Whigs did not recover from the internal dissension and disappeared. A new party arose once again, as the **Free-Soil Party** appeared as an anti-slavery party—setting the stage for the creation of the **Republican Party** that followed it. In addition, the American, or **Know Nothing Party,** appeared briefly as a powerful force. The Know Nothings were vehemently opposed to Catholicism and skeptical of immigrants. It was one of the first political movements that sought to preserve the country for what it saw as true Americans (those who had arrived before the current wave of immigrants). The Know Nothing party leaders attempted to use immigration and anti-Catholic issues as a way to push the slavery issue aside. However, the Know Nothings were also split between northern and southern wings and did not survive.

After the Civil War, the Republicans were dominant in the North while the Democratic Party was revived and became the major opposition party in the North and the South. From this period forward, these two parties have dominated the U.S. political system, although sometimes challenged by large third-party movements, such as the Populist Party. The **Populist Party** appeared in the late 1800s to represent small farmers and others who seemed to be poorly represented by the two major parties. The Populists gained control of some state governments, electing governors and Senators, and were powerful in other states. On the national level, the Populists fielded presidential candidates who carried states and gained electoral votes. Eventually, the Democratic Party changed some of its policies and attracted most of the Populists into the party.

> # DIDYOUKNOW?
>
> In 1872, Horace Greeley, a journalist known for his phrase, "Go West young man," was the joint presidential candidate of the Liberal Republicans and Democrats He ran against President Grant. He lost the election, and his 66 electoral votes were scattered among various candidates since he died three weeks after the election.

Between 1868 and 1932, the Democrats only won the presidency on four occasions. Grover Cleveland won two very close elections in addition to losing a close election in between his two terms of office. In 1912, the Democrats benefitted from a split in the Republican Party. The regular Republicans nominated William Howard Taft for a second term while the dissident Republicans and some Democrats formed the Progressive Party (commonly called the **Bull Moose Party**) that nominated dissident Republican Theodore Roosevelt. The Democrats nominated Woodrow Wilson. The race was basically between Wilson and Roosevelt. The Republicans split their votes, and Wilson became president. He was popular enough to win reelection in 1916 without any split in the Republican Party. After his two terms, the Republicans maintained control of the presidency. The Democratic Party remained the major opposition, although the **Progressive Party** in this period contested with the Republicans and the Democrats. The Progressives were located between the two major parties in terms of ideology. They were influential in a number of states but eventually faded from the scene, being absorbed by the local Republican Party in some states and the local Democratic Party in other states.

The Democrats surged into power after the Great Depression. From 1932–1964, the Democratic Party was the dominant party, controlling the political agenda and creating federal programs to offset the economic damage of the Great Depression. This period of dominance began with the election of Franklin Roosevelt as president. Roosevelt instituted the **New Deal**, an extension of the **Square Deal**, to promote economic recovery.

(The New Deal would later serve as the inspiration for Kennedy's New Frontier and the **Great Society** and **War on Poverty** programs of his successor, Lyndon B. Johnson.) The only breakthrough for the Republicans during this period of Democratic dominance came when they nominated Dwight Eisenhower for the presidency in the 1952 election. His personal popularity carried him into office, and the Republicans even gained control of the House of Representatives from 1952–1954.

In 1968, the national political system became more competitive between the two major parties as traditional regional party allegiances shifted. After 1968, the Southern states realigned and switched party affiliation from the Democrats to the Republicans; consequently, the South became a stronghold of the Republican Party. President Nixon had been able to capture the southern vote, which had previously been solidly Democratic. In fact, Nixon systematically formulated a southern strategy to persuade Southerners to vote Republican as a means to protect themselves from desegregation and lawlessness that had appeared with anti-war protests in earlier years and racially-motivated riots in major cities. Nixon's election also began the period of divided government with one party controlling Congress and another in the White House, which is still the norm today.

The trend in divided government has led many political scientists to believe that the party system has dealigned rather than realigned. Party *dealignment* means that people are gradually moving away from both major parties. At times third parties or minor political parties occasionally rise to challenge the two major parties. They rarely gain enough support to win, but third-party candidates do force particular issues onto the political agenda and allow Americans to express their discontent with the two major parties. It is worth noting that while third parties have appealed to the voters, often because they have a particularly popular candidate, no third party has had the staying power that the Populists or Progressive parties had in the past. Some third parties, at times, have been somewhat more effective on the state level where they have been successful in either electing candidates or swaying enough voters to change the outcome of particular elections.

Third parties tend to fall into one of three categories: ideological, one-issue, or economic protest. The ideological parties are the ones that feel that the major parties are not conservative enough or liberal enough. The Populist Party in the past would fall into this category, and the various socialist parties in existence clearly feel that the Democratic Party is not liberal enough. One-issue parties focus on a single issue such as the environment in the case of the **Green Party**. For a period there was an anti-abortion party that appeared in New York State that focused on that single issue. Other parties form to protest the nation's economic situation. The Tea Party as a movement clearly falls into this category, although it also has an ideological component.

Important Political Parties at the National Level	
Party	**Time Active at the National Level (Presidential Years)**
Major Parties	
Federalist	1788–1816
Democratic Republicans	1792–1828
National Republicans (split in Democratic Republicans)	1818–1836
Democratic (split in Democratic Republicans)	1832–present
Whig	1836–1860
Republican	1856–present
Minor Parties	
Anti-Mason	1832–1836
Liberty	1832–1842
Free Soil	1848–1856
American (Know Nothing)	1852–1856
Constitutional Union	1856–1860
Southern Democrats	1856–1860
Prohibition	1868–present
Liberal Republican	1868–1872
Greenback	1872–1884
Socialist Labor	1884–1976
Populist	1888–1908
National Democratic	1892–1896
Socialist	1896–1956, 1972–1996

(continued)

Important Political Parties at the National Level *(continued)*	
Bull Moose/Progressive	1908–1912
La Follette Progressive	1920–1924
Communist	1924–1940, 1964–1984
Union	1932–1936
States' Rights Democratic	1944–1948
Henry Wallace Progressive	1944–1948
Socialist Workers	1948–present
George Wallace/American Independent	1964–1980, 1984–1988
Libertarian	1968–present
Citizens	1980–1988
National Unity	1980–1984
New Alliance	1988–1996
Ross Perot/Reform	1992–2004
Natural Law	1992–2000
Constitution	1992–present
Green	1996–present

National Conventions

Party national conventions take place every four years. The main task of national conventions used to be to select the presidential and vice-presidential candidates for the party. In the past, conventions often performed the actual selection process, but more recently the winner has been known before the convention meets because the results of delegate selection in primaries and caucuses are known. By tradition, the presidential nominee now chooses a running mate. In some cases, the chosen running mate is known before the convention, and in other cases the choice is announced at the convention, which then ratifies the ticket.

The national conventions also write the official party platform. Different parts of the platform are important to different party members, and major disagreements can arise. The platform disagreements can also reflect the fact that delegates to the national conventions are likely to be more committed to the liberal or conservative ideologies of their party than the average supporter of their party. Consequently, the delegates take the platform statements very seriously. They are among the more conservative Republicans and more liberal Democrats around, and thus hope to tie their candidates to the platform and its more extreme views. As a consequence, the platform may appear to be somewhat extreme to many voters. The outcome of the platform debates is one part of the convention that is not known in advance. The party's presidential candidate will attempt to influence the platform to reflect his or her views since the platform can become an issue during the general election campaign. The candidate can emphasize some parts of the platform over other parts. The platform may also at times reflect the impact of a third party because one of the major parties may attempt to attract the votes of third-party supporters by incorporating some of the third party's key demands.

Election Laws

The details of elections laws are left to the individual states. As noted, the states can pass legislation that requires primaries or pass permissive legislation that gives the parties some options. There are variations among the details for primaries; this situation leads individual political parties within states organizing themselves to win the specific type of primary that is used. A closed primary is one in which only registered party members can vote. An open primary is one in which on election day, each individual voter decides which party primary he or she prefers to vote in. Louisiana has an even more open system. All candidates for an office—whether Democratic, Republican, or third party—run on the same ballot. If one receives a majority in the primary, he or she is elected. If no one receives a majority, then the two candidates with the most votes are placed on the ballot on Election Day.

The states also deal with details such as the legal requirements that parties must meet (for example, the process of funding for primaries) and other details of the election process. States can impose reasonable limitations on campaigning activities in voting areas. Most states, for example, prohibit active campaigning inside of polling areas. The states also determine the hours that the polls will remain open. Generally, polls will open at 6 a.m., but in some states they close as early as 6 p.m., while they are open until 9 p.m. or 10 p.m. in other states. Earlier closings result in somewhat lower turnout, which can affect the outcome of the elections. In addition, states provide systems for absentee voting or early voting. The details for elections can obviously vary greatly from state to state. Oregon is currently unique among the states because it has gone to a complete absentee voting system. Everyone who cares to vote does so via the absentee route.

TEST TIP

Be sure to include transition words and phrases in your essays. Words such as *then*, *next*, *because*, *since*, *in contrast*, and as a *result* help guide scorers through your argument and make your ideas clearer to the reader.

Interest Groups

Voter records have indicated that voters have become less active over the past few decades. While the 2008 election saw an increase in voter turnout, for many groups this increase was still down from the peak voter turnout of the 1960s and 1970s. Although voting levels have been on the decline, there has been an increase in interest groups and **political action committees** (PACs) over this time. Political action committees are the political arm of existing organizations or groups that try to influence politics. The PACs frequently are responsible for disbursing campaign funds to friendly candidates or for funding public campaigns for referenda and other public votes. Interest groups have been on the rise for the last three decades, and as of today, there are more than 20,000 of these private organizations in Washington. Interest groups represent bodies of people with shared interests who lobby legislators on behalf of their objectives. In this sense, interest groups are a part of both our democracy and bureaucracy. As the bureaucracy is not viewed kindly, Americans tend to view interests groups with the same skepticism and anger at a general level. On the other hand, Americans place a great deal of value on the interest groups that they belong to or ones that they agree with.

During election campaigns, candidates often levy the charge that "special" interest groups fund their opponents. The adjective "special" is used to indicate that the groups supporting the opponent are uninterested in the general good and welfare and want to get special favors from the government. In point of fact, all interest groups are special interest groups. They seek government actions that provide more benefits for some segments of the population, usually the members of the interest groups. Even if particular interest groups are entirely altruistic and seek to help the poor, homeless animals, or those with medical problems, and even if the goals of such interest groups are in the national interest, they are still defined as special interest groups.

Theories of Interest Group Politics

There are a number of theories that explain the activities of interest groups. **Pluralist theory** argues that interest group activity brings representation to everyone in society as groups compete with and counterbalance one another. This competition aids democracy because the groups allow people to organize themselves to try to change policies. People can be more effective as part of a group rather than as isolated individuals. Because hundreds of interest groups must compete for influence, no one group will dominate the others or the political system, even though all groups are not equal in power because of the different levels of resources at their disposal. The competition from different groups involves **countervailing power**, where the groups balance each other out. The activities of the groups ultimately are important for government because the activities influence policies that are in place.

Elite theory takes a different view of how policies are approved by government. Elite theory suggests that the decisions of the elite in society are more important than the views of the mass population. Society is divided along class lines, and an upper-class elite will have disproportionate power in the political system, regardless of the formal governmental organization. Those who believe in an elite interest group theory believe that while there are many interest groups, only a select few have any real power. They also believe that the system will provide special rewards to only a handful of elites, and the majority of the population will get very little from the system. Elite theorists do not argue that the people always lose in competition with the elites since that would eventually lead to the overthrow of the elite; instead, they suggest that the benefits of the system are heavily weighted toward the elite.

Hyperpluralism theory, or interest group liberalism, provides another explanation as to why the political system may not provide benefits for major groups of people. According to this theory, interest groups are so numerous and have such varied competing interests that effective coalitions of groups are difficult to form, and, consequently, no bills can garner enough votes in Congress to pass. The end result is policy gridlock. While pluralism states that several groups with a common goal would influence a policy through planned and effective efforts, hyperpluralism starts from a similar perspective but comes to a different conclusion. Although people who believe in pluralism are optimistic, hyperpluralism is a pessimistic view that suggests that it is impossible for the government to pass policies. In other words, hyperpluralists think too many cooks spoil the broth. The theory suggests that policymakers try to please every group and end up with a policy that pleases no one and improves little or nothing. It is important to note that if indeed hyperpluralism does exist, the winners in the system are those who benefit from the status quo. Some of the **gridlock** can come from groups that seek to prevent changes, and their policy objectives, whether elite-driven or pluralist, can be met by inaction.

(Special) Interest Groups	
Types of Organized Interest Groups	

Economic Groups

Farm Groups

National Farm Bureau Federation	National Farmers Union
National Grange	National Cattlemen's Association

Business Groups

National Chamber of Commerce	Business Roundtable
National Federation of Independent Business	Committee on Economic Development
National Association of Manufacturers	American Petroleum Institute

Labor Groups

American Federation of Labor–Congress of Industrial Organizations (AFL–CIO)	American Federation of Teachers (AFT)
United Automobile Workers Union (UAW)	National Education Association (NEA)
American Federation of State and Municipal Employees (AFSME)	Teamsters Union

Professional Associations

American Medical Association	Association of Trial Lawyers of America
American Bar Association	National Association of Realtors

Non-Economic Groups

Religious Groups

Ethnic and National Origin	Environmentalists
Veterans	Animal rights groups
Women	Fraternal

Various Single Issue Interest Groups

National Rifle Association	National Right to Life Committee

Range of Interests Represented

A wide variety of interest groups operate in the United States. Interest groups can be loosely grouped into four main policy areas revolving around economic issues, environmental issues, equality issues, and consumer interests. There are also single-issue groups that may focus on an economic issue or consumer interest, but they can also focus on some issue that does not conveniently fall into one of these categories.

Economic interest groups are undoubtedly the largest category. These groups represent business, labor, and farmers. In some cases they are fighting against regulations and tax increases; in other cases they want tax advantages, subsidies, and contracts for work. There are also economic interest groups that represent individual sectors of activity such as the auto industry, Silicon Valley, or aircraft production. Organized labor is the second-largest group. Unions seek to enhance the working conditions for organized labor and the labor force in general. Due to the aging of the baby boomer generation, AARP (the American Association of Retired People) is the single largest interest group in terms of membership. The most common type of interest groups active in Washington are linked to businesses trying to ensure that policies remain profitable for them and ensure that any new policy work is favorable for them.

Environmental interest groups are the fastest-growing type of interest group, favoring wilderness protection, pollution control, and renewable energy alternatives. These groups are also active in opposing policies that would damage the environment. They are opposed to factory farming because of the environmental deterioration that often results because of cruelty to livestock. Such groups oppose oil drilling in wilderness areas or unregulated drilling offshore. These groups are also concerned about endangered species in the United States.

Equality interest groups stem from social concerns of the people. These concerns typically revolve around civil rights, women's rights, and social welfare groups' concerns. These groups seek greater equality for black Americans, women, Hispanics, gays and lesbians, and other groups that have faced discrimination and other disadvantages in U.S. society. These groups can be litigious at times, especially if there is any perceived bias in the treatment in jobs, housing, and education that are available to members of the group.

Consumers' interests revolve around the safety of products that are used by all people. These interests look to create policy that will benefit the entire population. Their activities can be wide-ranging. Safety issues can involve automobiles with accelerators that stick, unsafe medications, food additives, and misrepresentation by mortgage companies in lending practices. Improvement in these areas could benefit the bulk of the population of the United States, but there will always be some individuals or groups, however small, that do not benefit from the efforts of this type of interest group. If safety concerns cause a factory to shut down, the people who lose their job may not benefit if they cannot find other employment.

Single-issue groups focus on one issue or a closely related set of issues. The National Rifle Association is dedicated to limiting any restrictions on the personal ownership of firearms. It becomes active any time gun-control issues come before Congress or state legislatures. The NRA has been quite effective in preventing the passage of legislation that it opposes. There are some elected officials who will not even raise the issue of gun control because of the NRA.

Activities of Interest Groups

Interest groups and the associated PACs will affect policy only to the extent that their activities provide elected officials with information and resources relevant to the official's prospects for reelection. These groups will support the status quo as long as their specific agenda items are being satisfied. Interest groups are often criticized for perpetuating a policymaking system heavily influenced by the ability to raise and donate money to candidates for legislative and executive office. The more money an interest group has, the more it is able to influence policy. It is important to note, however, that money is not the only way in which interest groups can influence policy. It is also important to note that interest groups also raise new issues for the political agenda. Interest groups, in fact, are a key source of ideas for the political agenda. While the items put forward for the political agenda may be self-serving for their members, they can also contribute to implementing good ideas and creating good policies.

There are many ways that interest groups attempt to shape political policies. These methods include lobbying, electioneering, litigating, and mobilization of public opinion. They normally have deep pockets and loyal constituents, which make them valuable allies for politicians.

Lobbying is a key activity of interest groups. Lobbying involves efforts to persuade elected politicians or bureaucrats to support the position of the interest group. Some groups rely on members to lobby with politicians. Others rely on professional lobbyists to attempt to persuade lawmakers to act on behalf of their group and the politician's constituents. The more a politician and lobbyist work together, the greater the influence the lobbyist has with that specific politician. Lobbyists serve as part of the bureaucracy and act as policy experts in their interest area. They also act as consultants on how to approach policy issues and debates, and mobilize support for previously loyal politicians during reelection. The information that lobbyists provide has to be factual, even if it is designed to present a particular viewpoint. Lobbyists do everything they can to maintain long-term relationships with politicians.

Interest groups also are involved in **electioneering**. Interest groups can endorse a candidate who supports their objectives and can work to get that candidate elected. The groups encourage their members and the public to vote for their candidate and use their considerable resources to help finance the candidate's campaign through PACs and other forms of support.

Interest groups also engage in litigation, using lawsuits to change policies that have already gone through the legislative process. Even the threat of a lawsuit may be enough to influence policymaking. Groups can file *amicus curiae* (friend of the court) briefs to state their side in a court case and assess the consequences of the decisions the court might make. Lawsuits can be used against companies, individuals, and other private-sector groups that are violating rules or regulations or are otherwise engaged in behavior that might be considered questionable. Interest groups have also sued the national or state governments to force them to enforce laws that have been passed or to challenge the way in which regulations have been interpreted or enforced by particular agencies.

What Interest Groups Do

Supply Credible information

Raise Public Support

Make Campaign Contributions

Employ former government officials who know how to lobby

Seize opportunities through protest

Supply the means for litigation

Lobbying

Electioneering

Interest groups can support their other activities by mobilizing public opinion. Interest groups try to influence the public because they know that politicians' careers depend on public opinion. Groups cultivate a positive image of themselves in the eyes of the public. They provide information to the public and, much like political parties, they perform an education function when they compete with each other. They can also use their considerable resources to give back to the community and spread a positive image of the role they play within the larger community.

Interest groups and associated PACs gained greater prominence with the passage of the Federal Election Campaign Act of 1971. With the passage of this act, PACs could legally donate more money than individuals could, and as a result, campaigns have focused upon PACs as a source of substantial sums of money. Thus, interest groups in general, and PACs in particular, have become increasingly influential in the recruitment and selection of candidates for political office. While they still do not directly place candidates in the primaries, the support of interest groups can be instrumental in gaining the nomination. The influence is perhaps less effective in general elections since both Democrats and Republicans will be supported by competing interest groups. Even though many critics contend that the PACs are controlling key political processes, others could contend that the PACs have balanced the influence political parties have enjoyed for decades.

TEST TIP

If you have a hard time understanding a question, try circling or underlining key words and ideas from the question stem. Then focus on defining or restating those parts in your own words to help you figure out the purpose of the question overall.

What Makes an Interest Group Successful?

Resources give interest groups power and influence. Many think that money is the only important resource for interest groups, but it is not the only one. The size of the group in terms of members or voters can be essential. It is important to distinguish between a potential group, which is all of the people who might be members of the group, and an actual group, which is all the people who actually join. In some cases, the number of people that interest groups might represent can be as important as the actual numbers. All other things being equal, in a competition between interest groups, a large interest group will defeat a small interest group if electioneering is a key activity. Smaller groups tend to be more effective when operating behind the scenes because organization is easier and participants are more focused on their cause. A member of a small group is more likely to be rewarded upon the group's success and is inclined to redouble his or her efforts to gain additional accolades from other members of the group.

Groups can also be more effective if the members feel intensely about issues. All other things being equal (such as equal numbers), a group with members committed to the issue will be more effective than one with members who are lukewarm. Commitment may mean that group members will volunteer to work for the campaigns of supportive politicians. Committed members will join demonstrations, launch e-mail campaigns, or undertake other actions to help further the objectives of the groups to which they belong. Single-issue groups often have such commitment on the part of their members, and commitment will increase the influence of the groups. Politicians respond to this type of interest group because members often vote according to a candidate's stand on the group's issue.

Interest groups may also command expertise or have access to knowledge. Environmental groups often have committed members who will organize and demonstrate, but they also can depend upon experts who provide information to legislative committees, bureaucratic agencies, or the public as well, by testifying as experts in court cases as to the damage that is being done to the environment. It is often thought that corporations can hire experts to present their side, but when groups get the expertise for free, they may be able to counterbalance the opposition. While expertise as a resource is difficult to quantify, it can be especially important in some contexts.

Money allows interest groups to maintain their organization and to pay lobbyists. Money is also available as contributions to politicians. Much PAC money tends to go to incumbents, so the financial contributions reinforce the incumbency advantage that is present in the system. Financial resources can also be used to mount publicity campaigns. All other things being equal, a richer group will be more influential than a poorer group, but other things are not always equal. Money does not always win. The tobacco companies spent huge amounts of money to prevent one of the first bans on smoking in public places in San Francisco. Yet an ad hoc group of committed activists won out in the public referendum on the issue. While candidates who get the most money often win elections, there are enough instances in which the largest spender loses to indicate that money does not necessarily buy an election.

Mass Media

The role of the media has evolved much like the government over the years. Alexander Hamilton, with his *New York Evening Post*, was not the first or last politician to create a newspaper to promote his own needs. There are endless tales of money-men, politicians, and newspapers that used conjecture and yellow journalism to achieve their goals.

The mass media includes newspapers, radio, television, and the Internet. They all have influence over public opinion. Politicians today have never been as visible or as able to reach so many constituents at one time. In the 21st century, any controversial action will be broadcast and re-broadcast on one or more of the many 24-hour news channels. For good or for ill, the media has the ability to sway public perception and help set the public agenda. American society has always used technology to help get items on the political agenda. Modern technology makes it very easy for citizens to begin to openly question what is in fact news and what is bias that reflects the political agenda of elites or other groups in society.

The media have undergone a series of transformations. The first important sources of information were party newspapers. Political parties created and controlled various newspapers that had small circulations, but the cost for the subscriptions was relatively high. These party papers were mostly shared amongst the political elites. A good example was the *New York Evening Post*, established, as we said, by Alexander Hamilton. Telegraphs gave daily newspapers greater access to news, and modern presses made mass readership and multiple editions of daily papers possible. The telegraph helped create the Associated Press in 1848. The press gained the reputation for its objective reporting and distribution of information. As the industrial boom created urban cities and larger readerships, daily newspapers grew to incorporate a general readership along with the elites. The newspapers' need to sell copies led to "**yellow journalism**," which was the creation of sensational stories without supporting facts to feed the gossip mills of the early twentieth century. A good example of yellow journalism was William Randolph Hearst's inciting, through misleading and exaggerated reporting, a war between the United States and Spain over Cuba.

In the latter part of the 1800s, the development of modern photography allowed for a new form of magazine, which provided visual images along with becoming an alternative source of news stories. As the middle class emerged with higher rates of literacy, distribution of magazines such as *McClure's* and *Atlantic Monthly* increased. These magazines were the opposite of sensationalist newspapers. Their reporters became known as muckrakers as they fully investigated their stories. A **muckraker** later came to mean a journalist whose intention was to expose corruption in society and especially in the political system. Radio came into existence in 1920 and was used most effectively by President Franklin Roosevelt to provide hope to the country after the Great Depression. Radio was a lifeline during World War II for the masses that needed to receive the news about the war. The influence of radio would rival print media until the large-scale adoption of television in the 1950s and 1960s.

Television shifted the focus from a politician's achievements or message and put more emphasis on appearance and performance than ever before. During the first televised presidential debate, John Kennedy used the new medium more effectively than Richard Nixon did. The Nixon-Kennedy debate was a tale of two debates. On the radio, listeners felt the seasoned Nixon clearly had won the debate. However, on television, Nixon came off as sluggish and nervous in comparison to Kennedy's charm and youthful handsomeness. Viewers of the televised debate felt Kennedy had won.

With the advent of cable television, viewers are able to select what information they do or do not want to see. This "narrowcasting" allows viewers to avoid content they deem unimportant, which also can limit the range of ideas they are exposed to. Viewers tend to find information that reinforces their preexisting attitudes. Also of relevance is the creation of party-aligned 24-hour news stations, which narrowcast information to feed the need of a particular political party. These stations are in many ways the modern equivalent of the newspapers that were affiliated with the early political parties.

The advent of the Internet and its growth has paved the way for the average person to become a reporter through blogging and other website authoring. The Internet allows for more easily accessible political information, but many people are not any more informed about politics than in previous generations. The greatest concern about citizen reporting is that current consumers of such information are unable to differentiate fact and real news from opinion.

Competition has become fierce between the different types of media: cable channels, print media, and electronic content over the Internet. This competition has also increased the pressure to break a story first, which has led to some concern about the way in which information is being gathered and disseminated. This competition has also eroded local news reporting. As a consequence, the national media has evolved and has taken on more active roles in disseminating news.

Development of Media Politics

Politics and the media have evolved, with both using the other to achieve its goals. At times, politicians have used the media to promote their own individual agendas, including positioning themselves to run for higher office. There have been times when the media have promoted their own agenda. The media are, of course, in a good position to inform the public about threats to freedom of the press. It is possible that the media might develop other political goals that could be advanced through newscasts or other programming.

Since 1996, the trend has been for a few corporations to consolidate ownership of most media outlets in the United States. These media empires include newspapers, as well as radio and television stations. These major corporations have the potential for significant control over information conveyed in the media. Traditionally, newspaper readers have tended to be politically informed, active citizens, but with the advent of television and the Internet, newspaper circulation has been on the decline, ceding greater influence to these new forms of media. Today, most Americans, especially the young, get their information from the broadcast media. The information they receive from these sources helps to form their opinions. This situation puts the corporations and the media in general in a position to shape public perception on national policy issues and the political agenda.

Newscasting is a business geared toward achieving high ratings. The higher the ratings, the higher the rate that networks can charge for advertising. This situation can have detrimental consequences for both the political agenda addressed in the news and for the political knowledge of Americans. Profits determine, or at least help to determine, what is reported as the news. The desire to enhance ratings and to increase profits can also lead to emphasizing sensational, unusual, or negative events. This type of news frequently receives more attention than more positive or everyday policymaking does and leads the public to believe that politics is scandalous and to distrust political leaders.

TEST TIP

It's okay to skip an item if you're unsure about it or would like to come back to it later, but be careful to also skip that line on your answer sheet so that you continue to fill in your answers on the correct line.

A major concern of analysts is the simplistic view that most broadcast media present. Often the content is based on information that is quick, provides little depth, and, at times, simplifies very complex issues to fit into specific time slots. The media also focuses the public's attention on politicians rather than on their policies and uses audio or visual clips (sound bites) of politicians to "create" a politician's persona. None of these approaches guarantees that the direct issues involved will be addressed or that the public will be aware of the complexities of those issues.

There have been three defining moments in American politics in the twentieth century that have influenced the evolution of the role that the media plays. The first was the use of the mass media by President Franklin Roosevelt in the aftermath of the Great Depression. He used press conferences and radio "Fireside Chats" to present his goals and opinions to the public and to convey a calm sense of purpose. He was a visionary in the way he used modern technology to his advantage.

Watergate and Vietnam changed the government's relationship with the press more than any other events. Watergate established investigative journalism as an important part of the media's role in the political system when the *Washington Post's* Bob Woodward and Carl Bernstein tracked down lead after lead to expose corruption in the Nixon White House. Watergate gave birth to the modern investigative journalist, who routinely attempts to expose and reveal political scandals. Investigative journalists generally remain skeptical of any information that modern politicians supply. There is an effort by both the journalists and the politicians, who attempt to set their agendas for their interactions, to not to appear as willing participants.

In general, there's no question that journalists and politicians need each other and that theirs is a symbiotic relationship. Clearly, the politician will be motivated to tell the best version of the story available—the one that makes him or her look good. Journalists trained in newsgathering, however, are looking to tell objectively the best version of the truth available. This often involves turning to multiple sources who have differing views on the events and issues of the day.

As was demonstrated in the revelations about the Watergate scandal, at certain key moments in the American experience, journalists have helped shape our history.

So it was with Edward R. Murrow, who in 1954 exposed the fear-mongering tactics of Senator Joseph McCarthy, who had gained a national sotplight with allegations of communist infiltration of U.S. government agencies, including the State Department, the Voice of America, and the U.S. Army. Murrow and his employer, CBS News, became targets of McCarthy, who, in his rebuttal to the March 4 *See It Now* report described Murrow as "the leader of the jackal pack." In the wake of the broadcast, public opinion shifted dramatically, with McCarthy's own words and pictures spelling his undoing.

Another seminal moment for the media came in 1968, when, after spending two weeks in Vietnam in the wake of the Communist uprising known as the Tet Offensive, CBS's Walter Cronkite delivered a rare broadcast commentary. He said the war was mired in stalemate and pointed to a negotiated peace settlement as the best way out. It was later reported that President Lyndon Johnson reacted by saying, "If I've lost Cronkite, I've lost middle America," which was a way of conveying that the president believed he'd lost a big swath of his political base. One month later, Johnson said he would not seek a second term.

Government and the Media

The media acts as a key link between the people and the government, and free-speech issues often arise. For example, at times, the government has attempted to pressure reporters to reveal their sources, but many times reporters keep their sources confidential. The journalist's right to protect his or her sources is not absolute. The government can imprison a reporter who is protecting a source of information if that information could influence or bear witness to a crime that was committed.

Because of the fine line between what is considered free speech and where that speech can be spoken, the federal government established the **Federal Communications Commission**. The FCC regulates interstate and international communications by radio, television, wire, satellite, and cable. It was established by the Communications Act of 1934 and operates as an independent regulatory agency. The FCC promotes competition, innovation, and investment in broadband services and facilities. It also is designed to ensure an appropriate competitive framework as the communications revolution continues to unfold. The FCC revises media regulations so that new technologies can flourish alongside diversity and localism. Or at least in theory.

In 1996, the Telecommunications Act was adopted to reduce unnecessary barriers in the communications industry. The act has allowed for cross-ownership and further allowed larger conglomerates to control larger numbers of media outlets. One media company is now allowed to own eight radio stations in large markets and unlimited national stations. This has led to the consolidation of ownership. To ensure the fairness during the political process and political campaigns, the FCC ensures that equal access is granted to political candidates, that commercial rates are not discounted for political allies, and any debates have to be open to all candidates.

Impact of Media on Politics

The media plays a gatekeeper role, helping to determine what subjects become national political issues, or in some cases, who becomes newsworthy. Coverage by the media can help project politicians onto the national scene. The media also provides information on possible candidates and their activities. The media, with the rise of investigative reporting, also investigates people in government, business, religion, sports, entertainment, and other fields of endeavor.

Since the writing of the Constitution, politics and the mass media have been intertwined. Traditionally, they have often worked together to communicate information to the public. Since Vietnam and Watergate, however, the media and politicians have often been in opposition, with members of the press seeking to expose scandals involving politicians or problems in the political system. The press has become more suspicious about the political motives of politicians and bureaucrats.

Today the media engages in investigative journalism, often with the intent of revealing political scandals. Mass media can have an enormous influence over public opinion and the agenda being set by the public. News organizations have some ability to select the issues that they will present and that they desire the public to become aware of. The media may indirectly be able to influence the political priories of the electorate. By **narrowcasting** for audience rating purposes or assigning importance to certain issues, the media can inundate the masses with their political agenda and help the electorate form an opinion on the subject being presented. The media has the ability to widely disseminate information and increase the attention that events and issues receive, or they can choose not to address certain things.

This process can have divergent effects. The intermingled relationship between PACs and conglomerates could have an effect on how the news reports pertinent information to the public. An example of this would be if ABC/Disney did not report about issues arising with the Disney Corporation, which had aligned itself with a PAC to influence new legislation for theme park rides while all other news organizations did extensive reporting.

Social Media and the Internet

The Internet has made political information easily accessible, but it also has given rise to new concerns. The electorate may be unable to distinguish fact from opinion (or even fiction) on some sites. While information is easily retrieved, it is often retrieved without any context. In recent years, the social media have connected protest movements to like groups around the world. A real concern here is if the masses are not well informed, it will be easier for them to be influenced by falsehoods and opinion-based reporting. As Mark Twain said, "a lie can travel halfway around the would while the truth is putting on its shoes."

Time for a quiz
- Review strategies in Chapter 2
- Take Quiz 3 at the REA Study Center
  (www.rea.com/studycenter)

Take Mini-Test 1
on Chapters 3–5
Go to the REA Study Center
(www.rea.com/studycenter)

Institutions of National Government: the Congress, the Presidency, the Bureaucracy, and the Federal Courts

The Three Branches of the Government: Legislative, Executive, and Judicial

As noted in Chapter 3, the Founding Fathers set up a relatively intricate division of powers among the three branches of government. The checks and balances system was designed to keep any one branch from becoming too powerful. The system was also designed to prevent the national government from becoming too powerful. For example, having the Senate elected by the state legislatures was in part designed to preserve the rights of the states in the new federal system.

Congress

After the failure of the Articles of Confederation and the unicameral congress, the framers of the Constitution set out to balance power between the states and the new federal government. They wanted to be sure that the national government was powerful enough to be effective but not so powerful that it could become tyrannical. To ensure this balance, the framers created a bicameral legislature through the Great Compromise. While the two-house legislature ensured that there would be balance between the large states and the small states, the arrangement also institutionalized differences in the legislature that were likely to make it less effective. Both houses must pass legislation in exactly the same form. If one house is opposed to a particular piece of legislation, then it can stop it. This need for approval by both chambers has meant that compromise is often essential, a fact that the Founding Fathers would likely regard with positive approval. This arrangement avoided placing too much power in the legislative branch. Further, each branch of the national government had its own defined roles and responsibilities.

The Founding Fathers expected that the division of power that they devised would leave Congress as the more dominant branch of the government. They expected Congress to

DID YOU KNOW?

Nebraska has a unicameral legislature with just one chamber.

respond to the people, but not very quickly, given the longer terms for Senators and the fact that they were selected by state legislatures. Some of the checks and balances in the system were clearly designed to protect the other two branches from Congress. Congress was initially the dominant branch for the first hundred years or so of the government, often overshadowing the presidency; John Quincy Adams did not feel it was a diminishment of his stature to serve in the House of Representatives after his term as president. Most of the nation's vexing political questions were decided by Congress. Today, this situation has changed, and leadership has shifted to the presidency and to some extent to the Courts.

TEST TIP

One-third to one-half of all AP questions revolve around the branches of government and their individual powers/functions as well as their creation and influence today.

Congress has a wide variety of duties. The most obvious, of course, is lawmaking, or legislating. Congress must pass the laws that govern the country. The legislative process is a more involved process than simply passing laws because Congress must also determine which laws should *not* be passed. The discussion of legislation often leads to the defeat of proposals, but that is part of the legislative process, as well. Congress also has oversight functions, which require it to look over programs to assess how well they are working. Congress also should monitor the activities of the president to make sure that the president's activities stay within the bounds of the Constitution and legislation. Congress is also involved in considering whether or not ideas should be discussed or debated in the legislature and even whether these ideas will become part of the national agenda as new programs administered by the government. Congress is in addition expected to represent the voters. Individual members of Congress have become quite adept at representing the voters in their district or state. Of course, as long as they do so effectively they increase their chances of reelection.

Organization of Congress

The basic requirements for serving in the House of Representative is that you must be 25 years old at the time you are sworn in (so you can actually be elected when you are only 24), a citizen of the United States for at least seven years, and a resident of the state you wish to represent. The Constitution does not actually require that members live in the district that they represent, but voters have come to expect that their representatives actually live within the district. There are 435 members of the House. The Constitution does not specify a minimum or maximum number of representatives other than specifying that each state have at least one. Every ten years, after the national census has been completed, the district lines are redrawn to reflect the current population distribution through a process called reapportionment. This can result in some states losing representation while others gain, but there will always remain 435 total representatives, as set by Public Law 62-5 on August 8, 1911, and in effect since 1913. During the redistricting process the controlling political party in particular states will attempt to draw the district lines to create the greatest political advantage and will try to include as many of the same party members or same political constituents in that general area. The districts within states have to be equal in population size so that every vote, in effect, counts the same. Besides the individual states, there are delegates in the House currently representing the District of Columbia, the Virgin Islands, Guam, American Samoa, and the Commonwealth of the Northern Mariana Islands. These delegates do not have voting rights but can otherwise participate in the activities of Congress. Members of the House serve two-year terms, and the entire chamber is up for reelection every two years, permitting at least the possibility of major changes in the makeup of the chamber.

The House has certain powers allocated to it. All tax legislation must start in the House. Disputes over taxes were central to the outbreak of the American Revolution, and the founders wanted such legislation to begin in the popularly elected branch of government. **Impeachment** proceedings must also originate in the chamber. If the House does not vote to remove someone from office and send the case to the Senate, no action can occur. Because of its size, the House has to have more formal rules than the Senate, and the House is generally more formal in how it operates.

Senators must be 30 years old when they are sworn in and a citizen of the United States for at least nine years. Like representatives, they must reside in the state in which they are elected. There are 100 senators today, reflecting the fact that each of the 50 states has two. The number of senators is obvi-

DIDYOUKNOW?

David (Davy) Crockett was a Representative from Tennessee for six years. He lost his seat after opposing President Jackson's Indiana Removal Act in 1832. After his defeat, he left Tennessee for the (then) Mexican province of Texas.

ously determined by the number of states admitted into the union. Given the smaller number of people in the chamber, the Senate operates more informally than the House of Representatives. Senators serve six-year terms, and the Founding Fathers felt that this longer term would permit them to slow down legislation that was too responsive to public opinion. In addition to the longer term, only one-third of the Senate is up for reelection every two years, meaning that there is limited possibility of major changes in just one election year—it would take at least two elections to bring about major changes in the makeup of the Senate. Senators were initially indirectly elected, but they are now directly elected by the people in all states.

The Senate has some special powers, just as the House does. It must approve treaties by a two-thirds vote of approval. All presidential nominations for cabinet-level positions, judges in the federal judiciary, and ambassadors serving in foreign countries must be approved by the Senate by a majority vote. The Senate also hears impeachment cases after proceedings are instituted by the House of Representatives. In its role as judge, the Senate can remove someone from office by a two-thirds majority vote. While tax legislation must originate in the House of Representatives, the Senate still must approve tax legislation, just as it must approve any other law. The Senate also has the principle of "unlimited debate," which is also called a **filibuster**, which suggests that individual members of the chamber can continuously debate a piece of legislation. No one senator can effectively use the technique, but a group of senators can be much more effective in tying up a potential piece of legislation. Actually, unlimited debate is a bit misleading since there is a way to limit debate. If 60 percent of the Senate (that is, 60 senators) votes to limit debate, there will then be a time limit imposed. Each senator then has only one more hour to debate the legislation before a vote can be taken. Of course, once debate is limited (this is called invoking **cloture**), most senators do not use their time. Once cloture is invoked, the passage of the legislation in question is all but inevitable.

There are some obvious differences between the two chambers of Congress. The workload for the average senator is heavier than for the average representative. Senators serve on two or three committees, while representatives only serve on one or, at the most, two committees. Senators represent entire states rather than one district. As a consequence, senators have to represent far more citizens than do representatives. As a result, a senator can be expected to deal with a greater variety of issues than a representative in most cases.

Congressional Leadership, 2012

Speaker of the House—John A. Boehner (R-OH)

House Majority Leader—Eric Cantor (R-VA)

House Minority Leader—Nancy Pelosi (D-CA)

President of the Senate—Joseph Biden (D-DE)

President pro tempore of the Senate—Dan Inouye (D-HI)

Senate Majority Leader—Harry Reid (D-NV)

Senate Minority Leader—Mitch McConnell (R-KY)

Parties are essential to the operation of Congress. The party that controls the most seats controls the leadership positions and has a majority membership on each of the committees where the initial work of Congress occurs. Currently (2011), the Republicans control the House of Representatives while the Democrats control the Senate. The Democrats are supported by two independents who caucus with the Democrats and vote with them on organizational issues.

At the beginning of each congressional term, the individual parties will meet in caucus to elect their respective party leaders. These include the Speaker of the House, the majority party leader, the minority party leader, and **party whips** respectively. The Speaker of the House is voted on by the House of Representatives, but the candidate of the majority party is assured of winning. The leaders of the majority party and the minority party are involved in all aspects of the legislative process. It is expected that they be strict advocates for their parties and their policy positions. The leader of the minority party is generally assumed to be the Speaker of the House in waiting should his or her party win control of the chamber in the next elections. It was no surprise that John Boehner became the Speaker of the House in 2011 after the Republicans won a majority of the seats in the 2010 election. Nancy Pelosi had previously been the minority leader for the Democrats before she became Speaker after the Democrats won a majority of the seats in the 2006 elections. She was the first woman to hold this position. The leader of the majority party is assumed to be next in line for election to head the House at some future point in time. The majority and minority whips are responsible for ensuring party discipline. They encourage party members to remain loyal to the party preferences when casting votes and to use their position to influence members when voting for new legislation. Whips also are expected to be able to "count votes" for proposed legislation and to ensure that their party members vote accordingly. In effect, their job is to "whip up the vote," as necessary. Party whips frequently move up into other positions when openings appear as the whip position is seen as a leadership test.

The Speaker of the House is the presiding officer of the chamber, although the actual job of presiding is often left to a junior member of the majority party since much of the position is ceremonial. Of course, if important decisions are to be made, the Speaker will personally preside. The Speaker also is responsible for assigning committee chairs and party positions. The majority leader and the party Steering Committee make committee assignments. By tradition, the minority leader and other leaders of the party are responsible for the committee assignments for their party, and the majority party does not interfere in that process. The Speaker is also responsible for scheduling legislation, but there are limits in the flexibility that the Speaker has. He or she does have some flexibility in terms of directing legislation to particular committees. The Speaker of the House is also the third person in line of succession to the presidency if the president should die or be incapacitated and there is no vice president. Since there is now a mechanism in place to fill a vacancy in the vice presidency, this aspect of the Speaker of the House position has become somewhat less important. It can be an awkward situation when the president and Speaker are from different parties, as was the case in 2011 with President Obama and Speaker of the House Boehner.

Senate leadership is somewhat different. There are two constitutionally mandated positions that are part of the Senate—the vice president and the president pro tempore (temporary). These positions are often ceremonial ones. The vice president has few powers as a presiding officer, and he can only vote to break ties. The president pro tempore presides in the absence of the vice president. Traditionally, the most senior member of the ranking majority party within the Senate fills this position. He frequently is not an active leader for his party. Even so, the occupant is next in line after the Speaker of the House to succeed the presidency should there be a vacancy.

The majority and minority leaders are the most influential leaders in the Senate. Their fellow party members elect them, and they can be replaced if they prove to be ineffective. The majority leader is very influential in terms of scheduling legislation for debate, but much of the scheduling is done in consultation with the minority leader. Since the Senate has the tradition of unlimited debate, the minority party and its leaders have significant influence in scheduling since a filibuster can block legislation, in many cases. At the very least, the minority party has the ability to slow down the legislative process. The leader of the minority party is often expected to be the spokesperson for his or her party and to provide the public and the media with the party's position on major legislation. He or she may also be called upon to rebut any presidential speech or address, although recently the parties have chosen a variety of spokespersons depending upon the issue addressed in the presidential speech.

There are also party whips in the Senate. Like the House party whips, their job is to ensure party loyalty as much as possible when it is time to vote on proposed legislation. Party whips try to guarantee that party members will be loyal when their votes are needed for legislation. Their influence on members of their own party may be limited, however; senators have longer terms and the next reelection campaign may be further in the future. It is also more difficult to pressure senators on account of the smaller size of the Senate. Every senator can potentially cast a deciding vote on a piece of legislation at some time in the future; thus, leaders of both the majority and minority parties have to be careful to not alienate members of their own parties. Out of necessity, they must plan for the future and act accordingly.

The most important **caucuses** that exist in Congress are the ones for the major parties. These meetings include all members of the majority party plus the rare independents who choose to meet with the majority or the minority. These meetings select leaders and can help decide policy stances on important issues. Since the major parties are not totally homogenous and reflect differing perspectives on major issues, determining a party stance within the caucus can often be a first step in determining the party position. There are other caucuses as well that represent different interests.

There are, for example, caucuses for women members, black members, agricultural interests, and more than a hundred others. Some of these groups are more active than others. These caucuses are usually bipartisan since they focus on a particular policy issue, and while the parties have differences, the members may have more in common with each other on particular issues than with their parties. A caucus of women members could have a different perspective on issues involving gender equality than other members of either party. Members from states facing water shortages could find much in common on pending legislation dealing with irrigation policies, independent of party.

TEST TIP

Remember that the multiple-choice section of the AP exam gives you 45 minutes to answer 60 questions. Plan to spend about 40 to 43 seconds on each question. Pacing yourself in this way will help ensure that you have enough time to comfortably respond to every item.

Committees and Subcommittees

Committees and subcommittees are an essential organizational fact of life for Congress. There are approximately 250 congressional committees and subcommittees, each charged with different functions, and each of these committees is made up of members of Congress. They are responsible for researching, assessing, and revising the thousands of bills that are introduced to Congress each year. They also conduct legislative oversight, which is the monitoring of federal agencies and their execution of the law. As the federal bureaucracy and government programs grew, the need for such legislative oversight also increased.

There are three types of committees in Congress. **Standing committees** are permanent committees present in each chamber. These committees are functional committees in that they handle specific policy areas, such as agriculture, finance, energy, and commerce. For the most part, the membership of these committees is proportional to the strength of the parties in the chambers. If the Republicans have 54 percent of the seats and the Democrats 46 percent of the seats, then the committee memberships reflect these percentages. The majority party chooses the committee chairs. Each standing committee is normally divided into subcommittees to better consider the legislation related to their subject area. Because they have legislative jurisdiction, standing committees consider bills and issues and recommend measures for consideration by their respective chambers. They also have oversight responsibility to monitor agencies, programs, and activities within their jurisdictions and in some cases in areas that cut across committee jurisdictions. The standing committees ensure that all legislation receives at least some consideration. There are far too many bills introduced into the House and the Senate for either chamber to consider the legislation. The committees are the workhorses of the chambers. The committees often eliminate proposals that have no chance of success or that duplicate another proposal. Standing committees inevitably have subcommittees. The committee may assign their subcommittees specific tasks such as the initial consideration of measures and oversight of laws and programs that are in the subcommittees' areas of expertise. The committee and subcommittees frequently hold hearings that are designed to discover facts or information relevant to pending legislation. Such hearings are also important for gathering information for the oversight functions of the committees. When there are concerns about wrongdoing somewhere in the government, the hearings can become investigations in which the people appearing before the committees or subcommittees are required to testify under oath and can suffer criminal penalties for lying under oath.

Standing Committees in Congress

Standing Committees in the Senate

Agriculture, Nutrition, and Forestry

Appropriations

Armed Services

Banking, Housing, and Urban Affairs

Budget

Commerce, Science, and Transportation

Energy and Natural Resources

Environment and Public Works

Finance

Foreign Relations

Health, Education, Labor, and Pensions

Homeland Security and Governmental Affairs

Judiciary

Rules and Administration

Small Business and Entrepreneurship

Veteran's Affairs

(continued)

Standing Committees in Congress (continued)

Standing Committees in the House

Agriculture

Appropriations

Armed Services

Budget

Education and Workforce

Energy and Commerce

Ethics

Financial Services

Foreign Affairs

Homeland Security

House Administration

Judiciary

Natural Resources

Oversight and Government Reform

Rules

Science, Space, and Technology

Small Business

Transportation and Infrastructure

Veteran's Affairs

Ways and Means

In addition to the standing committees mentioned in the box, both the House and the Senate have intelligence committees that are the equivalent of standing committees. These committees are designed to oversee the activities of the intelligence services of the U.S. government. They are small committees, and the members are chosen for their knowledge of intelligence activities and for their ability to be circumspect in what they divulge to the public or to other members of Congress. The committees of the House and the Senate often meet together with intelligence officials for briefings so that the officials do not have to repeat themselves. There are a number of other **joint committees** that handle administrative and other issues that Congress deals with. These actions require joint agreement between the two chambers in order for action to proceed. While these committees are often less prestigious than the standing committees (with the possible exception of the Intelligence Committees), they are essential for the successful operation of the government.

A third type of committee is the **select committee** (or special committee). Select committees are normally created by a resolution of the chamber that is seeking to establish the committee. These committees are established to handle specific issues that do not fit clearly within the existing structures of the standing committees or for special cases. Once the issues have been dealt with, the committees are disbanded, so they typically have a short life span. Perhaps the most important committee of this type was the Senate Select Committee on Watergate, which looked into the issues surrounding President Nixon's actions during the Watergate scandal. The Senate chose to establish a special committee with carefully selected membership to consider the issues. History shows that this particular committee proved to be up to the task.

There is another special committee that is sometimes used, especially in the House of Representatives. The House will convene as a **committee of the whole**, where the entire membership is considered part of the committee. This committee can operate more informally and requires fewer members to be present to operate. This procedure has allowed the House to monitor ongoing governmental operations, identify issues suitable for legislative review, gather and evaluate information, and recommend courses of action to their parent body.

Important Committees

The House Rules Committee is commonly known as "The Speaker's Committee" because it is the mechanism that the Speaker uses to maintain control of how legislation proceeds on the floor of the House. Until 1910, this committee was chaired by the Speaker. This committee reviews all bills submitted by all subsequent committees before they can be assigned time for debate on the floor. The "rule" that is assigned specifies the time allotted for debate. It also determines whether or not amendments are possible. A closed rule is one where no amendments are possible. An open rule permits amendments, although oftentimes an open rule will limit the number or type of amendments that will be allowed. The rule that is given has a major effect on the prospects for the legislation on the floor.

The House Ways and Means Committee is the chief tax-writing committee in the House of Representatives. This committee must approve all tax legislation, even that which has been considered by other committees. The Appropriations Committee deals with spending bills. Appropriations are the one type of legislation that goes to the floor of the House without the possibility of amendments. Many members of the House would hope to add pet projects to any spending bill, and there would be an endless list of potential amendments. Most of the detailed spending decisions are made in the committee and its subcommittees, providing the members with a great deal of influence.

The Rules Committee, Appropriations Committee, and the Ways and Means Committee are considered so important that they are exclusive committees in the House. Members that serve on these committees do not serve on other committees, which is a reflection of their importance. These committees rarely include any freshman members of the House. It usually requires years of service in the House before representatives can hope to gain membership on any one of these committees.

There are no exclusive committees in the Senate. There are far too few senators to staff all the standing committees if some of the senators were restricted to service on only one committee. The Finance Committee is considered one of the most important committees in the Senate and is equivalent to the House Ways and Means Committee, dealing with tax and revenue generation issues. The Senate also has an Appropriations Committee with duties that are similar to its House counterpart. The Foreign Relations Committee is the third committee that is considered quite important given the special duties that the Senate has in regard to foreign policy, including approval of treaties and appointments of ambassadors and key officials in the Department of State. While there are no exclusive committees in the Senate, it would be extremely rare for any senator to actually serve on more than one of these three committees.

Committee Service and Committee Chairs

Committee assignment can be very important for the members. Members of both the House and the Senate seek at least one committee assignment that will help them with the voters back home. If a congressperson is from a district or state with a large union population, he or she would attempt to get on the committee that deals with labor issues in his or her chamber so he or she can look after the interests of the union members who help to elect him or her. Members of committees can also demonstrate to the voters that they are in a position to look after the interests of their own district or state. When the Republicans and Democrats make committee assignments, they try to provide members with this advantage by giving each member at least one committee assignment. Members of Congress also try to attain a higher profile by getting onto an important committee such as the exclusive committees in the House or the three Senate committees. The higher the profile, the better it is for the member in terms of the publicity received. There is, of course, competition for the seats on the prestigious committees. Party leaders try to balance interests to support their members, but more senior members of the chambers have an edge in terms of getting choice assignments.

Committee chairs are quite important for the way in which committees operate. They have significant control over the agenda of the committee, and they can assign staff and support committee members who follow their lead or punish members who might disagree with them. They also have a great deal of influence over who can appear before the committee to provide information on pending legislation or to present proposals for new legislation. The chair is always the member of the majority party who has served the longest on the committee. The minority party member of the committee with the longest tenure on the committee is called the ranking member, and he or she leads the minority party in its discussions and assigns staff among the minority members. The **seniority** system was a formal rule once used to select chairs, but is no longer a requirement for selecting the chair, although it is still used as a tradition that is almost always honored. One advantage of this process is that it is automatic and avoids party infighting for leadership positions.

There are some important checks on the committee chairs. They must be approved by the party **caucuses**. While such approval has been present, a number of negative votes might indicate to committee chairs that they need to be less arbitrary in how they make decisions. There is always the possibility that a committee chair could be removed, but this has not happened since the 1980s. No senator or representative is allowed to chair more than one committee. If someone is the most senior member of two committees, he or she can choose which committee to chair, and the second most senior member of the majority party becomes chair of the second committee. The Republicans have recently decided to limit the time that members can serve as chairs of committees. This decision is a party decision rather than a formal rule.

The Makeup of Congress

The members of Congress do not reflect the U.S. population in all respects. The minimum age requirement means that the average age is higher than the age of the general population. White males dominate the membership, although the likelihood of a representative being a white male has dropped since 1950. There has been increased representation of both women and members of minority groups over time. In part, this change reflects changes in American society and the fact that in the southern states, black Americans have found it easier to vote. In terms of occupation, many members of Congress are lawyers, and others come from a business background. Given the total size of Congress, there is always some diversity in terms of the makeup of the membership. Members of Congress frequently serve multiple terms in the legislature. Prior to 1950, many legislators only served one term, but this situation has changed, and many now turn holding congressional office into a career, which has created limited turnover and also has raised concerns among the voters about the overall effectiveness of Congress, at times.

Party affiliations have been extremely important. Democrats have traditionally dominated Congress as they have controlled both houses (House and Senate) on many occasions and at least one house in others. In 1994, when the Republicans gained

DIDYOU**KNOW?**

In the 111th Congress (2009–2010), there were twenty-three Representatives and no Senators who had a Ph.D., and twenty-seven Representatives and one Senator who had only a high school diploma.

control of the House of Representatives, it was the first time in forty years that they had done so. They had previously gained control of the Senate a bit more frequently. From 2002 to 2006, the Republicans were in the rare position of controlling both chambers of Congress as well as the presidency. After the 2006 election, the Democrats won control of both chambers; however, they would lose control of the House of Representatives during the mid-term elections in 2010. Of course, changes in control of Congress should reflect changes in public opinion about the job that one party or the other is doing.

Getting Elected to Congress

Congressional elections are held every two years in November. Incumbent candidates, those already holding the office, win reelection approximately 90 percent of the time when they choose to run for reelection. Incumbency allows legislators (senators and representatives) to gain valuable experience and creates some stability in Congress. The high reelection rate and the stability of representation in the House is a cause of concern for some. The fact that reelection is almost automatic can mean that some members are protected from being forced to change their voting patterns to meet societal needs. The high reelection rate may also make it harder for constituents to create effective change. The same incumbency factor does not positively affect senators. They tend to have higher profiles, and as a result are more likely to be held accountable for public policy successes or failures. Further, making reelection of senators more difficult is the fact that their challengers are most likely going to be known within the political arena because senatorial races often draw former representatives or governors (quality candidates). While incumbency does not always help senators, it is worth noting that incumbents do enjoy narrow margins of victory. An example is the 2010 midterm elections, which saw a party shift within the House, but the same sentiment did not occur in the Senate, as the reigning party remained in power. Although incumbents get reelected with great regularity, there is significant turnover in Congress with time. In any given decade, about 50 percent of the members are new at the end of the decade due to retirements, defeats in elections, or individuals leaving Congress to run for some other office. The turnover in Congress is thus a gradual one rather than the more dramatic changes that some groups of voters desire.

Incumbents have a number of advantages when they seek reelection compared to challengers. Incumbents clearly benefit from their current position, as their congressional record allows them to demonstrate to their constituents that they can accomplish things in Congress. They can often publicize that they have been effective in getting federal money for local highways, parks, and other projects that benefit their districts or states. They can also demonstrate that they are effective in getting legislation passed that is beneficial to their district or states. With this record of service, incumbents are in a position to define their stance on influential issues and refine their public image. Challengers do not have a record that they can use, and they can have difficulty demonstrating how they would serve their state or district. Incumbents also use their challengers' lack of previous service as a cause for public concern. Also important to incumbents is their knowledge of the bureaucracy, which allows them to help their constituents navigate the bureaucratic red tape often encountered. Incumbents often have an advantage in attracting financial support when they seek reelection. Probably the biggest advantage they have when it comes to attracting funds is that they have already proven that they can win. Challengers often have to demonstrate that they might be able to win, which is a more difficult task.

Incumbents normally promote their positions to their constituents when running for reelection, and they also highlight that their challengers do not have such well-defined positions on the issues. Of course, it is possible that the incumbent's position does not sit well with the district or state, but individuals going against public opinion are not likely to last very long. Previous positions can be a liability if public opinion changes or the nature of the district is changing as people move out in or out of the area or the state.

Name recognition is extremely important to an incumbent. Sitting members of Congress have the opportunity to gain free publicity by virtue of their office. They also have a "**franking privilege**" which allows them to mail information to their voters for free (actually at government expense). This information supposedly is to inform the voters about what is going on in the nation's capital. What happens, of course, is that the mailings give incumbents a chance to promote themselves and increase their name recognition. Name recognition also helps in fundraising. The number of votes candidates receive is often proportional to the amount of money spent on their election advertising on television and the amount of public appearances they make. This requires large "war chests" to draw from, as the cost of purchasing airtime is quite expensive, but free airtime promoting new initiatives is just as good. This publicity is why incumbents try to be more publicly visible (for free) in the months before an election.

When voters are unsure of the candidates in certain races or are even less aware of the races themselves, they rely upon party labels when voting. This party identification can help incumbents within certain voting districts remain in office when their party dominates the district or state. Of course, party identification can assist relatively unknown candidates of the appropriate party as well, especially when an incumbent has retired and no candidate has name recognition or any other advantage.

While incumbency provides many advantages, defeating an incumbent is not impossible. At times districts are redrawn due to census data, changing a district's party makeup or redefining the socioeconomic makeup of the voting district. Sometimes incumbents run against other incumbents as would occur if a former governor were running for a Senate seat against the current incumbent. Also, any time there is a political scandal, the incumbent becomes susceptible to losing, as voters might consider the alternatives, especially if the scandal is egregious. Even so, incumbents who have been associated with scandals often manage to get reelected. Incumbents of the president's party can suffer if the president is unpopular with the general public. The unpopularity of President George W. Bush and his policies clearly hurt the Republicans in the 2006 elections, just as the unpopularity of President Obama led to the defeat of many Democratic incumbents during the midterm elections in 2010. Incumbency advantages are normally more pronounced in the House of Representatives. Senators have always been more susceptible to losing an election since they have a statewide voter base that makes it more difficult for them to appease everyone on key issues.

Voting in Congress

There are three common theories for how members of Congress vote on proposed legislation and how they try to affect government policies. One theory is that members will place more emphasis on representing the voters back home, even at the expense of party loyalty. Some issues are particularly important to voters in the member's home district or state, and reelection depends on the appropriate vote. It is difficult to imagine any member of Congress from Michigan voting against legislation that helps the auto industry or someone from an oil state voting to end subsidies to oil companies. This type of representational voting is probably more pronounced in an election year.

Representational voting would also include cases where individual members trade votes. They will vote for someone else's issue in return for support for their own issue. This is possible when the voters have no strong opinion on the legislation in question. Vote trading and mutual support is rather common in Congress. Vote trading in general came to be known as **logrolling**. If members cooperate, they can keep the log rolling and they all get legislation passed. When spending on "special" projects comes into play, the term that is frequently used is "**pork barrel**" legislation. More and more projects get added to the bills so that passage is easier. Such legislation does add to the costs of the final bills when they are passed. The addition of such projects frequently cuts across party lines, with both Democrats and Republicans getting their share of the projects. Members of the majority party fare somewhat better than members of the minority party, but both take advantage of such opportunities. Individual members sitting on committees often fare the best in terms of inserting special projects into pending legislation. (This is another reason why committee assignments can be so important.)

Legislators will vote along party lines when their constituents are not directly involved or party leaders have reached out to them for their support. This serves as a way for some legislators to garner support later on a matter that is important to their constituents. Party loyalty may help legislators attain positions on committees at a later time as well as raise their own profile. When the voters back home are not directly involved in an issue, legislators may vote on how they personally feel towards some legislation, which at times is in opposition the party position. The term "maverick" has begun to be used to describe members who cross party lines with some frequency when they vote. Of course, the voting behavior of such mavericks may be very reflective of the general views of the population in their district or state. It is unlikely that someone with very liberal attitudes would be elected from a conservative district or state. It is highly unlikely that the voting record of a maverick would dramatically contradict the attitudes of the voters.

Staff Support

Congressional members have a number of different staff members that assist them. Each staff member has varying responsibilities, such as researching legislation. In the twentieth century, congressional staffs grew, and while popular opinion generally indicates the public feels the staffs have grown too much, the staffs nonetheless perform many important tasks. They review legislation for the member and can research particular issues to help determine what the consequences of any legislation or program change could be. They are also instrumental in helping the member to reach out and respond to the concerns of voters from his or her district or state. Approximately one-third of a Congress member's staff works in the home district, and almost all have at least one full-time district office. Congressional committees also have their own staff, usually one for the majority side and one for the minority side. It is difficult, if not impossible, for members of Congress to keep up with the increased legislative work; therefore, they must rely heavily on their staffs.

The **Congressional Research Service** (CRS) is the public policy research arm of the United States Congress. As a legislative branch agency within the Library of Congress, CRS works exclusively and directly for members of Congress, their committees, and staffs on a confidential, nonpartisan basis. The CRS will research issues and provide information. This support function is particularly important in dealing with legislative proposals from the executive branch. Presidents and bureaucrats have access to a wide variety of information. The service does not recommend policy, but it does research facts and indicate the arguments for and against proposed policy. It also tracks the status of every major bill before Congress. The **Congressional Budget Office**

(CBO) also provides research support to Congress. The CBO provides economic data to Congress and advises Congress on the likely potential economic effects of different spending programs and associated costs. It also issues budget estimates on the prospects of deficits or surpluses and their likely size. The CBO tends to use conservative estimates. It appears to be a truly bipartisan agency since its estimates are almost always less optimistic than the estimates that presidents, whether Republican or Democrat, come up with.

Government Accountability Office (GAO) is another congressional agency. It is the audit, evaluation, and investigative arm of the United States Congress. It not only looks into cases of misspending or misallocation of funds but also evaluates programs to see how well they are working and what may be causing some of the problems that an agency or program is facing. It may undertake an investigation at the request of a committee, or it may use its own initiative to look into a program. As a consequence, the GAO may be in position to make recommendations on almost every aspect of government.

Types of Congressional Staff

1. Personal Staff—individuals who work for a member of Congress and are hired and fired by that member
2. Committee Staff—individuals who serve either party on congressional committees and are congressional employees
3. Leadership Staff—those who work for the Speaker, Majority and Minority Leaders, and Majority and Minority Whips in the House of Representatives, and the Majority and Minority Leaders and Assistant Majority and Minority Leaders (Whips) in the Senate
4. Institutional Staff—this includes majority or minority party floor staff and non-partisan individuals working for groups such as the Capitol Police
5. Support Agency Staff—non-partisan employees of the Congressional Research Service, Congressional Budget Office, and Government Accountability Office

The Congressional Process

Policy creation and the passage of legislation is a slow process for a variety of reasons. Final legislation can be entirely different from the idea initially presented. The slow process was originally intended to create a way to prevent hasty decisions from being enacted without due diligence being applied, especially since attitudes can change quickly on certain fiercely debated policy topics. These complicated steps were created to force bipartisan support and compromise to ensure that the proper action is being undertaken.

In order for any idea to become legislation, it has to go through a lengthy process. The bill has to gain a sponsor, as only members of Congress can submit proposed legislation. Once introduced into the House or Senate, the bill will go to the appropriate standing committee. The committee, including subcommittees, will consider the legislation. If the bill moves forward, it will go to the floor of the House or Senate for a vote. The bill will have to pass both chambers in exactly the same form. A **conference committee** may be necessary to deal with differences. If passed by both houses in the same form, the bill goes to the president for final approval as law. As the chart on "How a Bill Becomes a Law" demonstrates, this can be a long and complicated process. In point of fact, the chart could more accurately be labeled *how a bill does not become a law* since usually 90 percent of the bills proposed never make it though the process to become law (although parts of some proposals will no doubt have been included in successful legislation). The legislative process is so difficult that it is likely to be years before a new member of Congress is apt to be able to introduce a bill and see it all the way through the process.

How a Bill Becomes a Law	
Introduction	Only members of Congress can introduce legislation and in doing so become its sponsor. There are four basic types of legislation: bills, joint resolutions, concurrent resolutions, and simple resolutions.
Referral to the Committee	Bill must be referred to the correct standing committee based upon numerous procedural rules.
Committee Action	Once a bill is appropriately referred, it then must be reviewed and acted upon. If a bill is not acted upon, it officially is considered killed.
Subcommittee Review	Subcommittees review and study the bill while also opening the debate of the merits of the bill during official hearings. These hearings allow for interested parties to align with the bill and explain its importance or allow dissonance to be spoken and explain the adverse effects of the bill.
Mark-Up	The subcommittee after its review can amend the bill before allowing it to proceed to the larger committee. The subcommittee at this point can vote to terminate the bill after its review.

How a Bill Becomes a Law *(continued)*	
Committee Action to Report a Bill	Once returned from the subcommittee, the full committee can vote on the proposed legislation with subcommittee markups or can decide to further investigate the legislation and hold their own hearings and markups before voting on allowing this legislation to continue. This process is called "ordering a bill reported." The committee could also decide to terminate the bill.
Publication of a Written Report	Once the bill is reported, the chair of the committee asks for written reports on the legislation from all stakeholders. This comprehensive report identifies the scope of the legislation and how it affects current laws and programs. Dissenting viewpoints are also included in the written reports.
Scheduling Floor Action	After a bill is reported back to the chamber of origination, it is then placed in chronological order onto the schedules to be publicly debated and reviewed if and when the speaker and majority leader determine. In the House, the bill must also be sent to the Rules Committee where it will receive a rule that will govern its deliberation on the floor.
Debate	Members of both chambers are afforded appropriate time to debate and alter the legislation before voting unless the Rule attached to the bill indicates otherwise.
	The House has two readings of the legislation. After the first reading, the House allows for equal speaking time for both parties to debate the merits of the legislation. After the debate time has passed, a second reading is convened. At this time, legislators can offer amendments to the bill, debate, and vote. In some cases, amendments added during this phase make the legislation controversial "poison pill," and the bill is not voted out of the House.
	Senators are allowed to speak for an unlimited amount of time unless indicated otherwise by the unanimous consent agreement that accompanies the bill. Typically a senator is recognize to speak no more than twice in one day. A senator(s) is engaged in a filibuster when he or she exercises the right to unlimited debate, particularly as a means to stall the vote on a bill. When the filibuster has the support of a group of senators, it can prevent the passage of a bill, unless the filibuster is broken by others invoking cloture.
Voting	After the debate, the legislation is put to a vote with any additional amendments for the members present for voting on that day.
Referral to Other Chamber	When a bill is passed in only one chamber, it is referred to the other for its review. The conferring chamber can reject it, amend it, ignore it, or accept it.

(continued)

How a Bill Becomes a Law *(continued)*	
Conference Committee Action	If the other chamber makes minor alterations, the bill is sent back to the original chamber for approval of the changes. If there are large changes to the legislation, a conference committee is established to reconcile the difference between the House and Senate legislation. The conference committee managers prepare a report for both chambers if changes are needed during the reconciliation phase. If agreement is reached, a conference report is prepared describing the committee's recommendations. If agreement is reached on some areas, a new conference committee can be created to attempt to reach a final resolution. If the committees are unable to address the areas of concern, the bill will die. Both the House and the Senate must approve of the conference report before the legislation is allowed to continue.
Final Actions	After both the House and the Senate have approved the identical legislation, it is sent to the president. The president can sign the bill into law or decide to officially veto the bill. The president can also do nothing for ten days while Congress is in session, and the bill automatically becomes a law, or the president can "pocket veto" the bill by waiting ten days while Congress is *not* in session, and the bill automatically is terminated.
Overriding a Veto	As with any overriding of a veto in regards to laws, a vote is required with the requirement of a two-thirds majority.

Ethical and Effectiveness Concerns

The American people have had several historical concerns about Congress. One major concern was whether the members of Congress mirror public opinion or set public opinion. Later in this chapter, we will look at the judiciary's role in this issue. The Founding Fathers felt that politicians should transcend local politics and look to create a greater good. They believed compromise and debate would lead to fruitful discussion and resolution that would help the nation as a whole, not just certain sections of the nation. Another major concern has been the speed in enacting or altering any law. While it is an arduous process, it is one that allows for ample reflective time before making large-scale changes and one that the Framers wanted in the Constitution. Today the issue of special interests and the perceived power they have over elected officials worry many, as they see politicians being more in line with special interests to maintain power and reelection prospects.

Today, it seems that Congress is not performing very well, according to numerous public opinion polls. The general public has felt that the differing ideologies of the two parties have prevented action, especially since the Democrats control the Senate and the Republicans control the House. The parties' inability to agree on programs and solutions to economic problems has led to an all-time low approval rating. Traditionally, most have rationalized that lobbyists and interest groups do not hinder the political process, as they serve the people's wants and are comprised of the people who elect politicians. At some level, interest groups supply or furnish mechanisms that provide individuals with the opportunity to have their voices heard in government. With a divided and polarized Congress, however, the odds of any group creating a proposal that meets with success is very slim. Of course, it must be remembered that the failure to act can, in at least some circumstances, accurately reflect major divisions that exist within American society.

The President

The president of the United States is considered by many to be the most powerful individual in all of American politics. The presidency as a government institution has changed in various ways since the writing of the Constitution. At times the president has gained formal power, and at other times the president has lost formal power, albeit only to a limited extent. And still at other times, the president has lost favor with the public leading to changes in the office. When the Founding Fathers were developing the role of the president, they did not grant the office extensive powers, in part because the **Electoral College** was used to elect the president instead of a popular vote. It was expected that the president would be chosen from his peers. Popular vote, however, became important early on in the history of the country. While the Electoral College still exists, it merely serves to vote in accordance to the popular vote. The Electoral College is being modified in some states from a winner take all system to one that reflects the votes in individual districts. The Electoral System can result in a president winning the popular vote but losing the electoral vote, and therefore, the election. Even so, it is still important to understand that the people still do not directly elect the president but instead elect through proxy. As the United States has grown, so has the role and powers of the Office of the President. The office has evolved under a number of presidents to meet their needs or their perception of the needs required to defend the union.

Presidential Eligibility Requirements

The requirements for being president are not extensive. No person is eligible to be president, unless that person is a natural-born U.S. citizen, is at least thirty-five years old, and has been a resident within the United States for at least fourteen years. These eligibility requirements are specified in the U.S. Constitution, Article II, Section 1, Clause 5, which also provides a definition of who would be considered a natural born citizen at the time that the Constitution was ratified. The requirement that someone be a natural born citizen reflects the fear of some (at the time the Constitution was written) of there being a preference for a foreign-born member of a royal family popular with the people. The residency requirement also precludes someone who has lived abroad for most of his or her life from becoming president. Being a natural born citizen does not require that someone actually be born on U.S. soil. Being born in the United States or in one of its possessions does confer automatic citizenship. An individual is also a natural born citizen if one of his or her parents is a U.S. citizen, regardless of place of birth. Some observers raised questions about whether President Obama was actually born in Hawaii. His birth on U.S. soil was officially recorded by the State of Hawaii, but the argument actually "missed" the citizenship requirements because there never was any necessity that he had to be born on U.S. soil in order to be a natural-born citizen. There have been some suggestions that this requirement should be changed by constitutional amendment since it excludes prominent individuals who were born in other countries but have long been citizens of the United States and active in its political system.

The Electoral College

The Founding Fathers were suspicious of a strong executive. Their experience with the English system was one reason for this fear because the king and his advisers had a great deal of power. As a consequence, the President of the Continental Congress under the Articles of Confederation was given no real power. The experience with the Articles of Confederation convinced the Founding Fathers that they needed to avoid this other extreme of an executive who was far too weak. The Founding Fathers remained concerned about the president becoming too powerful, so the system of checks and balances was put into place to guard against this danger. The Electoral College was designed to provide one of these checks on the president.

As originally conceived, the president was to be chosen by the electors in the Electoral College. It was assumed that these electors would be prominent state leaders who would be knowledgeable about potential presidents. The electors would be able to avoid popular pressure to choose someone unsuitable for the office. The states had some control over the electors since they determined exactly how the electors were selected. Most were selected in some form of public vote, but in South Carolina, the state legislature chose the electors up until the Civil War. Each state had electors equal to its representation in Congress (two for the senators and one for each representative).

There was an additional check on the presidency with the Electoral College: the electors never meet in person; they cast their votes in their state capitals. At the time the Constitution was written, electors would be unlikely to know who the other electors were or how they would vote. There was the expectation that electors from the various states would be unlikely to focus their attention on just a few candidates. It was assumed that the electoral votes would be scattered among many different people, at least after the first election, when everyone expected George Washington to be victorious. This design of the Electoral College and the expectations about how it would work made it very likely that no one would ever receive a majority of the electoral votes, and the Constitution requires that any presidential candidate receive a majority of the electoral votes to win. There is no second vote in the Electoral College if no one receives a majority. The runoff procedure for selecting the president resides in the House of Representatives. If no candidate receives a majority, then the House elects the president. There is a twist to the election process. Each state has one vote, regardless of the number of representatives. The successful candidate has to win a majority of the states. This requirement treated each state as equal, which eased the concern of the smaller states. The Founding Fathers expected that the runoff procedure would frequently come into play. If the runoff procedure had come into play as anticipated, it would have meant that the legislative branch would have had a great deal of control over the president through the election process. As it turned out, the Electoral College did not work out as anticipated. By the time George Washington had finished his second term, political parties had come into being. The parties provided the necessary organization for the electors and have provided a means whereby the popular vote can be translated into a majority of the electors.

The Founding Fathers settled on a four-year term for the new office, which would require periodic renewal. George Washington did indeed easily win a majority of the electoral votes (in fact, he was twice elected unanimously). George Washington set the precedent of serving no more than two terms as president. This tradition

DIDYOUKNOW?

George Washington was unanimously elected President of the United States for two terms of office. When James Monroe ran for his second term, he swept every state, but one elector cast a vote for John Quincy Adams, thus preserving the distinction of unanimous selection for Washington.

was followed for many years, but it was not a formal rule. As a consequence, President Franklin Roosevelt would successfully run for election four times. His four elections led to the passage of the Twenty-second Amendment, which limited any candidate to two full terms or ten years maximum if the time in the office included less than half of the term for someone who succeeded to the office.

Presidential Powers: The Pardon

Article II of the Constitution gives the president a number of powers. The powers are in a variety of areas, some of which are more important for domestic concerns and others for foreign policy. The Constitution gives the president the power to grant pardons or clemency (reductions in sentences) for federal offenses. At the time the Constitution was written, the English monarch had the traditional power of the pardon. It seemed appropriate to place a similar power in the hands of the president. The power is solely in the hands of the president without any constitutional limits, although the president must be aware of the political implications of any pardon that would be controversial.

Presidential Powers: Military

The president serves as Commander-in-Chief of the armed forces of the United States. During the American Revolution, a committee of the Continental Congress attempted to serve as the de facto commander-in-chief on behalf of the larger legislature. This arrangement turned out not to be a particularly useful one. When the Constitution was created, this option seemed even less desirable since Congress would not be in session all of the time, and therefore would be unable to direct the military forces of the country. While the president is Commander-in-Chief, there were limits on the significance of the power in 1790. The Founding Fathers were suspicious of large standing armies; they saw them as a threat to liberty. So, they required that the appropriation of money for the military had to be done every two years—a constitutional requirement only for military spending. In this way, the size of the military could be kept small.

During the early days of the new nation, there was virtually no army. The American Legion has to be authorized specifically by Congress to deal with problems with the Indians in what is now Ohio (they refused to give up their land) because there was no other military force available. The Second Amendment guaranteed the states the right to maintain a militia. This amendment was a reflection of the fear of a standing army at the disposal of the *national* government. These local military forces reinforced federalism and provided a check on the president's ability to command military forces. The national government had to rely on these state militias as an army for much of the early history of the country. The War of 1812 and the Civil War were basically fought by such militias, although by the end of these conflicts (as opposed to the beginning), the armies were professional ones. The country did have naval forces, but navies by their nature are less threatening to a government than armies are. Naval commanders also have to operate with general instructions and a great deal of latitude in carrying out their missions given the limitations of transportation and communications in this era.

While the power to declare war belongs to Congress, presidents, in their capacity of commander-in-chief, can send troops into combat. Presidents have ordered military forces into combat many times throughout the history of the country. While many of these actions were not controversial, presidents have on occasion been able to use their power by threatening military action as a means of intimidating foreign countries. Presidents have actively supported military action to achieve foreign policy goals. President Monroe was apparently aware of Andrew Jackson's willingness to invade Spanish Florida in an attempt to deal with external support for Indian tribes and ultimately to suggest to Spain that it would be wise to sell Florida to the United States. President Polk helped to instigate the war with Mexico in 1846 when he ordered U.S. troops to a territory dispute between Mexico and the United States. Mexican troops were already present in the area, and the movement of American troops into what Mexico considered its own territory was quite likely to lead to an outbreak of fighting. This is exactly what occurred, and it provided the rationale for a declaration of war. This power of the president was important even before the United States had large military forces. Being commander-in-chief of the armed forces of a superpower provides the president with an immense amount of leverage in dealing with foreign countries and with using military force to achieve foreign policy goals. President Reagan launched air attacks on Libya, President George H. W. Bush liberated Kuwait, President Clinton launched air attacks against Yugoslavia over the situation in Kosovo, and a number of presidents have sent troops to Haiti to deal with unrest in that country.

A declaration of war under international law permits a country to undertake a variety of actions, but combat situations do not necessarily require a declaration of war. The United States fought wars in Korea, Indochina, Iraq (twice), and Afghanistan without a declaration of war. Congress usually has to support any long-term conflicts with grants. President Jefferson had no difficulty in gaining the necessary financial support for the conflicts with the Barbary Pirates. Congress passed the **War Powers Act** in the waning days of President Nixon's time in office in an effort to restrict the ability of a president to involve the United States in a long-term conflict without a declaration of war, but it has not been particularly effective. President George W. Bush involved the United States in combat in both Afghanistan and Iraq notwithstanding the War Powers Act. Of course, he did receive the necessary support from Congress for involvement in these conflicts.

Presidential Powers: Diplomacy

The United States gives the president a great deal of power in the area of foreign policy. The president (or his representative) accepts or rejects the credentials of foreign ambassadors sent to the United States. If the president refuses to receive the foreign ambassador, he has prevented the United States from opening diplomatic relations with the country. If the president accepts the credentials, there is not really anything Congress can do to prevent him from opening relations. The president also sends ambassadors abroad (subject to senatorial approval) and can recall ambassadors when he sees fit. These powers give the president a great deal of latitude in dealing with foreign countries, with very little oversight from Congress.

While the Senate ratifies treaties (with a two-thirds majority), it is the president or people chosen by him who negotiate the treaties. The Senate basically has the choice either to accept or reject what is presented to them. Often, the Senate will accept a less than perfect document if the overall treaty has value. Of course, the Senate cannot ratify treaties that are not presented to it, as in the case of executive agreements. Presidents have the power to negotiate **executive agreements**, which are agreements that are negotiated between the president and the head of government (prime minister, president, king, etc.) of another country. Unlike treaties, executive agreements are not subject to approval by the Senate. Executive agreements are much more common than treaties, but the vast majority of executive agreements are used to implement treaties, so they are therefore a logical extension of treaties. Even though most executive agreements are related to treaties that have been approved, they can be used to get around congressional oversight in the area of foreign policy. Of course, if arrangements that a president makes require funding, Congress will ultimately have to approve what is being done as it must provide the necessary financial support. Treaties ratified by the Senate supersede any existing law, whereas executive agreements do not, therefore, legislation might need to be passed for executive agreements to be fully implemented.

The power that the president was given in the Constitution was not excessive in the context of 1790. While early presidents had great discretion and power, the new United States was not a major actor in the world. U.S. foreign policy, of necessity, would be reactive in those days since the United States was a minor power on the world scene. Presidents could only initiate policies within a very limited range. Today, of course, the United States is a superpower, and the president has much greater potential to use the powers that the Constitution gives to him. In addition, foreign policy is much more important today than it was two centuries ago. The United States is part of the global community and highly involved in world affairs.

Presidential Powers: Administering Programs

The Constitution calls for the president to faithfully execute the laws of the land. The president is considered to be the head of the bureaucracy. Of course, the president cannot be expected to micromanage nearly 3 million civilian employees and hundreds of programs, even if he did not have any other duties. Other officials have to be concerned with the day-to-day direction of government programs. Many of these key officials are people nominated by the president, and they can reflect his views to at least some extent. Presidents can, however, affect the administration of programs in a number of ways. Most of these nominations are subject to approval of the Senate. The president can make recess appointments if Congress is not in session in order to staff positions in the government. In the early days of the Constitution, this power was more important. Today, with Congress virtually in constant session, the opportunity for recess appointments is greatly diminished. His appointees can change the orientation of government agencies by general or specific directions they give.

A president, for example, can influence programs directly or through his appointees. He could direct key appointees, for example, to have government agencies pay more attention to environmental concerns or to give less attention to such issues. Presidents can also issue **executive orders** that can influence government programs or affect society. Presidents in many cases in the past used executive orders to further equality for black Americans. President Truman desegregated the armed forces, and Presidents Eisenhower, Kennedy, Johnson, and Nixon followed up with changes in rules and procedures that they felt could help promote greater equality.

Presidents frequently appoint commissions to study situations and to make recommendations. Some **presidential commissions** carry great weight with their recommendations, either with politicians or with professional groups. Other commissions issue findings that go virtually unnoticed. Of course, a president can choose to give great weight to some recommendations and to publicize those findings. Actually, presidents (or their advisers) may be able to "stack" a particular commission with individuals whose views are already known. The likely conclusions or recommendations from the panel of experts are already known in advance for all practical purposes, but they can be used. Many commissions are designed for even-handed fact gathering, but even these commissions reflect the interest or the attention of a president who feels that some work is necessary in a particular area (as opposed to some other area).

Presidential Powers: Presidents and Congress

Though not a member of the legislative branch, presidents have a key role to play in the legislative process. Presidents do have some legislative roles specified in the Constitution. The president has the **veto** power when considering legislation passed by Congress. The president can return the legislation to Congress with an explanation as to why he is unwilling to accept it. Such vetoes are difficult to override given the substantial majorities that are required. The Founding Fathers gave the presidency the veto power as a means of defending the office against the dangers of an overbearing Congress. Presidents have used the veto power in efforts to protect the office from Congress, but not always successfully, such as when Congress overrode President Nixon's veto of the War Powers Act. If Congress has adjourned, however, a president can simply not sign the legislation and it is considered to be vetoed, since he cannot return it. This procedure used when Congress has adjourned is called a **pocket veto**.

The Constitution also requires that the president provide Congress with information on the state of the union, which is now known as the **State of the Union Address**. The president is also tasked with making recommendations for congressional actions. In 1921, Congress passed a bill requiring the president to prepare a budget annually to present to Congress, thereby increasing his legislative input in a very direct fashion; the budget is obviously a key document and statement of purpose and priorities for the government. In point of fact, the president has increasingly become the source of major pieces of legislation that are prepared in the executive branch and sponsored by a cooperative member of Congress.

In the United States government, executive privilege can provide the president with a means of resisting congressional actions or provide a base for bargaining. **Executive privilege** is the power claimed by the President of the United States and other members of the executive branch to resist certain subpoenas and other interventions by the legislative and judicial branches of government. The concept of executive privilege is not mentioned explicitly in the United States Constitution, but the Supreme Court of the United States ruled it to be an element of the separation of powers doctrine and/or derived from the supremacy of the executive branch in its own area of constitutional activity. The Supreme Court confirmed the legitimacy of this, but only to the extent of confirming that there is a qualified privilege. Presidents and other officials have been forced to turn over information to Congress. President Nixon was required to give the Senate select committee complete access to the Watergate tapes. The top officials of the Environmental Protection Agency appointed by President Reagan also had to turn over materials that eventually led to criminal charges being filed against them. President Bill Clinton even had to turn over to a special investigator some communications between him and lawyers working in his office. Neither the lawyer-client privilege nor executive privilege worked to keep these documents from public view.

Impoundment is the power of the president to withhold some or all of the funds appropriated by Congress from federal departments or agencies for particular programs. While many presidents used impoundment to postpone spending for projects that were not ready for additional funding, other presidents used impoundment to undercut programs they disagreed with. In response to President Nixon's impoundments in 1972, the **Budget Reform Act of 1974** was passed. The act requires presidents to notify Congress of funds they do not intend to spend. Congress must agree within forty-five days to delete the item.

TEST TIP

In May 2010, over one-quarter of a million students took the AP U.S. Government and Politics exam. Just over 51 percent of those students scored a 3 or above.

Presidents have some limited powers over Congress that go largely unused in current times. A president can call Congress into extraordinary session during times of emergencies. This power is much less relevant in a time when Congress is virtually in continuous session. The president also has the power to determine when Congress can adjourn in cases where the House and Senate cannot agree on a time of adjournment. Again, in modern times, with Congress in continuous session, adjournment is not an issue. In addition, the two chambers have not had significant disagreements on times of adjournment, and Congress as an institution has avoided giving the presidency such external control.

American elections often produce divided government because of the nature of the election process. A divided government is one in which different parties control different portions of the executive branch and the legislative branch. This situation can lead to periods of paralyzed legislation and inaction. Periods of unified government often do not yield any different results, however, because at times the two branches act in opposing ways, balancing the needs of the federal government and the needs of constituents. Further, the president has a national constituency while Congress is a conglomerate of local interests. In the 2008 election, voter dissatisfaction with the policies of a unified Republican Congress and presidency led to a Democratic landslide that united the legislature and the presidency under the control of the Democrats. In the 2010 midterm election, however, voters left Congress divided between the two parties. In 2010 and 2011, the president and Congress have been unable to resolve many issues, and while the public has perceived this as counterproductive, it is the essence of the separation of powers that the framers created. Americans increasingly look to the president for leadership and hold the president responsible for problems, successes, and failures in the nation.

Presidents rely heavily on how the public perceives them, and persuasion can be a formidable political tool for presidents. Presidents traditionally have three varied groups of people they need to persuade and influence—their fellow politicians, party activists, and the general public. The different target audiences require different approaches. The president needs the cooperation of the politicians with legislative initiatives. Party activists are important for nominating candidates and mobilizing support. And of course the general public provides the votes that will keep the president in office for a second term and increase the number of supporters in Congress.

Shortly after taking office, presidents try to transform their popularity within the country into congressional support for their new programs. Politicians running for reelection have used these early days in a presidency to attach themselves to any new initiatives in order to remain aligned with the positive feeling the public has toward the newly elected presidents In recent years, this has become more difficult to achieve because party members who have tried to ride the **presidential coattails** (members of Congress being elected based on the president's popularity) seem to have had less success because constituents have been less likely to support such politicians. In any event, Congress attempts to avoid the political risks of opposing a popular president by passing more of that president's legislative agenda. This cooperation, however, does not insulate Congress if those programs are ill conceived or poorly received by the public. The impact of presidential popularity on getting legislative proposals passed is difficult to measure. Some presidents have been hugely popular and successful at enacting new legislation while others have not been so successful. Ultimately, a president will not be judged favorably or negatively if able to get many, only a few, or no bills passed by Congress. What will determine their situation is the public perception of them. The key to enacting any legislation is the timing of proposing a bill. A president is generally most popular immediately after he is elected, the "honeymoon period" or the first 100 days in office. Most will decline in popularity as their term continues because policy takes time to enact and takes even longer before creating any significant change.

Some presidents have enjoyed prosperous periods because of unpopular legislation-enacted during a previous presidency. It is also possible that new presidents will suffer by comparison if they take office after a very popular president. Even popular presidents can suffer a loss of public support if they are faced with an economy facing difficulties, a political scandal, or involvement in an unpopular war. National emergencies, such as the attacks on September 11, 2001, can give the president at least a temporary spike in popularity stemming from what is know as the "**rally around the flag effect,**" which raises nationalism amongst citizens and translates into support for the government—allowing elected officials to act on behalf of a unified public for the good of the country.

Presidential Powers: Public Opinion

Public support for the president factors heavily on public approval rating. Legislators are likely to vote in favor of the initiatives of a president who has a high approval rating—a situation that grants the president leeway in pursuing policy goals presented during the election campaign. Legislators are more apt to vote along with the president if they are confident that those who elected the president will view all presidential allies as favorable candidates in future elections. If a president does not have public support and suffers a low approval rating, creating new policy will be difficult, as legislators will attempt to distance themselves from a particular president and vote along party lines or constituent ideologies.

Since the time when Franklin Roosevelt was so effective in mobilizing public support with his fireside chats and other activities, presidents have cultivated a favorable public image and approval rating to help achieve platform program goals and political party agendas. As stated previously, a favorable image or approval rating is vital when attempting to create support. In order to create a favorable approval rating, it is important for presidents to understand how it is created. Presidents have become quite adept at using the media to enhance their image. When presidents have the opportunity to announce positive news, they do so early in the day so as to have the announcement available for the evening news. They will announce bad news, or perhaps have it announced by the press secretary, late in the day or even on a Friday afternoon, which is a day on which fewer people watch the evening news. In effect, presidents can time announcements to maximize or minimize impact, including the impact on approval ratings.

Presidents have a unique advantage over any other politicians in that they can command media coverage of press conferences. While not all people in the nation will watch such conferences, many will, and the president has great control of what is said. When presidents (and other politicians) take questions at press conferences, they usually know which reporters are likely to ask friendly questions and which ones are likely to ask hostile questions. Needless to say, presidents prefer to field friendly questions—or at least less hostile questions—when given the choice. Presidents also have an opportunity to attempt to use the media to mold public opinion through private interviews granted to major media figures. They can be sure that the interviews will get major coverage on the network that does the interview and even some coverage on the other networks that report on the interview. Although it is always possible for a media outlet to take comments in the interview out of context, the negative consequence of such an action would be no more interviews. The media, as a consequence, present the material fairly because it is in their long-term interest to do so.

While presidents have an opportunity to use the media to present their point of view and to attempt to appeal to the public for support, the media in the United States has become selective in its interpretations of government actions and increasingly likely to present more liberal or more conservative points of view. Radio talk shows frequently contain large amounts of political information that has either a liberal or a conservative slant. For example, Fox News has become well known for following a conservative agenda in terms of the presentation of the news, especially with regard to the political commentators who appear on the network. Some TV shows provide more liberal commentary, such as John Stewart on Comedy Central's *The Daily Show*. Other networks have been charged with being too supportive of liberal views, either because they do not present the conservative view out of liberal bias or because they avoid bias altogether.

Media commentaries on presidential actions and public appeals can influence public opinion. Oftentimes, commentaries simply reinforce existing positions. Interestingly enough, the early newspapers in the United States were highly partisan in their viewpoints and were frequently identified with one or the other of the major parties in the United States. It was only much later that newspapers began to seek to be more neutral in their coverage and to separate news from commentary (with commentary being reserved for the editorial pages). The identification of particular radio programs, TV channels, and newspapers with one party or general ideological viewpoint (such as the generalization that conservatives listen to Rush Limbaugh, and liberals listen to John Stewart) is in some ways a return to past practice.

Presidential Programs

Presidential relationships with Congress and with the public often depend on their vision of what the government should accomplish while they are in office. The twentieth century has seen presidents run for the office with a platform that details what they would attempt to do if elected. These promises form the blueprint for presidential programs. The trend of presenting a coherent plan of action began with President Theodore Roosevelt's **Square Deal** and eventually evolved into Franklin Roosevelt's better-known **New Deal**. These plans were not just catchy slogans but contained reasonably coherent plans for future policies. As a result, modern presidents have begun to create programs that they can enact in the first hundred days of their election. Some presidents have created large-scale programs and reforms for all aspects of society and have run on those issues while others have concentrated on a few reforms or initiatives and have delivered on them. In any case, a president's success in enacting these programs has shown to be related to their chances of being successful at winning a second term as president.

Presidential Power over Time

While the presidency has come to be seen as the most powerful office in the national government, this was not always the case. Prior to the Civil War, most presidents did not have an opportunity to introduce policies and exert power. George Washington, of course, was quite important as the first occupant of the office who helped to set the broad outlines of what was possible or preferred for all future occupants. Thomas Jefferson used the military and diplomatic powers of the office to deal with the Barbary Pirates and to purchase Louisiana, but his greatest impacts on the early country perhaps came with his activities before he became president. Given his own views of the limited role that government should have, he did not implement any major domestic policy programs that he hoped to implement. All of the early presidents were also constrained by the limited military power and limited diplomatic influence of the United States. The relative weakness of the presidency and its earlier occupants is perhaps best seen by the fact that many presidents either did not seek to run for a second term or were not re-nominated by their own party. It is hard to envision a modern-day president who would not seek a second term. In fact, Lyndon Johnson is the only modern-day president who chose not to seek another term due to the unpopularity of the Vietnam conflict and his own declining popularity. Abraham Lincoln was a powerful president during the Civil War out of necessity. After the Civil War until almost 1900, the pattern reverted to weaker presidents who did not have major domestic agendas and a country that was less involved in world affairs.

Today, of course, the office is much more powerful. International affairs are much more important to the United States, and the Constitution has given the presidency a great deal of power in this area. The relative freedom in foreign policy evolved during a period where the country and the presidency were weak—circumstances that no longer exist—but the freedom of action continues. In domestic affairs, the complexity of issues often requires that the response to problems has many parts. It is essential that someone make a decision as to what a complex policy approach to a problem should look like. It is difficult for 535 members of Congress to formulate a complex plan; it is much easier for the president since he does indeed have the final word. As a consequence, the presidency has a much greater role to play in formulating legislation, and the complexity of programs that are passed provides opportunities for interpretation when programs are being implemented.

Impeachment

Impeachment is Congress's greatest control over what a president can do. Popular presidents are less vulnerable than unpopular presidents to the impeachment process because members of the House and the Senate are sensitive to public opinion, which has an effect on their reelection prospects. The Constitution sets forth the process for impeaching a president who has abused his powers or committed a "high crime or misdemeanor" worthy of removal from office. Presidents can be removed only if the House votes articles of impeachment and if two-thirds of the Senate votes to remove them from office. If the Senate hears impeachment charges, the Chief Justice of the Supreme Court presides. It was deemed inappropriate to have the vice president preside over such a hearing given his personal stake in the outcome.

TEST TIP

Before you begin writing your response to an essay question on the AP exam, create an outline of your thoughts. Your outline should include a thesis statement and the main points you wish to include in your essay. To help organize your essay, you may wish to divide up your ideas paragraph by paragraph or list them in the order in which you plan to discuss them.

Only two presidents have gone through the impeachment process, though neither was removed from office. President Andrew Johnson was tried but not convicted in 1868. The impeachment charges against him were clearly politically motivated. Evidence of crimes and misdemeanors was limited, at best. He was unpopular with radical Republicans in Congress at the time since he attempted to continue Lincoln's plans for a gentle reintegration of the South back into the Union. However, Johnson lacked Lincoln's stature and suffered from the disadvantage of being a southerner (from Tennessee), a former Democrat (who strongly supported the Union), and not being well-liked by the Republican congressmen. Although he was not removed from office, the vote was close to the necessary two-thirds majority. The failure to remove him from office, however, does speak well for the process, as enough senators were unwilling to remove him from office on trumped-up charges. President Bill Clinton was impeached by the House of Representatives even though not a single article of impeachment received even a majority vote in the Senate in 1999. Notwithstanding Clinton's questionable personal choices, his biggest problem was his general unpopularity with Republicans in Congress. President Richard Nixon is often thought of as the third president impeached, but he actually resigned as the impeachment process was gathering steam. The House was prepared to vote on articles of impeachment, and it was clear that there would be a majority vote for at least some of the articles of impeachment, if not all of them. It was less clear whether two-thirds of the Senate would have voted to remove him from office.

The Presidents: How They Got There

Previous service in offices such as governor, member of Congress, cabinet member, or vice president has helped many win the presidency. Previous political experience is obviously a plus for the nation's chief executive. Service in Congress can provide members with knowledge of the legislative process, and depending upon committee assignments, even some detailed knowledge about foreign affairs. Many presidents have also served terms as governors of their states. President Truman moved up from the vice presidency but had also served in the Senate. President Nixon had served in the House of Representatives and had previously been vice president. Gerald Ford had long served in the House of Representatives before becoming vice president. Barack Obama and John F. Kennedy served in the Senate, as had Lyndon Johnson before becoming vice president. More recently, individuals with experience as governors, such as Jimmy Carter, Ronald Reagan, George W. Bush, and Bill Clinton, have become president. George H. W. Bush had served just two years in the House of Representatives but had served as ambassador to China in addition to being the CIA director, among other posts, before becoming vice president.

A number of other presidents have used a military career as a starting point to begin a political career. In fact, voters in the United States have frequently had a preference for former generals. George Washington, James Madison, and James Monroe fought in the Revolutionary War. Both William Henry Harrison and Andrew Jackson fought in the War of 1812 and against the Indians. Zachary Taylor was a victorious general from the Mexican War. Ulysses S. Grant, Rutherford B. Hayes, and James A. Garfield served in the Civil War. Theodore Roosevelt enhanced his political prospects by service in the Spanish-American War. Dwight Eisenhower was the commander of the Allied forces in Europe during World War II. Some of these individuals also served in other political positions in addition to military service. Eisenhower was the last career military person to reach the presidency.

Vice Presidents and the Line of Succession

The congressional role of the vice president is relatively limited to presiding over the Senate and casting an occasional tie-breaking vote, which has happened 244 times to date. Vice President Cheney cast a large number of such votes when the Senate was evenly divided between Democrats and Republicans in 2000. His vote determined the chairs of all the Senate committees, and he was involved in other key votes. His presence was less necessary after 2002 when the Republicans gained a larger majority. The extent to which vice presidents participate in the White House is left up to individual presidents. Franklin Roosevelt was famous for ignoring his vice presidents. When Harry Truman was vice president, he did not even attend cabinet meetings. He also was not aware of the fact that the United States had developed an atomic bomb. To date, no vice president has redefined how the role operates within the federal government, although some, such as Vice President Cheney, have clearly been influential advisers. The key constitutional role of the vice president is to be ready to assume the presidency should something happen to the president.

The Constitution was incomplete in one sense with regard to the vice presidency: while the vice president moved up if the president died in office or was removed by impeachment, there was no provision for filling a vacancy in the vice presidency. This shortcoming did have consequences. Prior to 1963, eight presidents died in office (from illness or assassination) and their vice presidents became president. In all eight cases, the vice presidents were able to complete the term of office. In seven other cases, the vice

DIDYOU**KNOW?**

When John C. Calhoun was vice president he resigned from the office since he felt that he had too little influence with President Andrew Jackson.

president died in office, but the president served out his term. Andrew Jackson's vice president in his first term, John C. Calhoun, resigned from the vice presidency because his advice was being ignored, but Jackson finished the term without a vice president. Probably the closest the country came to having both offices vacant was when Chester A. Arthur was vice president. President Garfield had been assassinated early in his term. Arthur took over, but by the end of the term, he was suffering from poor health, and he did not survive very long after his return to private legal practice.

Since the Constitution was silent on vacancies in the vice presidency, it was up to Congress to establish an order of succession. The **Succession Act of 1886**, which followed upon earlier acts, established the line of succession to the powers and duties of the office of President of the United States in the event that neither a president nor vice president is able to discharge the powers and duties of the office. It is perhaps not surprising that the law was passed in the session of Congress after President Garfield's assassination and Arthur's move to the presidency. The current Presidential Succession Act includes amendments passed in 1947. At first, the Secretary of State was next in line for the presidency should the president and vice president die. This is understandable since many of the initial presidents had served in as Secretary of State before ascending to the position of presidency. Being Secretary of State was seen as a necessary requirement to being elected following the Washington and Adams presidencies as five of the next six presidents held that distinction and seven out of the first fifteen. The concern over this was that the president had the ability to pick his own successor. There was also concern because the Secretary of State was not an elected position, and there was no public input. The amendment in 1947 made the elected Speaker of the House and the president pro tempore next in line ahead of the secretary of state. The concern there is that many were given those roles and positions because of seniority, not ability to lead (more of an issue in the case the president pro tempore since the Speaker of the House had to demonstrate leadership abilities within his or her own party to achieve that position). The Speaker and president pro tempore at least, however, had the positive advantage of having been elected to public office.

Members of the cabinet are only in the line of succession if they meet the eligibility requirements. All of them are at least 35 years old, but some cabinet members have been naturalized citizens

DIDYOUKNOW?

William Henry Harrison caught pneumonia on inauguration day and died six weeks later, never really serving any time in office.

(Secretary of State Henry Kissinger, for example). When that is the case, the line of succession skips over them. The order of succession among the first cabinet members was based on perceptions of relative importance—hence the Secretary of State coming first. For departments that were established later in time, the position simply reflects the date of the establishment of the department. The Secretary of Homeland Security is last since it is the youngest cabinet level department, not because it is considered to be the least important cabinet level department.

Line of Succession	
Office	**Current Officeholder (2012)**
President of the United States	Barack Obama (D)
1 Vice President of the United States	Joe Biden (D)
2 Speaker of the House	John Boehner (R)
3 President pro tempore of the Senate	Daniel Inouye (D)
4 Secretary of State	Hillary Rodham Clinton (D)
5 Secretary of the Treasury	Timothy Geithner (I)
6 Secretary of Defense	Leon Panetta (D)
7 Attorney General	Eric Holder (D)
8 Secretary of the Interior	Ken Salazar (D)
9 Secretary of Agriculture	Tom Vilsack (D)
10 Secretary of Commerce	Gary Locke (D)
11 Secretary of Labor	Hilda Solis (D)
12 Secretary of Health and Human Services	Kathleen Sebelius (D)
13 Secretary of Housing and Urban Development	Shaun Donovan (D)
14 Secretary of Transportation	Ray LaHood (R)
15 Secretary of Energy	Steven Chu (D)
16 Secretary of Education	Arne Duncan (D)
17 Secretary of Veterans Affairs	Eric Shinseki[I]
18 Secretary of Homeland Security	Janet Napolitano (D)

The Twenty-fifth Amendment resolved lingering ambiguities about presidential and vice presidential succession. It specifies that in case of a vacancy in the vice presidency, the president will nominate a new vice president, subject to confirmation by a majority vote of the House of Representatives and a majority vote of the Senate. When President Nixon's vice president resigned, he nominated Gerald Ford to be his new vice president. When Ford became president following Richard Nixon's resignation, he nominated Nelson Rockefeller to be his vice president, and Rockefeller was approved by both houses of the Congress. Because of past concerns, the Twenty-fifth amendment definitively establishes the line of succession in case of presidential resignation, conviction during impeachment, or death. The amendment also defines what happens if the president is incapacitated, providing an opportunity for the vice president to temporarily fulfill the duties of the president so that there is someone available to make the necessary decisions.

The Executive Branch

The president's closest assistants have offices in the White House. Titles vary from administration to administration, but in general, the men and women who hold these offices oversee the political and policy interests of the president. They are not confirmed by the Senate and can be hired and fired at the president's will. There are three ways that presidents can organize their personal staff. Some elements are organized in a hierarchical fashion, with assistants reporting up a chain of authority to a chief of staff who thus controls access to the president. Other advisers and key assistants have regular access to the president in what can be considered a circular arrangement because there is no hierarchy. Finally, there are frequently ad hoc arrangements in which a president uses committees and informal groups of friends and advisers in dealing with issues or specific situations.

The cabinet is composed of the heads of the executive branch departments. There are currently fifteen major departments. Although not explicitly mentioned in the Constitution, every president has had a cabinet. The secretaries often become advocates for their departments, but they also serve as the president's person who is supposed to implement his policy preferences. At different times, the heads of other agencies, such as the chief of the Environmental Protection Agency, have been elevated to cabinet-level status. Some cabinet departments and secretaries are inevitably closer to the president than others because of a personal relationship with the president or because of the inherent importance of their office relative to other positions. Most of the people filling the cabinet level positions are nominated by the president but subject to confirmation by the Senate. These individuals nominated by the president also serve at his pleasure, meaning that he can request their resignations any time that he likes.

The bureaucrats that work for the federal government are part of cabinet level departments, other agencies, and regulatory commissions. All of these agencies are technically part of the executive branch, as are the employees that work with them. These agencies in question have a great deal of autonomy. The employees are protected against being fired for arbitrary reasons or for political reasons, which means that it is difficult to fire them. They work for the government as a career, and they will see presidents and secretaries come and go. The various agencies also develop close links with congressional committees and subcommittees that help protect them from negative presidential actions.

Independent regulatory commissions are also part of the bureaucracy in the executive branch. These multimember commissions or boards regulate some aspect of the economy. For example, the Securities and Exchange Commission oversees operation on Wall Street; the Federal Communications Commission deals with television and radio station and to a limited extent, the Internet; and the Nuclear Regulatory Commission provides for safety in the nuclear industry. While the members of the commissions are nominated by the president and subject to senatorial approval, once they are in office, they serve fixed terms rather than at the pleasure of the president. They can only be removed by the impeachment process. The fixed terms were designed to make the members of the commissions relatively immune to political pressure from either the presidency or Congress.

The basic job of the bureaucracy is to carry out the programs that are passed by Congress and administered by the president. It is up to the president and his appointees and congressional committees through oversight to make sure that the programs are operating as they should. The agencies and the programs frequently come under fire from the public for wasting money and undertaking silly projects, but it must be remembered that the elected politicians are charged with establishing these programs and making sure that they work well. In many cases, pork barrel considerations in the passage of the legislation are responsible for some of the wasteful spending that is present with bureaucratic programs. To some extent, the bureaucrats working in the various agencies are not responsible for problems that exist since they are simply carrying out instructions from the elected politicians. Of course, in other cases, where agencies have a great deal of discretion, the bureaucracy shares part of the blame for the problems that exist in the administration of programs.

The Executive Office of the President

President Franklin D. Roosevelt created the **Executive Office of the President** (EOP) in 1939 to provide the president with the support that he or she needs to govern effectively. This group of positions includes the White House Office. The EOP has responsibility for tasks ranging from communicating the president's message to the American people to promoting U.S. trade interests abroad. The heads of many of the elements of the EOP are subject to presidential nomination and must be approved by the Senate.

Principal Elements of the Executive Office of the President:
Council of Economic Advisers
Council on Environmental Quality
Executive Residence
National Security Staff
Office of Administration
Office of Management and Budget
Office of National Drug Control Policy
Office of Science and Technology Policy
Office of the United States Trade Representative
Office of the Vice President
White House Office

The **National Security Council's** major function has been to advise and assist the president on national security and foreign policy issues. The Council also serves as the president's principal arm for coordinating these policies among various government agencies. The **Council of Economic Advisors** provides advice on economic concerns and issues. The **Office of Management and Budget** manages various agencies to ensure that policies are implemented and reviews the budgetary implications of the implementation of these programs and legislation. It has had major responsibilities for helping the president prepare the budget that is submitted to Congress. It may suggest to departments and other agencies what levels of expenditures they should request, and it does review those requests. The White House Office includes important personal and political advisers. This office takes care of the president's political needs and manages the press and media contacts.

Additional Entities within the White House Office
Domestic Policy Council
Office of National AIDS Policy
Office of Faith-based and Neighborhood Partnerships
Office of Social Innovation and Civic Participation
National Security Advisor
National Economic Council
Office of Cabinet Affairs
Office of the Chief of Staff
Office of Communications
Office of the Press Secretary
Media Affairs
Research
Speechwriting
Office of Digital Strategy
Office of the First Lady
Office of the Social Secretary
Office of Legislative Affairs
Office of Management and Administration
White House Personnel
White House Operations

(continued)

Additional Entities within the White House Office *(continued)*
Telephone Office
Visitors Office
Oval Office Operations
Office of Presidential Personnel
Office of Public Engagement and Intergovernmental Affairs
Office of Public Engagement
Council on Women and Girls
Office of Intergovernmental Affairs
Office of Urban Affairs
Office of Scheduling and Advance
Office of the Staff Secretary
Presidential Correspondence
Executive Clerk
Records Management
Office of the White House Counsel

The Federal Judiciary

The Founding Fathers understood the need for an independent judiciary that would be able to make decisions that would not be influenced by politics in any direct fashion. Article III of the Constitution deals with the judicial branch. It is much shorter than the articles dealing with the legislative and executive branch. The Founding Fathers were less specific about the courts in part because they knew what a court and legal system were and in part because they were less concerned about the judiciary becoming the dominant part of the national government or dominating the states. The judiciary, in fact, has usually been considered the weakest branch of the three. Because the Constitution created a federal system, the judicial system is a dual one, with both national courts and state courts. While each court system is responsible for hearing certain types of cases, neither is completely independent of the other, and the two systems often interact.

How the Federal Courts Developed

The Founding Fathers of the Constitution did not initially give the judiciary much power, and they probably would not recognize the judiciary's more active role in policy-making that has developed over time. There was a discussion at the Constitutional Convention about what the judicial system should look like. One group wanted a fully developed national court system that would deal with issues arising out of national laws. A second group wanted one high court to deal with major issues or issues between the national government and the states but would depend upon the state court systems to try cases involving national laws. Since the two groups could not decide on which approach to take, they opted to let the new government make the decision. Therefore, Article III requires the creation of a Supreme Court and such lower courts as Congress may decide to establish.

The new Congress quickly made the decision to establish a full national court system when it passed the Judiciary Act of 1789. This act established thirteen district courts in main cities, served by one judge apiece, and three circuit courts to cover the other areas of the eastern, middle, and southern United States. The act also established the Supreme Court, with a Chief Justice and five Associate Justices, as the highest court of appeals. The creation of a national court system provided a safeguard against state courts refusing to effectively deal with national laws that the local state leaders disagreed with.

While Congress established the court system, the new judges had to decide cases that would come before them in the context of the Constitution and national laws. The new courts also relied on established legal precedents, which were drawn mainly from the British legal system and British **common law** that relied heavily on previous practice when the law was silent on an issue. Once **judicial review** was established as a judicial power, the courts were able to determine whether actions of the other branches of government or the states were in accord with the Constitution, providing the courts with significant interpretative power.

The idea of judicial review was discussed in Philadelphia at the Constitutional Convention. A number of states had mechanisms for reviewing governmental actions to determine whether they were in keeping with the state constitutions. Some of these methods involved judges, and others did not. No consensus developed among the delegates; consequently, they provided no direct mention of judicial review or how it would operate. Judicial review and the role of the courts were left to evolve over time. This development of the national judiciary and its role in the government can be conveniently grouped into three eras. The first era, lasting until the end of the Civil War, shaped the relationship between the states and the national government and helped to define judicial review. The second era dealt to a great extent with issues of economic regulation by the national government between 1865 and 1936. The third era beginning in 1936 has been characterized by decisions that have dealt with questions of political liberties.

The First Era: Defining the System

The first era for the judiciary was a formative one that helped to establish the framework for the new political system and for the role of the courts within that system. *Marbury v. Madison* is the critical case for the establishment of judicial review, but the first Chief Justice, John Jay, helped set the stage. Jay had served as President of the Continental Congress under the Articles of Confederation, but he was a supporter of the new Constitution (and a contributor to three of the Federalist Papers). There were a number of cases while he was Chief Justice that served as a preview for *Marbury v. Madison*. In one early case, the Supreme Court ruled that Georgia was subject to the jurisdiction of the Supreme Court, dealing with one key issue related to the division of power under federalism. In another situation, President Washington asked the Supreme Court for an **advisory opinion** on legislation being debated in Congress. He wanted to know whether the Court thought the legislation would be constitutional. It is instructive that the first president looked to the Court for advice on a question of constitutionality. Jay's response was to refuse to issue an advisory opinion on the grounds that it would be a violation of the idea of separation of powers for the judiciary to intervene in the legislative process at that stage. He suggested President Washington seek such an advisory opinion from the Attorney General. The refusal to issue the advisory opinion placed a limitation on the judiciary, but it also suggested that the president and Congress should not interfere with the normal activities of the judiciary except when directly permitted by the Constitution. In another case, Congress attempted to have veterans of the Continental Army petition the courts to determine whether they were qualified for pensions. The Supreme Court declined to hear the case because the law as written would permit the president or Congress to reverse a court decision and because the law violated the doctrine of separation of powers as defined by the Constitution. This decision was also a limitation on the judiciary since it remained uninvolved in the issue, but it again was a decision that emphasized the independence of the judiciary and suggested that the Supreme Court did indeed have the power to determine what would and what would not be constitutional.

Jay resigned from his position on the Supreme Court in order to serve as governor of New York. It was under John Marshall, the third Chief Justice, that the key case of *Marbury v. Madison*

DIDYOU**KNOW?**

John Marshall never attended law school. He learned the law as an apprentice.

was to be decided. The Marbury case was linked to the change in the presidency from John Adams and the Federalist Party to Thomas Jefferson and the Republican Party (or Democratic-Republican Party as it would be known, and then the Democratic Party). Adams remained in office until March of 1801 (the Twentieth Amendment changed the date of the inauguration of the president to January). During this time, he was busy filling offices in the national government using his powers of appointment. William Marbury received an appointment as a justice of the peace in the District of Colombia. Adams had filled out the paperwork for Marbury's appointment, but he had not had a chance to deliver it. The paperwork had not been delivered when Thomas Jefferson assumed the office of president, with James Madison as his Secretary of State. Jefferson accepted that Adams should appoint good Federalists while he was in office, but disagreed with the last minute appointments—the appointees were known as **midnight appointees** because Adams was busy doing paperwork up until his last hour in office. John Marshall, a recent appointee as Chief Justice, had not been able to deliver all the paperwork while he was still Secretary of State. Marshall assumed that the new Secretary of State would deliver the paperwork as a matter of routine. As a consequence of the disagreements over the appointment of these midnight judges, Jefferson and Madison refused to deliver the commission authorizing Marbury to take up his office. Marbury then sued to force Madison to give him the paperwork.

A position of justice of the peace in Washington, D.C. would not seem like an office worth a major lawsuit, and in many respects, it was not. The suit was an effort by some members of the Federalist Party to embarrass the new president and his administration. The new administration and its new majority in Congress proceeded to revise the laws in order to delay the hearing of the case. Marshall and his colleagues on the Court had been discussing the principle of judicial review and were looking for cases to build upon the earlier decisions of the Supreme Court. Marbury's suit, however, placed the Court and its new Chief Justice in an awkward position. If the Court accepted Jefferson and Madison's refusal to deliver the paperwork, the judiciary would indicate its weaknesses relative to the other two branches. On the other hand, if the Court ruled that Madison should deliver the paperwork, it had no effective way of enforcing that decision, which would also demonstrate the weakness of the judiciary. The situation was very much a political struggle between Federalists and Republicans, and the Supreme Court was caught up in the struggle.

In 1803, the case was heard by the Supreme Court. Marbury had filed for a **writ of mandamus**, directing Madison to deliver the paperwork in keeping with the requirements of the Judiciary Act of 1789. One section of this act specified that the Supreme Court would have original jurisdiction to hear cases involving writs of mandamus. Marshall and the Court asked and answered four questions in this case. The first question was whether or not Marbury had a right to the paperwork, and the answer was a definitive yes. The second question was whether or not there was a legal way to enforce the right, and the answer was again yes. A third question was whether Marbury used the correct legal remedy when he asked for a writ of mandamus, and the answer was again yes. The final question was whether or not the Supreme Court could issue the necessary writ. The Court answered this question in the negative. The decision of the Court said that it could not issue the writ because only the Constitution could give the Supreme Court original jurisdiction in a case. The section of the Judiciary Act of 1789 that gave the Supreme Court original jurisdiction conflicted with the Constitution. Since the Constitution was the supreme law of the land, this section was invalid, because no act of Congress could change the Constitution. The decision also made it clear that it was the duty of the Supreme Court to determine whether laws passed by Congress were constitutional or not. The power of judicial review was later used to determine whether actions of presidents and the states were constitutional or not. Marshall and his colleagues had managed to turn a dangerous position for the Supreme Court into a positive benefit for the institution. Since the Supreme Court ruled that it did not have the power to issue the writ of mandamus, Marbury did not get his commission as a justice of the peace.

Jefferson disagreed with Marshall's reasoning in the case, but was forced to accept it. It is interesting that James Madison never provided any open disagreement that the Supreme Court had the power to use judicial review, and given Madison's role at the Constitutional Convention, his silence on the issue is strongly supportive of the view that the Supreme Court was expected to use this power, which was not more firmly established. The political confrontation did not end with the decision. Jefferson and Marshall, even though they were cousins, had become political adversaries. Marshall was one of the few prominent Virginians to stay with the Federalists after Washington had retired. In 1805, Jefferson had sufficient support in the House of Representatives to impeach Associate Justice Samuel Chase, who had signed the Declaration of Independence and was a stalwart Federalist. Jefferson wanted to remove him for political reasons, although Chase had also made himself vulnerable due to arbitrary decisions he had made while involved in cases. The House did vote on articles of impeachment, but the Senate failed to vote to remove Chase from office. It was obvious at the time that Marshall would have been the next target if Jefferson has been successful. Had Jefferson been successful in removing Chase and then Marshall, the independence of the judiciary would have been severely compromised.

McCulloch v. Maryland was another early case that had major constitutional implications when it was heard by the Supreme Court. James McCulloch was the Chief Teller (branch manager) of a branch of the first national bank of the United States located in Maryland. The state had levied a tax on the bank, and McCulloch refused to pay the tax, arguing that states could not tax federal property. There were broader constitutional issues involved as well. There were some who opposed the establishment of the national bank because nowhere in the Constitution was the right to establish a national bank mentioned. These people argued, as a consequence, that the national bank was unconstitutional. A second group noted that Article I, Section 8 of the Constitution, which contained a list of things that Congress could do (the **enumerated powers**), ended with the phrase "and to make all laws which shall be necessary and proper for carrying into execution the forgoing powers, and other powers vested by this Constitution in the Government of the United States, or in any department or officer thereof." They argued that this "necessary and proper clause" or "**implied powers**" clause permitted Congress to create a national bank since the enumerated powers included mentions of creating a currency and establishing the national credit, and a national bank was one means of doing so. This group thus argued for a broader interpretation of the power of the national government to undertake actions and policies.

When the Supreme Court decided *McCulloch v. Maryland*, it answered the following. First, in regard to the right of states to tax federal property, the Court denied this right. It noted that "the power to tax is the power to destroy" and that letting states tax federal property would permit the states to negate national policies. State laws could not be used to overturn national laws (at least if the national laws were constitutional). Second, it noted that the national bank was allowed under the Constitution as a necessary and proper choice of Congress. In addition to affirming the specific issue of the national bank, the Court also indicated that a broader interpretation of the implied powers clause was going to be used as opposed to a strict interpretation. This decision set the stage for many later rulings based on the implied powers clause. The decision also indirectly indicated that state laws were subordinate to the Constitution.

Another case that helped to set the stage for the future dealt with government regulation of trade. The Constitution clearly prevented the states from interfering in either international trade or interstate trade. New York granted a company a monopoly to operate steamboats on the Hudson River, which was wholly within the confines of New York state and thus did not constitute interference in either international or interstate commerce. In *Gibbons v. Ogden* (1824), a challenge was mounted to the monopoly because the effect of the regulation was to provide an advantage to the New York company at the expense of companies in other states. The largest cost of transporting goods is the loading and unloading. The New York monopoly required that a producer in Connecticut would use the New York company rather than ship with a local company that would then have to unload in New York city to reload onto the New York steamboat, a circumstance that was too expensive to contemplate. The Supreme Court ultimately accepted the challenge to the New York company's monopoly since it did indeed interfere with interstate trade indirectly. The Court also found that the state regulation was in conflict with national licensing regulations and that preference had to be given to the national regulations as the Constitution gave preference to the national government in the area of trade. This decision clearly established the authority of the national government to regulate trade in an expanded context and to prevent even indirect state interference.

TEST TIP

When writing your essays, be sure to use neat, legible handwriting. Printing may be a better choice than writing in cursive if your handwriting tends to be messy. The essay graders cannot grade what the essay graders cannot read!

John Marshall continued as Chief Justice until he died in 1835. For more than three decades, he led the Court in helping to establish many of the key principles for the judiciary in the new government. The Supreme Court had become the source of much of the interpretation of the Constitution and had matured as an important branch of the national government. Although Marshall was not the first Chief Justice of the Supreme Court he was clearly the most important early Chief Justice, notwithstanding the early efforts of John Jay to stress the independence of the judiciary as the third branch of government. The Court was also strengthened by the failure of Jefferson to win his attempts to control the Court by removing justices that did not agree with him politically. Marshall's successors in the position of Chief Justice were not as effective in their decisions.

One of the key Supreme Court decisions after the death of Marshall was *Dred Scott v. Sandford* (1857). Roger Taney had become Chief Justice. Dred Scott was a slave who had frequently lived in free states or territories while being owned by a military officer. After the death of the officer, he sued in a number of cases to establish his freedom because he had lived in a free state. The final case made its way to the Supreme Court from Missouri. While the case was complicated in a number of respects, the Court ruled that Scott was still a slave. It initially held that Missouri law determined Scott's status under Missouri law. Taney, however, carried the case further, apparently in an attempt to put to rest the whole issue of slavery that had complicated politics in the country for decades. His decision led the Court in ruling that slaves, former slaves, and the descendents of slaves could not be considered citizens of the United States under the Constitution. As a consequence, they had no standing to sue. The Court upheld the institution of slavery and went on to declare the Missouri Compromise of 1820, which established which states and territories would allow slavery and which would not, as unconstitutional and therefore invalid. This was only the second time the Court overturned an act of Congress (*Marbury v. Madison* being the first). The decision failed to put the slavery issue to rest and actually increased animosity between the North and South. The decision is usually credited with increasing tensions over slavery and contributing to the outbreak of the Civil War. When the Court overturned the Missouri Compromise, it undermined a major political compromise that permitted the individual states to deal with slavery in different ways. This decision made political compromises over slavery between the North and South, if not impossible, much more difficult than it had been in the past.

The Civil War dealt with the issue of slavery for all practical purposes. The Thirteenth, Fourteenth, and Fifteenth Amendments were passed. The Thirteenth outlawed slavery throughout the country. Such an amendment was necessary since slavery was still possible in some slave states (Maryland, Kentucky, Delaware, and Missouri) that stayed in the Union. The amendment also did away with the three-fifths compromise requiring former slaves to be counted as a full person for purposes of assigning seats in the House of Representatives. The Fourteenth Amendment, among other issues, made former slaves citizens of the United States, in effect reversing the Dred Scott decision. The Fifteenth Amendment allowed Congress to support voting rights for former slaves. By and large Congress declined to exercise this authority until the 1960s, but the amendment did provide a basis for some activities in the efforts to generate greater equality for black Americans almost a hundred years later. In order to be readmitted into the Union, the former Confederate states were required to ratify these three amendments, which forced them to officially accept the end of slavery.

The Second Era: Economic Regulation (1865 to 1935)

The basic issues of the division of power among the branches and between the national government and the state governments had largely been resolved with the end of the Civil War. The War itself shifted power to the national government. In the years that followed, the Supreme Court was involved in decisions dealing with regulation of economic activities. Issues dealt with the role of states in regulating commerce and what regulations were permitted to the national government.

A large number of the decisions that were made in this period protected the property rights of individuals, disallowing government activity that would threaten those rights. *Lochner v. New York* (1905) dealt with a New York law that limited the hours that a baker employed by the owner could work to 10 hours a day and 60 hours a week. The Supreme Court overturned the labor law as an unnecessary violation of the right of the employer and employee to negotiate a contract for employment. In *Adkins v. Children's Hospital* (1923) the Court overturned a federal minimum wage law for women on basically the same grounds. While the Court in this era did not always overturn laws that favored employees, the trend against government supervision, particularly by the federal government, was pronounced.

In *Schechter Poultry Corp. v. United States* (1935), the Supreme Court continued to protect property rights against government regulations. In this particular case, the Court overturned federal regulations of the chicken industry as a misuse of the commerce clause of the Constitution. The case was not a complete negation of the right to regulate commerce, but the company in question was considered to be too small to require that it adhere to the new government regulations. The case threatened much of the New Deal legislation supported by Franklin Roosevelt. The decision was one factor in Roosevelt's effort to pack the Court with judges who would agree with him. The effort to make the Supreme Court more amenable to the New Deal did fail, but it also led to a new era in which the Court was more accepting of government involvement in the economy and passage of regulations dealing with national commerce.

The Supreme Court in this era decided an additional important case that did not affect economic regulation directly. In *Plessy v. Ferguson* (1896), the Court dealt with the issue of segregated facilities for blacks and whites that were present in many southern states. Homer Plessy intentionally sat in a "whites only" car in a Louisiana railroad where segregated cars were required by law, and he was arrested. His case was eventually appealed to the Supreme Court, which ruled that his rights were not violated and that the Fourteenth Amendment did not apply in this case because while the facilities were separate, they were equal in quality. The decision basically set the stage for the states that desired to do so to continue to require racial segregation. The **separate but equal doctrine** would have been sounder in theory if the facilities for whites and blacks were actually equal. In fact, the facilities available to black Americans were often greatly inferior, but *Plessy* served as a reason to not challenge the validity of mandatory segregation for many decades.

The Third Era: Increased Rights (1936 to Today)

Beginning in 1936, the Supreme Court began to reduce its rulings against government regulation and eventually accepted many of the New Deal programs. Today, there is recognition of a greater need for government regulations in terms of health and safety. The Courts have accepted the right of labor unions to exist. The transition away from the second era was a gradual one, but which would appear to have resulted in permanent changes.

The more modern period was one in which the judiciary began to deal with cases that extended personal rights and liberties in a variety of areas. A number of cases provided greater protection in the areas of civil liberties that are detailed in Chapter 8. More and more personal freedoms were protected against limitations by the states as well as the national government. There was a steady increase in the protections provided to individuals who were suspected of crimes. Defendants in criminal cases gained additional rights such as greater guarantees against self-incrimination, prohibitions on the use of evidence illegally obtained by the police, the right to have a lawyer during a trial, and other protections.

The Courts also became heavily involved in the civil rights struggle of black Americans. A series of court cases attacked the system of inequality that existed. Court cases first undermined state laws that required segregation. Mandatory segregation laws were declared unconstitutional in *Brown v. Board of Education of Topeka, Kansas* (1954). This decision basically overturned *Plessy v. Ferguson* by stating that separate facilities were inherently unequal. Later cases attacked other aspects of education and promoted more equal treatment of black Americans. In some cases, the decisions required an end to discrimination by private entities. Labor unions were required to end discriminatory practices because the right to collectively organize was guaranteed by law and with the protection of the law came responsibilities. The move to end discriminatory practices extended to other groups, including women, Hispanics, and other minorities that attempted to gain the same benefits as black Americans.

A controversial area that the Supreme Court became involved in was the ongoing abortion debate. The issue involved, what one side argued, were the rights of women against, what the other side argued, were the rights of the unborn. The issue was one that elected politicians found difficult to deal with since any decision would risk alienating one side or another in many districts and states. Different states had greatly differing laws. Some were extremely restrictive of when abortions could be performed, and others permitted abortions under a wide variety of circumstances. In *Roe v. Wade* (1973), the courts addressed the issue that the elected politicians had managed to avoid. In the decision, the Court created a national standard that permitted abortions in the first trimester, gave the states more influence in the second trimester, and that allowed states to prohibit abortions for most reasons in the last trimester. There continue to be issues related to abortion that come before the Court, including the consideration that medical advantages have changed the time at which a fetus could be considered viable. These changes are important since *Roe v. Wade* used viability as one basis for distinguishing between the different trimesters of a pregnancy.

Federal Court Structure

As noted, the first Congress decided to create a complete system of federal courts to deal with the application of national laws. The basic courts in the judiciary include the District Courts, the Circuit Courts of Appeals, and the Supreme Court. In addition, there are a number of specialized courts that have been created. Congress has also provided the equivalent of state courts for federal territories such as the Virgin Islands and American Samoa.

There are 94 district courts in the United States. Each state has at least one district court, and the more populous states have a number of courts. Puerto Rico and the District of Columbia also have a district court. The district courts are considered courts of first instance, or original jurisdiction. These courts hear criminal and civil cases for the first time. These are the courts that deal with issues of guilt or innocence or determine damages or changes in behavior that would be required in civil proceedings. These courts also deal with bankruptcy, although most bankruptcy proceedings are handled by magistrates attached to the court rather than in a courtroom proceeding. Although only 94 district courts exist, the districts have multiple judges assigned to them.

There are thirteen Circuit Courts of Appeal in the national system. Eleven of these courts cover distinct geographic areas. The twelfth covers the District of Columbia and some additional territories. The last is the Circuit Court of Appeal for the federal district that hears appeals on certain types of cases. The Circuit Court for the District of Columbia may also have certain types of cases directed to it rather than to one of the geographical courts. The number of judges on each circuit varies. The Circuit Courts with larger workloads have more judges. A Circuit Court of Appeals, as the name implies, only hears cases on appeal. The job of the court is not to make judgments of innocence or guilt but to determine whether or not there were procedural errors committed by the judge in the District Court. If the Court of Appeals determines that there was some type of error in the lower court, it will send the case back to be retried. Sometimes the decisions to exclude certain evidence from the trial may be equivalent to acquittal, but it is very rare for a directed verdict of an acquittal to be made. If the Circuit Court determines that a criminal sentence or damage award is too high, it may require changes without requiring a retrial. Since the Circuit Court reviews the judgment of a lower court, it is always a panel of judges that hears the appeal. The panel is usually three judges, and they will vote on a decision with majority vote ruling. On particularly important cases or a case with an especially important principle being decided, the entire circuit may rule on the appeal.

The Supreme Court is the highest court in the system. It does have original jurisdiction in selected cases such as those involving treaties, foreign ambassadors, and disputes between the states. Most of the cases that come before the Supreme Court are on appeal. There

DIDYOUKNOW?

There have been as many as 10 justices on the Supreme Court to reflect the number of circuits. The number was reduced by attrition at a request made by Chief Justice Chase in 1866.

are so many appeals, however, that the Court could not possibly hear them all. If four of the justices think that a case raises an important constitutional issue, then the Court will agree to hear the case. The Supreme Court primarily deals with such constitutional issues and attempts to provide examples for future cases. The Supreme Court inevitably has to hear a case when more than one Circuit Court of Appeal has heard a case and arrived at a different opinion. Under these circumstances, it is essential for the Supreme Court to provide a final judgment as to which interpretation will be the law of the land. When the Court hears a case, a decision is made by majority vote. Normally the justices provide one or more opinions as to why they ruled the way they did. A majority opinion indicates why the Court took the position that it did. Those who voted on the other side will provide one or more minority, or dissenting, opinions detailing why they disagreed with the majority. It is also possible for justices who voted with the majority to write a concurrent opinion explaining that while they voted with the majority, they did so for different reasons. Although the actual vote is important for the persons involved in the case, the principles laid out in the opinions provide guidelines to the lower courts and elected officials as to what the key constitutional issues are and what will be acceptable in the future.

Congress has set up specialized courts to deal with tax cases, customs issues, and disputes over copyrights and trademarks. These courts deal with highly specialized types of cases, and it has made more sense to have courts that can focus on these types of issues. The territorial courts are more general courts that deal with everyday issues related to local criminal laws and civil codes. There are also military courts that deal with offenses within the armed forces. Some types of appeals can go from the military courts to the civilian system.

While the state courts are basically separate systems that deal with the state laws and state constitutions, there is a connection to the federal courts. When an individual has appealed a case all the way to the state supreme court and

DIDYOU**KNOW?**

Texas and Oklahoma have two high courts—one to hear criminal cases and one to hear all other cases.

lost, he or she can appeal to the U.S. Supreme Court if he or she can make a case that the state courts have violated her or his rights under the U.S. Constitution or that a constitutional principle has been violated. There are, in fact, many such appeals from the state high courts, but only a handful are heard. If the appeal does not reach the Supreme Court directly, at times a case may be filed in a district court if a claim can be made that the state authorities violated a basic civil liberty guaranteed by the Constitution. In either event, the Supreme Court can overturn state laws and even provisions of state constitutions if they contradict basic rights that are in the Constitution.

Jurisdiction and Cases

Courts in the federal judiciary hear a wide variety of cases. Some of those cases come directly from the Constitution. Chief Justice Marshall used constitutional jurisdiction in the case of *Marbury v. Madison* to clearly establish the right of judicial review and the extent of the power of the courts. There are cases that clearly fall under the jurisdiction of federal courts that are listed in the Constitution, even if some of those cases are heard in lower courts rather than originating with Supreme Court. Most of the constitutional issues involving whether the national government or the state governments have the power to act in specific areas have been resolved over the course of time. Previous Supreme Court decisions have laid the groundwork for issues between different states as well. As noted previously, state laws and constitutions can also come into play if there is the possibility of these laws and constitutions violating basic principles of the national constitution.

Once a case is brought to the Supreme Court, lawyers from both sides submit written briefs that provide pertinent information on the case, give a synopsis of previous lower-court rulings, present both sides of the argument surrounding the case, and that explain the precedents involving the case. The briefs obviously also suggest why the justices should vote a particular way in the case. Oral arguments are then presented that the justices can stop at any time to ask clarifying questions. Fifty percent of the time, the Court is hearing a case in which the national government is either the defendant or the plaintiff. This requires the third ranking office in the Justice Department, the **Solicitor General** of the United States, to appear before the court. The government has a great deal of discretion in determining which cases it will appeal. Written briefs frequently include **amicus curiae** briefs (which are friends of the court briefs submitted by parties interested in the outcome of the case) and even oral arguments may be offered by a "friend of the court," rather than lawyers directly involved. After briefs are submitted and oral arguments are heard, justices develop their opinions and decisions. Clerks for the justices review past case law and begin to formulate and draft opinions, which are then circulated amongst the justices. The justices then meet in conference to exchange their own ideas, arguments, and opinions. After these meetings they vote and record the decision on the case and then the decision is published.

Issues involving treaties also fall under the jurisdiction of the federal courts. Any case involving the direct interpretation of a treaty is likely to be dealt with by the Supreme Court. It is also possible, however, for conflicts to appear in which state laws or national laws are in possible conflict with the provisions of a treaty. These kinds of cases may actually start in a district court or even in one of the specialized courts. Regardless of where the case is heard, clear priorities exist. If there is a question of the treaty conflicting with the Constitution, then any provisions of the treaty in conflict with the Constitution would be declared invalid. If there is no conflict with the Constitution, and it is unlikely that the Senate would ever approve a treaty that clearly violated the Constitution, then the treaty takes precedence over national laws, state laws, and even state constitutions.

Federal courts get most of their immediate jurisdiction from national laws passed by Congress. When Congress passes laws, the assumption is that any violation of those laws will be dealt with by national courts. Any questions of interpretation of those laws will also be dealt with by the national courts. District courts, of course, are the initial courts to deal with these issues. The vast majority of these cases do not involve any constitutional issues or any questions, and the judgment of the court is the last word in the case. A smaller number of cases advance to the Circuit Courts of Appeal and are dealt with there.

State courts primarily have jurisdiction based on their own state laws and constitutions. The state constitutions take precedence over state laws, and local governments have to adhere to the state constitutions and adapt to state laws. Judges in state courts have to be aware of decisions from the Supreme Court that could have an effect on their interpretation of state laws. State courts have overturned laws on the basis of conflicts with the U.S. Constitution. The effects of decisions of the Supreme Court also influence how state legislatures write laws as they attempt to avoid challenges to the laws on the basis of the U.S. Constitution.

Civil suits can occur in state or federal courts depending upon the issues and the location of the people involved. The procedures are similar in both court systems. In civil suits. the government may be prosecuting an individual or company for violating government regulations or seeking to force someone to stop an action that infringes upon the rights of others. The goal of the civil suit often is to bring about a change in behavior. The government can also be the target in civil suits. In civil suits. the parties involved are known as litigants. The **plaintiff** brings the charges (this name is listed first in the name of the case). The **defendant** is the party who has been charged (this name is listed second). Plaintiffs must have **standing to sue**, or sufficient legal reason to bring charges. Plaintiffs in a **class action suit** sue on behalf of all citizens who are in the same situation. Civil suits often seek monetary compensation for loss of income or for other damages suffered.

In matters of criminal law, the government is always the plaintiff charging the defendant or defendants on behalf of the public. In a case where the federal government is prosecuting violations of federal laws, the U.S. attorney in each district serves as the government's lawyer. In criminal cases, an individual or company is being prosecuted for illegal activities. Attorneys present a case in court. Every citizen is guaranteed a lawyer in a criminal case. **Public interest lawyers** and **legal aid groups** may represent low-income people in some civil and criminal cases. State and local governments hire **public defenders** to represent low-income defendants in criminal cases. Usually people with more money can hire lawyers with more time and resources, and therefore may have an advantage. Sometimes civil suits are brought against the government. Such civil suits usually are not about money. The government has been sued for failing to enforce environmental laws or providing benefits to someone who can argue that they deserve the benefits. In these cases, U.S. attorney in the district has to serve as a defense attorney for the government or government agency that is the defendant in the case.

When important legal principles are involved in a criminal or civil case, other parties may become interested. Interest groups of all types become involved with court cases to influence decisions about the law. They may have their lawyers take up a litigant's case because they think the decision will have an effect on their group or its members. They often submit amicus curiae briefs to influence a judge's decision in cases where the

Types of Cases Heard in State and Federal Courses

State Courts	Federal Courts	State or Federal Courts
Crimes under state legislation	Crimes under statutes enacted by Congress	Crimes punishable under both federal and state law
State constitutional issues and cases involving state laws or regulations	Most cases involving federal laws or regulations (for example, tax, Social Security, broadcasting, civil rights)	Federal constitutional issues
		Certain civil rights claims
Family law issues		"Class action" cases
Real property issues	Matters involving interstate and international commerce, including airline and railroad regulation	Environmental regulations
Most private contract disputes (except those resolved under bankruptcy law)		Certain disputes involving federal law
Most issues involving the regulation of trades and professions	Cases involving securities and commodities regulation, including takeover of publicly held corporations	
Most professional malpractice issues	Admiralty cases	
	International trade law matters	
Most issues involving the internal governance of business associations such as partnerships and corporations	Patent, copyright, and other intellectual property issues	
Most personal injury lawsuits	Cases involving rights under treaties, foreign states, and foreign nationals	
Most workers' injury claims		
Probate and inheritance matters	State law disputes when "diversity of citizenship" exists	
Most traffic violations and registration of motor vehicles	Bankruptcy matters	
	Disputes between states	
	Habeas corpus actions	
	Traffic violations and other misdemeanors occurring on certain federal property	

groups themselves are not litigants. These briefs attempt to influence the outcome by explaining the possible effects of the judge's decision, bring new points of view to the case, or provide additional information not presented in the case. The federal government and state governments can also submit them. When federal courts are considering cases involving the imposition of capital punishment in a particular state, other states often file such briefs; a federal decision to overturn capital punishment would affect other states. A decision about which crimes are eligible for capital punishment or whether there was great freedom to impose such punishment would also affect existing practices in other states. Private groups opposed to capital punishment in general would weigh in with facts and information demonstrating that capital punishment is excessively cruel, that people convicted and sentenced to death may be innocent, or other facts supporting their point of view. The National Rifle Association will often file an amicus curiae brief in cases where the right to possess firearms or the requirement of registering firearms is an issue.

The Politics of Judicial Selection

According to the U.S. Constitution, the president shall nominate all judges and justices of the Supreme Court. The Senate has to confirm these nominees with a majority vote. As a political party member, the president traditionally nominates members of his or her own political party for Supreme Court positions with only an occasional nomination of someone from the opposing party. Presidents assume that members of their own party will have the same general views as they do. Party issues can make the nomination process contentious at times, especially when the president and a majority of the Senate are of different parties. Even when the Senate is controlled by the opposition party, the confirmation process for many judges is relatively routine. Simple party membership or general affiliation has not been enough by itself to make nominations contentious in the years since World War II.

One tradition regarding nominations is **senatorial courtesy**. Senators from the president's party review an appointee for a federal district court in their state; senators can "blue-slip" a nominee, in effect preventing the nomination from proceeding forward. This practice has been criticized because it gives senators virtual veto power in the nomination of judges. On the other hand, it involves the legislature in the staffing of the judiciary instead of giving the president a freer hand in nominating judges. Many presidents in fact use the appointment of judges and U.S. attorneys as a means of bargaining with Senators for support for other issues. The president will let the Senators suggest names, and in turn the Senators will provide support for important legislation.

Senatorial courtesy is not an issue for nominations for the Circuit Courts of Appeal or the Supreme Court.

Another concern is the use of the "**litmus test**," a test of ideological purity used by recent presidents in making nominations. Presidents may demand that the nominee have a similar view to their own on a key issue. At times it appears that a litmus test appeals to supporters of the party and is a way of pacifying a particular group within either the Democratic or Republican Party. Senators may also apply similar litmus tests for confirmation of judges. Traditionally, presidents seek judicial appointees with similar political ideologies to sit on the Court in hopes that they will support any programs or actions of the administration's that are challenged. They want allies in case there are possible questions of constitutionality. Of course, if a president is approaching the end of his term, it is unlikely that a recent nominee will have much opportunity to agree or disagree. Presidents can also regard the appointment of justices to the Supreme Court as a way to have a lasting impact on the political system long after they are out of office. During the confirmation process, candidates can be asked to state their judicial philosophy but are not required to respond to specific cases or how they would rule.

Presidents spend a considerable amount of time when they select nominees for the Supreme Court or even the Circuit Courts of Appeal since these judges will be making decisions that will establish precedents for the future. Even though nominees for the Supreme Court are carefully scrutinized before they are set forward by the president, he sometimes will choose a nominee who does not share his ideology or views on particular issues. Part of the problem is that it is difficult to predict how a justice will actually vote. Many nominees have previous service as a judge on a lower court (state supreme court, Circuit Court of Appeals), and her or his decisions can be reviewed. Of course, this previous service can be misleading since the decisions on these courts reflect the constraints of the current Supreme Court or state constitutions. Once on the Supreme Court, the justices are freer to use their own interpretations. Presidents have also appointed individuals whose basic background has been political. Politicians, of course, have a record that is easy to observe. But politicians also have to get elected in order to build a political career, and a politician may be forced to make decisions that are popular with the voters, even if he or she happens to disagree with some parts of that decision. President Eisenhower thought he was appointing a relatively conservative individual when he made Earl Warren his choice to be the new Chief Justice. Warren was a mainstream Republican who had served as California's Attorney General and Governor. He seemed to have the appropriate ideological credentials. He turned out to be quite liberal in his views when he no longer had to seek public approval.

Some nominees for the Supreme Court have faced difficult confirmation proceedings. In one case, President Nixon had his first two nominees with conservative backgrounds fail in the Senate. One of them had a poor record on civil rights, which forced his withdrawal in an era when there was still support for civil rights. A second nominee had a very undistinguished record as a district judge. On his third try, he nominated Harry Blackmun, whose conservative credentials were impeccable, and Blackmun was accepted by the Senate by a 94–0 vote. Obviously, conservative ideology was not in and of itself a bar to acceptance. President George H. W. Bush nominated Clarence Thomas who was known to be very conservative. His nomination was not facing any difficulties until charges of sexual harassment were raised against him. Even with these charges and a hearing on them in the Senate, he was approved. President George W. Bush nominated Harriet Miers for the Supreme Court. Her background was in corporate law and she lacked any experience as a judge. She had very little courtroom experience. Her background was questioned by many Republicans in the Senate as well as by Democrats, and President Bush withdrew her nomination. Robert Bork was a very controversial nominee put forward by President Reagan. He was very outspoken in his views, often arguing that the Supreme Court had made numerous mistakes in its decisions in the previous 20 to 25 years and suggesting that it was necessary to reverse these decisions. His nomination resulted in great opposition in the Senate. Even though he was the flag bearer for very conservative Republicans, his views did not sit well with more moderate Republicans and clearly not with Democrats. When it was obvious that his nomination would fail, it was withdrawn. These examples demonstrate that the Senate does have criteria that it uses when reviewing nominees for the Supreme Court. Clearly, the Senate expects some demonstration not only of competence but also of excellence in some fashion since the Supreme Court is the highest court in the land. Nominees who have not been accepted have often failed on this count. Robert Bork is clearly the only recent nominee who has failed to win approval on the basis of his ideology. It is possible that the sitting members of the Supreme Court may have been relieved to avoid a colleague who had spent much of his career criticizing their decisions.

When presidents and others look at potential nominees, they evaluate them in a number of ways. Conservatives want judges that are judicially restrained and believe in strict construction (interpretation) of the Constitution. Strict construction and judicial restraint are not the same thing. Loose construction and strict construction refer to how a judge views the power of all branches of the national government. A strict constructionist would limit what the government could do (no national bank allowed) while a loose constructionist would permit the government to do much more (broad interpretation of the implied powers clause). Judicial restraint suggests that a judge should limit the power of the judiciary to intervene in the affairs of the other branches or a state. This judge would defer to the other branches in their choices with great regularity. Judicial activism refers to a judge who would actively seek to involve the courts in making decisions. Robert Bork, for example, was a firm supporter of a strict construction of the Constitution, but he was very much appeared to be a judicial activist who would intervene as much as necessary to impose the judiciary's view on the other branches.

Judges in state courts obtain their positions in a variety of ways. In some states the governor will nominate individuals subject to some form of legislative approval. In other states, the judges are elected just like any other government official, including being identified as Democrats or Republicans (or even some third party). In some states, judges are elected, but it is a non-partisan ballot; party identification is not allowed. Other states use a variation of the system developed by Missouri. The governor appoints a nominee from a short list prepared by a committee, usually a non-partisan one that looks at the nominees based on their record. Within a limited range of nominees the governor does have an opportunity to choose individuals who seem to share his ideology. The judges are then subjected to a public vote after a number of years in office. If the public accepts them, they continue to serve until retirement. If the public rejects their continuation in service, they are removed and the vacancy is filled in whatever way is set in place.

Selection of Judges	
The Constitution states that federal judges are to be nominated by the President and confirmed by the Senate*.	State court judges are selected in a variety of ways, including • election, • appointment for a given number of years, • appointment for life, and • combinations of these methods, that is • appointment followed by election
They hold office during good behavior, typically, for life. Through congressional impeachment proceedings, federal judges may be removed from office for misbehavior.	State judges may serve for fixed terms, during good behavior (sometimes until a specified retirement age), or subject to elections or public approval in elections.

*Confirmation of district judges is determined by senatorial courtesy, in which Senators in the state where the district is located has a significant influence in appointing judges.

TEST TIP

In recent years, the AP exam has asked questions about which judges were nominated by which president and who was chosen or not chosen. Be sure to research all those justices that have been tabbed or appointed for the past 30 years.

The Courts as Policymakers

The federal courts have the power to make public policy in three ways. Judges can interpret the constitution or laws. Judges frequently interpret laws, many of which are vague in some areas because of the compromises that were necessary to get the legislation passed. In some cases, the judges or justices see a challenge to the law on constitutional grounds. If they interpret the law to mean "A," then it is unconstitutional. On the other hand, if they interpret the law to mean "B," it will be acceptable on constitutional grounds. The interpretation may not exactly be what Congress intended, but the law remains on the books. In this particular example, no law is declared unconstitutional, but the courts may have altered it to make it constitutional. In other cases, many interpretations of the law may be constitutional and a court is simply forced to make a choice from among the options as to what is possible or not possible. If they get it wrong, the legislators can provide the necessary clarity.

The courts can extend the reach of existing law. Existing law may affect books and newspapers, and it is extended to cover the electronic media and then the Internet. Both federal and state courts have to deal with criminal activity where existing laws do not exactly mention more modern ways of stealing money, extorting individuals, or otherwise using modern techniques to gain financially at someone else's expense. Brokerage firms on Wall Street manage to find ways around existing laws and regulations in terms of some of the practices that they follow.

Finally, they can design remedies that involve judges in administration or in continuing legal oversight of previous decisions. Judges were often involved in designing remedies for racial balance in schools that were required by their own decisions or decisions of other courts. In other cases, judges have had to approve (or not) remedies that states, companies, or individuals come up with to meet the requirements of previous decisions. The choices that are made have obvious consequences for the policies involved.

The types of cases accepted by the Supreme Court shape policy simply by the selection process that is used to choose cases to hear and render decisions about the issues involved.

The Supreme Court has a distinct process it follows when making decisions, and those decisions are based heavily on precedent and the interpretation of the Constitution. In some instances, the Court rules on the basis of **stare decisis** (to let the previous rulings stand). The Court often strives to clarify ambiguities in the law and create the legal precedent for other courts to follow. After the court renders its decisions, the decisions must be translated into policy. Policymakers, the president, lower courts, lawyers, and administrators are responsible for this aspect of the process. During this process, the public will become aware of any changes that affect their rights as citizens. The spread of the news would commonly involve the media to highlight the changes as they begin to go into effect.

Many of the Supreme Courts have made influential decisions that have changed public policy. Marshall and his colleagues increased the power of the court with the *Marbury v. Madison* decision. As a long-serving Chief Justice in the first days of the new country, the decisions of his Court were bound to set the stage for much of what was to follow. The Court under Chief Justice Taney with the *Dred Scott* decision demonstrated the negative effects that a decision could have on the political system. The Supreme Court in the Franklin Roosevelt years eventually supported the New Deal and the other programs that were designed to revive the American economy. The Warren court was extremely active in expanding civil rights with a series of rulings. The Court also provided a series of decisions that provided more rights for defendants in criminal proceedings. The Burger Court that followed made the *Roe v. Wade* decision that is still a source of controversy for many in the United States. The Rehnquist court overturned the line-item veto that had been passed by Congress, primarily because it transferred legislative power to the executive branch, and such transfers are unconstitutional.

Checks on Judicial Powers

Individuals who have disagreed with particular decisions of the Supreme Court or a series of decisions by the Court have often claimed that the Court has overstepped the bounds of its powers and that the country is being governed by the nine justices. For example, white southerners were outraged by the decisions of the Supreme Court in supporting civil rights for black Americans. This argument fails to recognize that the Founding Fathers placed a substantial number of checks on the judiciary just as they provided protections to the courts with service during time of good behavior to prevent undue political influence.

There are a number of major checks on the judiciary. The president and the Senate have high degree of control over the makeup of the judiciary. While the nature of a person appointed to a judicial position cannot always be predicted, this requirement does provide a major control on the courts. Through the appointment process, Franklin

Roosevelt eventually had a Supreme Court that supported New Deal legislation with little dissent. Congress controls the number of courts and their jurisdiction. While jurisdiction is not generally used to control what the courts do, Congress can send messages to the judiciary by failing to provide new positions or judges and leaving the existing judges to deal with the workload. Although Congress cannot reduce the salaries of sitting judges, they are not required to keep salaries on a par with inflation or similar to pay levels in the private sector. The legislature can alter legislation in response to Supreme Court decisions in an attempt to undo the decision. In extreme cases, the Constitution can be amended to reverse a decision of the Supreme Court, as happened with the Sixteenth Amendment that permitted Congress to create an income tax. The courts also labor from the disadvantage that they have to depend upon the executive branch, the Congress, and the states to implement whatever decisions they do make. Sometimes the implementation is slow and at other times virtually nonexistent. The Supreme Court has to take into account the need for implementation when it makes its decisions.

The Court also has to take into account public opinion. In theory the Court could make any decision that it wanted to, but public opinion provides limits on the decisions that can be made because it affects the general acceptance of the decision and the willingness of other branches to imple-

DIDYOUKNOW?

Earl Warren, known as a liberal Chief Justice of the Supreme Court, was Attorney General of California during World War II and argued for the relocation of American citizens of Japanese ancestry to camps in the interior of the country.

ment the decision. Desegregation decisions were possible in part because public opinion had reached the point where repression of black Americans in the South was no longer acceptable to the rest of the country (and to many in the South as well). In 1942, the United States relocated citizens of Japanese ancestry to camps in the interior of the United States. A number of challenges to the relocation made their way to the Supreme Court by 1944. The decision was going to be a difficult one. The courts normally defer to the president during times of war, and President Roosevelt supported the initial decision made by the military commander of the western United States. Congress was highly supportive as well. Public opinion was overwhelmingly in favor of the relocation. Under these circumstances, the Court would have found it difficult to find in favor of those who were challenging the operation. The Supreme Court found technical reasons to reject the cases at the time, thus supporting the president and Congress and avoiding a decision that would be unenforceable and would not be supported by the public. In 1946, the Court, in dealing with similar cases, basically ruled against the decisions to relocate these American citizens, which is now generally recognized as having been a major limitation on their civil liberties. This particular case illustrates the very real nature of the limitations that exist on the judiciary. Some of those limitations are part of the system of checks and balances, but there are the additional constraints that come from public opinion and the need for implementation that also prevent judicial tyranny.

Time for a quiz
- Review strategies in Chapter 2
- Take Quiz 4 at the REA Study Center
   (www.rea.com/studycenter)

Public Policy

Policymaking basically consists of determining what belongs on the political agenda or determining what issues the American public cares about. It is important to understand that political ideologies, special interests, political parties, and the media play a large role in how the public-policy agenda is set. Also playing an important role are the three branches of government, each of which has its own political roles in the policymaking agenda. Political parties also have a role to play in the process. There are four areas where the federal government makes domestic policy decisions. The areas are economic policy, social welfare policy, healthcare, and the environment. The economy has long been an area in which the government has been involved. The second area of activity, social welfare, became more important after World War I and evolved even more during 1950s and 1960s. The last two areas are newer areas of policy concern, and they are still evolving. These evolving policies and the groups that are involved in them sometimes have implications for the bureaucracy because new programs can increase the size of government. Foreign policy is obviously another area of special importance for the national government.

Policymaking in a Federal System

The most basic question, of course, is who is responsible for policy making in any area of activity? At some level, the answer is "anyone and everyone," but there are three main types of actors who drive policy: interest groups or the public in general, institutions of government, and the media.

Interest groups consist of citizens who seek to combine their resources and efforts in order to better affect policymaking. At times the groups are clearly special interest groups with singular missions. Interest groups can be unions, businesses, or other economic groups that want to gain influence within the government and by doing so would also increase the government's assistance or support for their group. Policy making might include new activities that the group wants government involvement in while in other cases, an interest group might want less government involvement if that is what would provide them an advantage.

The three branches of government are all potentially important in policymaking. Congress of course is almost always responsible for policymaking since programs normally require authorization and funding. The president is responsible for implementing policies and programs. The president can influence the implementation of certain policies or even attempt to implement some policies on his own, as a number of presidents did with executive orders in support of more equal rights for black Americans. The judiciary may become important if the policies raise constitutional issues or require legal interpretations.

The media has become important for policymaking, as well. The media's help to get items on the agenda and can be important in terms of focusing attention on the legislative process when legislation is being debated. The role of the media has increased as new forms of transmitting information have become available. Some media outlets have focused on particular target audiences as they have become more specialized, which creates an opportunity for mobilizing interest groups.

The Formation of Economic Policy Agendas

Political agendas change along with popular interests, government action or inaction, critical events, interest of the elites, and the media. There are four agents that can be involved in the formation of economic policies. Most social welfare programs will help large numbers of constituents (for example, social security) and may rely on numbers for support. Client politics involve the small groups or unions that would benefit from the programs; the policy may favor the group while the general population could be positively or negatively affected. Most of the time the client groups do not have the large resources of many interest groups, but the constituents served may be important for a politician.

Interest groups can be involved in forming economic policy. They involve smaller numbers of citizens than is the case for some of the social welfare policies. Some policies can be cost restrictive in that they insulate individuals from some of the costs of activities, while others are cost escalating except that the costs are likely to fall on others in the system. These policies do not revolve around the larger population and the use of lobbying techniques to mobilize support will be an underlying driver of any agenda. Businesses normally seek to benefit from subsidies, protection against foreign imports, government contracts, or other favorable arrangements with government agencies. These groups may use their political influence to pursue the creation of policies that please the populace and that may add popular support to their lobbying techniques (for example, solar panel developers who use concerns about **global warming** to get support for their production).

The deficits of the past few decades have raised ongoing policy debates for parties and citizens, yet the surpluses of 1999 and 2000 created controversy, as well. Republicans wanted to return the 1999 surplus to the public, while Democrats wanted to use it for new programs. Both sides got some of what they wanted in 2001. Republicans enacted one of three large tax cuts implemented since World War II. Democrats received the assurance that tax cuts would end in 2010, and spending on federal programs was increased. As 2010 came to a close, a divided congress and the executive branch had long and contentious negotiations revolving around the ending of the tax cuts as well as the increased spending on federal programs. The spirited political debate was a direct consequence of the fallout from the economic troubles that have plagued the United States starting in 2007. These economic problems themselves derived from earlier changes in policies where financial institutions had gained greater freedom from regulation that permitted risky mortgages and other investments. These concerns have led to low voter approval of the president and the Congress as a whole.

One thing that politicians understand is the importance of pocketbook issues during elections. Voters often see connections between their own economic circumstances, the president, and the nation as a whole. Incumbents are concerned when economic conditions worsen, such as the average income for Americans declining. When voters blame the elected officials, they tend to vote politicians out of power. The opposite can be said when economic conditions have gotten better, and incumbents can ride the wave of success. Challengers during times of worsening economic conditions evade responsibility and use their opponent's records as an explanation for the problems that the voters are facing. Also important are candidates who take strong positions in favor of benefits (for senior citizens who are members of the AARP) in order to gain more votes. They do not always know how to produce desirable economic outcomes to make all constituents happy. It is their hope that aligning with enough voters on this issue will mean a victory on election day.

Economic Theories

When they are struggling over the politics of taxing and spending, competing politicians offer conflicting recommendations, in part because they may have different political ideologies. Their recommendations tend to include taxes, debt, and introducing new programs or eliminating old ones because of cost. Each politician offers their own interpretation and economic rationales to support financing their policy changes in the ways they want to.

Monetarism is a set of views based on the belief that inflation depends on the amount of money printed by the government. It was proposed by Milton Friedman from the University of Chicago, who argued that based on the quantity theory of money in circulation, the government should keep the money supply steady, expanding it slightly each year mainly to allow for the natural growth of the economy.

Keynesian economists believe that aggregate demand is influenced by a host of economic decisions—both public and private—and that sometimes the economy behaves erratically. Derived from the work of the English economist John Maynard Keynes, Keynesianism assumes that the health of the economy depends on how much of their income people save or spend. The theory holds that government should create the correct level of demand. One way in which the government can create this level is by increasing spending, which may mean a larger deficit, when the economy is doing poorly. The increase in government spending will increase demand, which will help to revive the economy. The other belief of Keynesian economics is that the government should increase taxes and pay down the deficit when the economy is booming in order to avoid an overheated economy.

Supply-side economics is a school of macroeconomic thought that argues that economic growth can be most effectively created by lowering barriers for people to produce (supply) goods and services, such as by lowering income tax and capital gains tax rates and by allowing greater flexibility by

DIDYOUKNOW?

Politicians have been accused of being one-handed Keynesian economists. They are willing to do deficit spending during slowdowns, but they are unwilling to increase taxes and reduce spending during economic boom times.

reducing regulation. According to supply-side economics, consumers will then benefit from a greater supply of goods and services at lower prices. The growth in the economy will produce additional tax revenues that will make up for the lower taxes. **Reaganomics,** set in motion by President Ronald Reagan in 1981, was a program for economic recovery that had four major policy objectives: (1) reduce the growth of government spending, (2) reduce the marginal tax rates on income from both labor and capital, (3) reduce regulation, and (4) reduce inflation by controlling the growth of the money supply. Reagan wanted to reduce the size of the federal government, to stimulate economic growth, and to increase military strength. His approach did rely on supply-side economic ideas to some extent. One consequence of the approach was an increase in the deficit.

Economic policymaking is complicated, and a number of actors are involved in the process. Congress is the most important player in economic policymaking, since it approves all taxes and almost all expenditures. The **Council of Economic Advisers** (CEA) is part of the Executive Office of the Presidency. The CEA includes professional economists who are generally in agreement with the economic theory subscribed to by the current president. The CEA forecasts trends and analyzes issues to aid the president in policymaking. It also prepares the annual economic oversight report that the president sends to Congress. The **Office of Management and Budget** (OMB), also part of the Executive Office, is the largest component of the Executive Office of the President. It reports directly to the president and helps a wide range of executive departments and agencies across the federal government implement the commitments and priorities of the president. The OMB prepares estimates of amounts to be spent by federal government agencies, and it negotiates with these departments and agencies to determine their respective budget requests.

The Secretary of the Treasury is one of the principal economic advisers to the president and plays a critical role in policy making. He brings an economic and government financial policy perspective to issues facing the government. The Secretary of the Treasury is responsible for formulating and recommending financial, economic, and tax policies on the domestic and international levels. The Secretary also participates in the formulation of broad fiscal policies that have general significance for the economy and management of the public debt. The Secretary oversees the activities of the department in carrying out its major law-enforcement responsibilities that include activities, serving as the financial agent for the United States government, and in minting coins and printing currency.

The **Federal Reserve Board** (FRB or the Fed) was created on December 23, 1913. It consists of seven members of the Board of Governors and divides the country into twelve districts with a Reserve Bank for each district. Members are appointed by the president, confirmed by the Senate, and serve nonrenewable fourteen-year terms. The chairperson of the Federal Reserve serves for four years, and he or she can be reappointed. The members are removable for cause—they can be impeached. The job of this bureaucracy is to use **monetary policy** to maintain employment, keep prices stable, and regulate interest rates. The Federal Reserve Board also supervises banks, provides financial services, and researches the United States economy and the economies in the surrounding region. The Federal Reserve acts independently of both the executive and legislative branches. The most important role the Federal Reserve serves is to regulate the supply of money both in circulation and through reserve rates, the price of money in the form of interest rates and inflation rates.

Economic Policy and the Budget

Until 1921, there were many years in which there was no federal budget. A national budget was dependent upon Congress passing one. Even after presidents began submitting budgets to Congress after 1921, congressional committees continued to act on the budget independently as the presidential budget is only a guideline, and like any other piece of legislation, it is subject to modification by Congress. The Congressional Budget Act of 1974 established procedures to standardize the budgeting process and streamline the process.

Currently, there is a sequence for the budget process:

- The president submits the budget.

- The House and Senate budget committees study the budget after receiving an analysis from the Congressional Budget Office (CBO).

- Each committee proposes a budget resolution that sets a total budget ceiling as well as ceilings for each of several spending areas.

- Congress is expected to adopt these resolutions in order to guide its budget debates.

- Congress considers appropriations bills (bills that actually fund programs within established limits) and sees whether they are congruent with the budget resolution.

The process can be a lengthy one, and in many years the budget is passed in increments rather than as a unified document. The budget proposed by the president and the one passed by Congress, however, represent a statement of policy goals and priorities for the government.

The economy and the government have been linked since the creation of the Constitution, which gave the federal government control over international and interstate commerce as well as other powers. The American economy is based on capitalism and a laissez-faire marketplace, but the economy is defined as a mixed economy because of the regulatory role the government has developed over the years. Today, one of the largest concerns of the American economy is the growth of corporations that have begun to operate within the global economy.

Unemployment and inflation are two major economic concerns. Levels of unemployment or inflation can be responsive to the actions undertaken by the Federal

Reserve System as part of the board's vision of monetary policy. The monetary policy is set by presidential appointees, but the actions do not necessarily reflect the ideology of the current president—although the policy can alter with different presidents with different economic goals. Unemployment occurs when there are more job seekers than jobs. Since the recession in 2008, the unemployment rate has been used to determine the strength or weakness of the economy. Traditionally, Democratic presidents have been more concerned with keeping unemployment down, even at the cost of inflation. Inflation occurs when prices rise and is measured by the CPI, or consumer price index. Republican businesspeople traditionally are most concerned with the cost of goods and services provided to the general public as a means to determine the strength of the public to purchase goods at lower prices. Normally, Republican presidents have been more concerned with keeping inflation down even at the cost of unemployment. The changes in the party affiliation of the presidency keeps the system of checks and balances relevant, but it also hurts the economy as a whole since most presidents who install new policies will often not be in office when the changes take effect, and the following president (whether of the same or different party as the outgoing president) will gain the notoriety, for good and ill, from the previous administration's policy.

TEST TIP

Eliminating answer choices one by one can be slow going. To help you work more quickly, you may want to come up with your own answer to the question before reading the answer choice. Then, select the choice that most closely matches the answer you came up with.

Areas of Economic Policy

The government tries to control the economy through agencies such as the Securities and Exchange Commission, the Treasury Department, and Federal Reserve Bank. The unemployment rate and inflation are major concerns. Monetary policy is one mechanism and **fiscal policy** (running a surplus or deficit) is another. With an economy based on various economic principles like capitalism and laissez-faire, there is a fine line between enacting new policy and reforming older policy to meet the needs of the various interested groups (not interest groups). The unemployment rate concerns the larger population in terms of job creation, but the coalition of groups supporting the Democratic Party is concerned with large unemployment.

This coalition is made up of labor unions, the working class, and other groups for which jobs are very essential.

Conflicting views about job creation lead to various policy initiatives being suggested. Some believe higher taxes will lead to greater government surpluses which can offset job loses, while others advocate for lower taxes, which should lead to greater business surpluses and the ability to hire more workers. The Federal Reserve role interprets the unemployment rate along with the inflation rate to determine the monetary policy they will adapt to control inflation and unemployment. The Fed attempts to remain neutral from party politics, but political ideology does appear when a new chairperson is chosen, as they may make concessions to remain in their position. Although monetary policy is used to monitor and to attempt to control the amount of money in circulation, the integration of the U.S. economy into the world economy creates difficulties for the successful application of any policy. It is now more difficult to regulate the American economy because other countries may undertake policies that are not in alignment with the American policies.

If interest rates are lowered, businesses will be encouraged to borrow money for expansion, thus increasing employment. If interest rates increase, there will be less borrowing, but the higher rates may increase inflation because the cost of necessary borrowing to do business will be higher. The government may sell bonds or treasury bills, which provides a safe investment while increasing the amount of money in circulation in the United States. The government can also use fiscal policy in an effort to direct the economy. What sometimes creates difficulties is that the politicians are following a fiscal policy that is in conflict with the monetary policy of the Federal Reserve Bank. The two parts of the government are not always on the same page.

Other Policies the Affect Economic Policy

The **Federal Trade Commission**, which was created in 1914, has as its purpose the prevention of unfair methods of competition in commerce. The creation of the FTC was part of the battle to "bust the trusts," or the major monopolies that existed. Over the years, Congress passed additional laws giving the agency greater authority to police anticompetitive practices. In 1938, Congress passed a broad prohibition against "unfair and deceptive acts or practices." This part of the mandate of the FTC is to prevent false advertising. In later years, Congress directed the FTC to administer a wide variety of other consumer protection laws that concerned telemarketing and guarantees of equal access to credit. In 1975, Congress gave the FTC the authority to adopt industry-wide trade regulation rules. All of these activities can have an impact on the economy. Regulations can raise the costs of business, and there is a possibility that regulations could interfere with sales or activity. Other regulatory commissions can have similar effects, and these regulations in the aggregate can have important effects, for good or ill, on the economy.

While the U.S. Department of Agriculture is primarily responsible for food safety, the Food and Drug Administration is responsible for protecting the public health by assuring that foods are safe and properly labeled with regard to food additions (Red Dye Number 2, for example). The FDA is more involved in making sure that human drugs, veterinary drugs, and vaccines and other biological products and medical devices intended for human use are safe and effective. The FDA is also responsible for protecting the public from electronic radiation, assuring that cosmetics and dietary supplements are safe and properly labeled, and for regulating tobacco products. The FDA also tries to help the public get the accurate science-based information they need to use medicines, devices, and foods to improve their health.

The relationship between labor and the government has had effects on the economy. Prior to the twentieth century, the government traditionally favored business over labor. In the twentieth century, labor won some economic protection of the law, including the guaranteed right to collective bargaining, unemployment compensation, a minimum wage, a variety of safety standards, and a regular workweek. Collective bargaining provides representatives of employees (unions) and employers a method to negotiate the conditions of employment, normally resulting in a written contract setting forth the wages, hours, and other conditions to be observed for a stipulated period. The Social Security Act of 1935 created the Federal-State Unemployment Compensation Program. The program has two main objectives: (1) to provide temporary and partial wage replacement to involuntarily unemployed workers who were recently employed; and (2) to help stabilize the economy during recessions. Unemployment benefits are payments made by the state or other authorized bodies to unemployed people. Benefits may be based on a compulsory insurance system. Depending on the state rules and the status of the person, these sums may be small, covering only basic needs (thus a form of basic welfare), or may compensate the lost time proportionally to the previous earned salary. Minimum wages are determined by acts of Congress. The Department of Labor ensures that they are paid. Currently the federal minimum wage for covered nonexempt employees is $7.25 per hour, effective July 24, 2009.

Social Welfare Policy

The United States has two types of social welfare programs, and they revolve around the income of an individual. **Social Security** and **Medicare** are called entitlement programs and are available to anyone, regardless of income. Public funds, which draw upon previous individual contributions, must pay for these benefits regardless of national debt or any effort to determine if people are entitled to receive them. The other type of social welfare programs revolves around an individual's income. If the income falls below a certain threshold established by policy (a means test), people are eligible for the benefits. These programs were all developed at different times. The public often insists that only those who cannot help themselves should receive some form of assistance. The United States has been slower than most advanced countries to embrace such social welfare policies. It was not until the reinterpretation of the Constitution in the 1930s that the federal government was allowed by the Supreme Court to enact social welfare policies. State governments and private enterprises often play a significant role in administering programs in the United States, and there is some variation in terms of the benefits that someone will receive.

Significant Social Welfare Programs

There are a number of important social welfare programs. The Social Security Act of 1935 was developed during the Great Depression. President Franklin Roosevelt created programs that would provide insurance for the unemployed and elderly. The Social Security Act required workers and employers to contribute to the system and to later benefit from it. The system was in effect a government pension fund. Not all individuals received pension payments equivalent to the money that was paid into the system. Those who lived for longer periods of time often received more, and the system subsidized those with very low incomes. The unemployment provisions were designed to give those temporarily out of work sufficient income to survive on. When the Great Depression hit the United States, private charities were unable to provide sufficient assistance for the large numbers of unemployed and for the elderly who needed help. The second program developed at this time provided assistance for dependent children, the blind, and the elderly. In this instance, taxes were used to provide the funds of the programs.

The Social Security Act in 1935 did not include any provisions for medical care in order to ensure its passage. After the death of President Kennedy, President Johnson was able to initiate the war on poverty. One of the results of the war on poverty was the Medicare Act of 1965. This new legislation applied only to the aged (those over the age of sixty-five), so that the costs of the program would be limited. The program only covered hospital bills and not doctors' bills. The lack of coverage for the doctors' bills meant that doctors would not be subject to any government regulations. Eventually **Medicaid** was added to the system. This program made medical care available to those who were otherwise too poor to receive such care.

One part of the Social Security Act received enough negative attention to force its demise. The **Aid to Families with Dependent Children** (AFDC) was scarcely noticed when it was enacted in the 1930s. Initially the AFDC involved giving federal aid to support existing state programs. It allowed states to determine what constituted need, to set benefit levels, and to administer the program. The program became less acceptable to the public over the years. Many viewed the recipients as undeserving, and after 50 years it was reworked into the **Temporary Assistance for Needy Families** (TANF) program. This program provided federal assistant to the states to provide the necessary resources.

Entitlement Programs

Entitlement programs are ones that guarantee access to benefits based on established rights or by legislation. A "right" is itself an entitlement associated with a moral or social principle such that an "entitlement" is a provision made in accordance with the legal framework of a society. There are a wide number of entitlement programs in existence that cover many segments of American society. Income tax laws provide significant benefits for large groups of people. Students in colleges receive reductions in the amount of taxes due for tuition. There are tax credits for child and dependent care that reduce the amount of federal incomes taxes that are due. By far the biggest tax break in the federal income tax code is the exemption for the interest included in mortgage payments made on homes. The home mortgage exemption is essentially a subsidy for home ownership as it reduces the taxes that homeowners owe. It was designed to encourage home ownership and has been quite successful in doing so.

Other programs grant assistance as a matter of entitlement. Veterans of the armed forces are entitled to a wide variety of benefits as a consequence of their service to the country. Individuals are automatically eligible to receive social security benefits or survivors' benefits. Unemployment benefits are available to those who lose their jobs through no fault of their own. Medicare is also available to everyone that reaches age 65.

TEST TIP

Even though you will complete the multiple-choice portion of the exam using a pencil, bring a couple of pens with black or blue ink to write your essays. Pens write more quickly and don't require sharpening.

Means-Tested Programs

Some programs are **means-tested**, which means they require a determination of whether or not an individual or family is eligible for help from the government. Usually such programs depend on proof that one's income is below a certain level. Income refers to the amount of money a person receives in the form of wages or from other sources. Wealth refers to the assets a person amasses over time. Wealthy people in essence could have low incomes but have large assets to sustain them. A philanthropist who is retired, for example, is a wealthy person, and their wealth allows them to sustain what they want and to provide for others, but would preclude them from qualifying for any means-tested program of assistance. The distinction between *income* and *wages* becomes important for the social security program. Wages earned on a job are taxed to provide funds for payments. Income, which could come from investments, a trust fund, or other sources, is not taxed to provide social security benefits, although it does count for calculations of state and federal income taxes.

Most of the means testing is based on a **poverty line**. Government agencies determine a poverty level based on the total cost of all the essential resources that an average human adult consumes in one year. The poverty line is adjusted for the size of the family. The poverty level has to be adjusted as costs rise. This explains how inflation could be destructive to society by threatening families in distress. The official poverty line is periodically adjusted, of course, to reflect changes in the level of inflation, but there is often a lag before the adjustment catches up with reality. There has also been an increasing problem with the feminization of poverty. More and more women have become heads of households and the sole wage earner. When poverty statistics are analyzed, this group of women represents a disproportionate percentage of the poor who are eligible to these programs.

There are a variety of important means-tested programs. Medicaid, unlike Medicare, is one such program. **Supplemental Security Income** (SSI) provides additional benefits to social security payments to those who can demonstrate particular kinds of need. Food stamps are available to those with limited income as are the school breakfast and lunch programs for children from low-income families. **Head Start** is a program for pre-kindergarten students from low-income families. There are assistance programs for those who need help in paying their heating bills. There have also been a variety of programs that provide housing assistance for those below a particular income level. This type of housing assistance totals a much lower level of expenditures than the taxes that are not collected due to the home mortgage exemption provisions of the federal income tax code.

Social programs have become a major component of government programs. How they will continue to fare depends on future presidents, members of Congress, interest groups, and voters. Means tested programs that focus on those in need have not always been popular, and there are very few who want to completely do away with all of these types of programs. In some cases, the opponents of these programs want to tighten the means testing to limit those who are eligible. Entitlements have come under increasing fire from conservative groups, some Republicans, and those who identify with the Tea Party. They want taxes reduced and are willing to cut the benefits received by those receiving payments from the programs. Reducing payments to those who have already retired, as would be required with reductions in social security, is difficult, so much of the focus is on reducing future payments to everyone or reducing the cost for future retirees.

Social Welfare Programs

The first social welfare program that was part of a broader policy approach was the **Square Deal** that was instituted under President Theodore Roosevelt. His domestic program was based upon three basic ideas: conservation of natural resources, control of corporations, and consumer protection. The Square Deal is important not only because it was the first such program, but also because the **New Deal** has been at times considered to be an extension of the Square Deal.

The Great Depression had devastating effects in virtually every country, rich and poor, and all of their citizens. Personal income, tax revenue, profits, and prices dropped, while international trade plunged by more than 50 percent. Unemployment in the United States rose to 25 percent and in some countries rose as high as 33 percent. The severity of the crisis required some form of new approach. In 1932, the first presidential election after the onset of the Great Depression, Franklin Roosevelt easily defeated the incumbent President Herbert Hoover. President Roosevelt was able to create his New Deal, which was designed to revive the U.S. economy. The New Deal also weakened the laissez-faire basis of the American economy.

The New Deal was a series of economic programs implemented between 1933 and 1936. The programs were not enacted without controversy. President Roosevelt was forced to re-conceive some of his ideas in order to avoid opposition from the Supreme Court. While some of his programs, such as the **Civilian Conservation Corps**, were temporary measures designed to put people back to work, other programs remain with us today. The social security system, the **Securities and Exchange Commission**, and the Federal Housing Administration all date from this period. The Tennessee Valley Authority was created during to bring cheap electricity to the southeastern United States in order to permit electrification and industrialization and to revive an area that had been hit harder by the Great Depression than most other areas of the country. The **Federal Deposit Insurance Corporation** (FDIC) was created to end runs on banks and to stabilize the banking system. No private insurance company was willing to issue insurance to such a troubled sector as banking. The FDIC program has been extremely effective from the outset since it mitigates the worst consequences of bank failures. The National Labor Relations Act and the Fair Labor Standards Act provide protection for the rights of unions to organize and provided some protection to working-class individuals.

The **Great Society** was a set of domestic programs in the 1960s promoted by President Lyndon B. Johnson and fellow Democrats in Congress. Two main goals of the Great Society social reforms were the elimination of poverty (**War on Poverty**) and the end to racial injustice. The War on Poverty was a set of forty programs that were intended to eliminate poverty by improving living conditions and enabling people to lift themselves out of the cycle of poverty. There were an abundance of acts passed during Johnson's term in office. There were also education programs. There were sixty separate bills that provided for new and better-equipped classrooms, minority scholarships, and low-interest student loans. This period also saw other new programs designed to improve the environment and to improve air, land, and water quality. The Head Start program was designed to help four- and five-year-old children from disadvantaged families start school on an even basis with other youngsters. Drawing upon the inspiration of New Deal programs such as the Civilian Conservation Corps, a **Jobs Corps** was created to provide skills for young men and women to give them an appropriate background to become productive members of the workforce.

Health Care

Health care policy has become part of social policy in the United States. The United States has a mostly privatized health-care system, with 46 percent of the country's total health bill paid for by government. Private insurance companies cover one-third, and

Americans pay nearly one-fifth of their health care costs out of their own pockets. Since 1965, Medicare has provided hospitalization insurance, short-term nursing care, and inexpensive coverage for doctor fees for elderly Americans. The cost of health care in the United States has steadily increased in the past few years, mostly because of the cutting-edge technologies used. There have been new drugs developed, and their cost has been very high in part because of their newness and the cost of research and development. The cost of the new drugs has been of little concern because most of the cost is paid for by the government, employers, and insurance companies.

America does not have a universal health care policy. People do not have equal access to health care because much of the care is in the private sector. The average person receives healthcare benefits through their jobs. Employers and companies feel that much of the cost burden for healthcare for full-time employees is being passed on to the companies. Part-time employees are often not entitled to such benefits, and many small companies cannot afford the rising costs of healthcare and may be faced with terminating some employees to meet the increasing costs. It should be noted that the companies that provide health insurance for their employees do receive tax breaks to offset their costs. Others in companies with no benefits must pay for their own health care. Those who become unemployed have to depend on their own resources or government assistance. If none of these options are available, they will not receive any health care.

The largest percentage of Americans without insurance comes from minority families and lower-income families. As a result, they receive poorer health care and have much lower life expectancies. Increasing costs have priced others of the market for health care. The costs for government programs such as Medicare and Medicaid have resulted in demands for reductions in their overall cost, which reduce the amount of health care available for the elderly and the poor.

Lobbyist representing various aspects of the health care profession and elderly patients attempt to pass the increased costs of new medicines and techniques off to Medicare. It is important to emphasize that the elderly population in America is a strong voter block so their concerns will influence policy above public perception and agenda. Workers in low-paying careers, young college graduates, and the unemployed have a very hard time securing health insurance. Their plight, however, is lost on the public at large because of the perception from the media and a variety of interest groups that the insurance programs for those who have existing coverage will suffer if insurance benefits are extended. Other strong lobbyist groups representing business owners and corporations have tried to slow the rising costs that businesses have to pay. In turn hospitals and doctors have been left with few options. They can either pass the cost on to patients or they can offset cost in some other fashion.

Opponents to any healthcare reforms or new management styles in the healthcare system claim that any bureaucratic control of insurance to pay for healthcare would lead to rigid rules for doctors to follow, make if more difficult for patients to see specialists, and sometimes would deny them the opportunity entirely. Further, the opponents claim it would mean that the receipt of recommended treatments would take longer. They also imply that in some instances, the age of the patient could determine how much the appropriate treatment would cost or how much of the cost would be covered. Of course, many involved in the healthcare industry would be disadvantaged by changes. Insurance companies would lose money, and doctors and hospitals are concerned about lost income, as well.

When President Clinton first came into office, he attempted to overhaul the healthcare system in an effort to provide healthcare for more people. His effort failed due to the mobilization of opposition to reform by doctors, hospitals, and medical insurance companies. Other opposition came from those who did not want additional government programs on general ideological principle. President Obama was more successful in pushing a plan through Congress that would eliminate some of the inequity in access. He faced some of the same groups that had earlier opposed President Clinton. The opponents have mounted court challenges to aspects of the healthcare plan and in some cases have received some positive rulings (for them) on the constitutionality of President Obama's healthcare plan. Ultimately, the Supreme Court will have to determine whether or not the provisions of the plan are acceptable or not.

Tax Policy

Social welfare policy is influenced by the types of taxes that are administered. The impact of the home mortgage interest exemption has already been mentioned. How a government chooses to raise money through taxes will influence personal income levels and potentially the economy as a whole. There are ideological differences as to what types of taxes should be used: progressive, regressive, or fixed. Some of the differences are based on economic issues, and some are based on social policies.

A **progressive tax** is one that takes a larger tax percentage from the income of high-income earners than it does from low-income individuals. The United States income tax is considered progressive because the more a person earns, the higher the tax percentage. The U.S. income tax system has a number of exemptions and loopholes, however, which make the overall tax levels less progressive. A **regressive tax**, in contrast, imposes a greater burden (relative to resources) on the poor than on the rich. There is an inverse relationship between the tax rate and the taxpayer's ability to pay as measured by assets, consumption, or income. The more you earn, the less you pay. A fixed tax rate or flat tax rate is the same for all taxpayers regardless of the income of the individual.

While income taxes are progressive taxes, other taxes tend to be more regressive. All states rely on property taxes for local funding. Property taxes tend to be somewhat regressive overall. Property owners pay the property taxes directly (and can reduce their federal income tax bill by writing the payment off). Many states also rely on sales taxes as a source of revenue. These taxes range from less than 1 percent to more than 10 percent. Sales tax is collected by the seller at the point of purchase. Sales taxes are used to help offset the local government budget burden without increasing other various state taxes on residents. Sales taxes are considered to be regressive because those with lower levels of income end up paying a higher percentage of their income in sales tax than do the wealthy.

The distribution of the tax burden via progressive or regressive taxes can affect social policy. If taxes are progressive, funding for a variety of programs by the government are, in effect, funded by wealthy individuals. If taxes are flat or regressive, more funding comes from the less well-off. Conservatives argue that lowering the tax rates on the wealthy will make funds available for economic investment. This investment will increase economic growth and create more jobs, which will assist everyone, and will therefore reduce the amount of money spent on social welfare programs. Liberals argue that progressive tax rates help to fund social welfare programs that keep money in the pockets of the less well-off. These individuals will use the money from these programs to buy food, clothing, and shelter, providing a stimulus to the economy in a variety of areas. The debate about the best approach to take in social and economic terms continues.

TEST TIP

Not sure where to start in a free-response essay? Construct a straightforward, one-sentence response that directly answers the question posed. This sentence can now act as your thesis statement.

Environment

Environmental policies raise concerns about the benefits they create and how they are going to be paid for. Controversies often surround environmental policies because of scientific uncertainty about the nature and extent of the problems. Differing scientific options can make solutions to environmental problems uncertain. The scientific uncertainties (or arguments that there are scientific uncertainties) have led to a number of political features that make environmental policy different from other policies. As a result, conflicts between the government, businesses, and the public arise about how to preserve the environment

In entrepreneurial politics, an unorganized public will benefit from the efforts of a well-organized group. The issues of **global warming** and preserving endangered species reveal the workings of entrepreneurial politics. The scientific community has reached near consensus about global climate change, even though some doubters remain. Build-up of carbon dioxide and other gases in the atmosphere has increased the temperature of the Earth. Such global warming can reduce the ice caps leading to coastal flooding and changing weather patterns. The Kyoto Protocol was developed to address concerns about global warming. Signatories to the protocol pledged to support the lowering of carbon dioxide by 30 percent. Businesses raised concerns about the unintended consequences of such protocols since they may have severe negative effects on the economy; therefore, the United States did not initially sign the protocol. The Obama administration, however, believes the innovation necessary to meet the Kyoto goals will spark economic growth and has attempted to implement policies that will achieve the protocol's goals.

The Endangered Species Act of 1973 passed due to the efforts of well-organized environmentalists. The act forbids killing a protected species and prohibits actions that would adversely affect the habitat of an endangered species. Concerns about endangered species have led to continued doubts about the negative consequence that the Alaskan pipeline could have. Those opposed to the act argue that the legislation has slowed the ability of businesses to develop areas of the country where these protected species reside.

Pollution as a Trigger

The **Environmental Protection Agency** (EPA) was created during the Nixon administration. Environmental groups had pushed for a number of years for such an agency. The EPA is one of the largest federal regulatory agencies. It is charged with administering policies dealing with land use, air and water quality, and wilderness and wildlife preservation. The duties of he EPA have expanded over the years to deal with many problems.

Concerns over environmental quality arose because of increasing pollution of water, air, and land. As a consequence, public pressure for programs to improve these conditions increased. Efforts were made to clean up waterways with some success. Water treatment plants for urban areas became more efficient and industrial discharges were better controlled. Other sources of water pollution remained more difficult to control, but there were many areas where virtually dead rivers and lakes were restored.

Some pollution issues might be resolved if the United States relied more on renewable energy resources. Currently, only about 7 percent of the energy used in the country comes from renewable sources like wind and solar power. Greater reliance on renewable energy would not only help to ease paying for the high cost of oil, but could reduce global warming and ease the effects of pollution. Conservation measures would work in the same way to reduce energy usage, pollution, and global warming.

The Clean Air Act of 1970 was passed in response to air pollution that sometimes became so bad in some areas that it was a health hazard for some people with compromised breathing systems. Air pollution can come from fixed points—factories and especially utility plants—and from mobile sources—cars and trucks. Coal fired utility plants created problems with direct air pollution and with acid rain that damaged forests and lakes in distant areas. The Department of Transportation was initially charged with the responsibility of reducing automobile emissions. Efforts to reduce emissions from automobiles ran into opposition from the auto industry, and many of the timetables for the reduction of such pollution were pushed into the future. The EPA dealt with problems from industries and utility plants. Much of the pollution was related to the use of coal, which accounts for 90 percent of the country's energy resources. Much of the coal being burned contributed to chemical buildups in the air. Coal mining was also dangerous for the workers because of accidents and the danger of black lung disease. The EPA was able to reduce the release of pollutants. Stack scrubbers that are designed to remove chemicals from the smoke stacks and other plant modifications were used, and many plants began to use cleaner coal from mines in the western United States. In 1990, Congress passed a reauthorization of the Clean Air Act with amendments (Comprehensive Environmental Response, Compensation, and Liability Act), which significantly increased the controls on cars, oil refineries, chemical plants, and coal-fired utility plants, as well as permitted utility plants to use emissions trading (plants that were able to reduce emissions by more than the requirement could transfer the reductions to plants that had not been able to do so).

Land pollution was often considered a lesser issue for many years. In 1977 and 1978, however, it was discovered that a suburb of Buffalo, New York called **Love Canal** had been built on land that had formerly been used as a toxic waste dump. As the investigation proceeded, it was discovered that families in the suburb were suffering from excessive numbers of illnesses related to the toxic wastes from the ground and groundwater. The whole suburb was evacuated, and the slow process of cleanup began. The families who had lived there continued to suffer from the ill effects of toxic waste exposure. The experience of Love Canal led to the passage of the Superfund, which was designed to clean up similar toxic waste sites throughout the country. It has been a slow process to first locate all the sites and then to clean them up.

Industrial farming is another area of pollution concern. The concentration of animals in closed quarters has had negative effects on surrounding lands due to inadequate waste disposal. The inadequate waste disposal also leads to pollution of waterways and the contamination of groundwater. These farms also pollute the air with noxious odors, and there are adverse health consequences for those who live near factory farms, including increases in upper respiratory.

Foreign and Defense Policymaking

The goal of foreign policy is to achieve peace and prosperity in the international community. Foreign policy is typically a struggle to achieve a middle ground between political idealism and political realism. The Constitution divides the foreign policy powers of the country between the president and Congress, which invites conflict between the two groups. Overall, however, the president is clearly the more important branch in the area of foreign policy.

The president is the commander in chief, but Congress appropriates money for foreign and military operations. Congress also has the ability to curtail economic aid to other countries, for example, although they rarely do so for fear of angering constituents. The president appoints ambassadors, but the Senate confirms them. The president negotiates treaties, but the Senate must ratify them with a two-thirds vote. Presidents can use executive agreements to avoid Senate confirmation, and the president can often conduct diplomacy that requires little funding with a relatively free hand. Although Americans often think the president is in charge of foreign policy, only Congress can regulate commerce with other nations and declare war.

The Supreme Court has attempted to clarify the constitution, ruling that the federal government has foreign policy powers beyond those specifically enumerated, but the Court has refused to delineate which branch is supreme in the case of war powers. To address this concern, Congress attempted to limit the president's control of the use of military force by passing the War Powers Act in 1973. It contained a couple of important provisions: The president must report all commitments of troops in hostile situations within forty-eight hours, and the president may make only a sixty-day commitment of troops unless there is a declaration of war that has gained approval from Congress. Ultimately, the War Powers Act had little impact on presidential military actions. Every president since its passage has sent troops abroad without congressional approval.

Important Military Interventions since 1960

Year	Intervention
1961	U.S.-sponsored invasion of Cuba at Bay of Pigs
1961–1975	U.S. troops in Vietnam
1962	U.S. naval blockade of Cuba to prevent installation of Soviet missiles
1965	U.S. occupying troops in the Dominican Republic to block takeover by leftist political forces
1980	Unsuccessful military effort to rescue U.S. hostages in Iran
1981	U.S. military advisers in El Salvador to help the government
1982–1989	CIA support for antigovernment guerrillas in Nicaragua
1983	U.S. Marines in Lebanon as peacekeeping force
1983	U.S. invasion of Grenada to oust pro-Cuba government
1984	U.S. minesweepers in the Red Sea to clear mines
1987	U.S. Navy to escort tankers through Persian Gulf
1989	U.S. invasion of Panama to oust dictator Manuel Noriega
1991	U.S. troops, together with those from other countries, to force Iraq to end its invasion of Kuwait
2001	U.S. supports Northern Alliance in Afghanistan in war that ends Taliban regime
2003	U.S. invasion of Iraq

The Defense Budget

The peacetime military was very small until 1940. After World War II, the rise of communism and the Soviet threat left the United States struggling with the role of the most powerful military power. The United States had to fight battles to contain the communist/Soviet threat, and after the Korean Conflict in 1950s, the military did not decrease in size for decades. The Cold War military was designed to repel Soviet invasions around the world. Levels of military spending reflect the public's general support of the military in the postwar period as needed by the president, though there was a decrease in its size during the tenure of President Clinton. It began to grow again after the terrorist attacks of September 11, 2001.

Foreign policy has become crucial to governmental affairs in the past century, as the United States made the transition from isolationist country to world superpower. In this global era of high-speed connections, brief but deadly missile strikes, and free trade, it is apparent that this policy area will continue to hold an important place on every politician's agenda and in the public's mind, as well. American foreign policy is conducted mostly by the president and the executive branch, though Congress has some important responsibilities. The president serves as chief diplomat and as commander-in-chief of the armed forces. He negotiates treaties, makes executive agreements, and appoints ambassadors. He can act quickly and decisively.

The bureaucratic arm of foreign policy is the State Department. The Secretary of State is the president's top foreign policy adviser. American embassies fall under the jurisdiction of this department. The Department of Defense works closely with the State Department in matters of national security. The Joint Chiefs of Staff represent each branch of the armed forces in an advisory committee to the president. The **Central Intelligence Agency** collects information in other countries and coordinates the activities of other intelligence agencies to help the State and Defense Departments and the president make policy decisions. It sometimes plays a covert role in the governmental affairs of other nations. Congress helps to oversee foreign policy, authorizes declarations of war, and appropriates funds for national security.

The United States became involved in the Vietnam War to contain the spread of communism in Southeast Asia. The conflict resulted in massive troop commitments and heavy bombing of North Vietnam. Images of the war, its devastation, and casualties were broadcast into homes nightly by television. These images, increasing casualties, and the length of the conflict in addition to doubts about the quality of the government of South Vietnam sparked mass anti-war protests across America. Many Americans began to view the government with some skepticism. Vietnam had broader effects on policy as seen in the government's reliance on détente (peaceful agreements), which, for example, brought greater cooperation between the United States and the Soviet Union. Hostilities between the two countries and the Cold War came to an end with the fall of the Soviet Union in the late 1980s, but international relations have yet to peacefully stabilize.

Since the attacks of September 11, 2001, much of the focus of foreign policy has been on defeating terrorist groups that threaten the United States. The U.S. military involvements in Afghanistan and Iraq were a direct consequence of these efforts. The length of the military involvement with casualties and high costs eventually made these conflicts unpopular. While the threat of terrorism has been limited to some extent, it has clearly not been eliminated. It is not likely to be eliminated in the immediate future as new situations and new groups appear with some regularity.

As the most powerful country in the world, the United States has been involved in many international organizations. The United Nations remains the most important. The United States is particularly important in the United Nations since it has a permanent seat on the Security Council, and like Britain, France, Russia, and China, it can veto any action of the Security Council that it does not like. The **North Atlantic Treaty Organization** has been a key defensive alliance since the end of World War II. It joins the United States, Canada, and most European countries in a mutual defense treaty. The United States has similar arrangements with countries in Latin America, Japan, Australia, and New Zealand, among others.

The International Economy

The growth of the global economy has led to an increase in international trade over the past two decades. International economic interactions have become much more important for the United States and its general prosperity. What happens elsewhere in the world has positive or negative effects on the United States. International economic treaties have been created to address issues of international trade through such ideas as most favored nation status, where equitable trade and tariff policies are observed by foreign nations. The use of tariffs has declined to help free trade among nations. However, the trade imbalance that the United States has faced in recent years is a concern for some.

While all aspects of foreign policy can have significant effects on citizens of the United States, economic and trade policies can have the most direct effect on individual pocketbooks. Interest groups, including labor unions and businesses, are quite active in lobbying Congress to try to arrange changes in trade policies and other types of economic activities involving foreign countries. Some groups want closer ties with the global economy, and other groups seek to weaken such linkages. The World Trade

Organization (WTO) has provided structure to international trade and other forms of international economic activity. The United States has been a strong supporter of the WTO, in part because the organization has provided support for many activities that are important to the United States, such as protecting intellectual property rights (copyrights and trademarks) and making foreign investment easier.

Protests against free trade have become commonplace due to fear that weaker developing countries will be exploited by foreign governments and international businesses. In addition, the rise of developing nations has made the economy interdependent, and this has had an effect on the supplies and cost of energy. The Organization of Petroleum Exporting Countries (OPEC) and other petroleum exporting countries have benefited as demand and price have steadily increased in the past two decades. The end of the Cold War has limited the ability of the United States to gain economic concessions from its allies since these countries are much less likely to need U.S. military protection. The recent global economic problems have highlighted the interconnectedness of economic activities in various parts of the globe and made economic recovery in the United States and Europe more difficult.

Time for a quiz
- Review strategies in Chapter 2
- Take Quiz 5 at the REA Study Center
  (www.rea.com/studycenter)

Civil Rights and Civil Liberties

Liberties and Rights

Although the terms **civil rights** and **civil liberties** are often used interchangeably, it is important to understand the difference between them. *Civil liberties* are the rights and freedoms provided by the government, or what Locke defined as a natural right to life, liberty, and property. The Constitution (actually the **Bill of Rights**) was specifically designed to enumerate the civil liberties to which every individual is entitled and to ensure that these liberties are protected. In theory, these rights were supposed to be available to all citizens. The actual content of these liberties and how they have been applied to people in the United States has evolved over time.

Civil rights, on the other hand, protect an individual from discrimination and guarantee his or her freedom from unwarranted infringement by governments and private organizations. The civil rights struggle by black Americans and their supporters was started so that they would have the protections and liberties that the Constitution and Bill of Rights were supposed to provide. While the civil rights movement for black Americans is perhaps the best known civil rights movement, many other groups in the United States have struggled to achieve equal treatment and avoid discrimination based on group characteristics.

Civil Liberties

Civil liberties are defined as liberties or freedoms granted to the people by the Constitution, by common law, or by legislation. The Constitution and common law both provide a solid basis for civil liberties. Common law has had well-established practices, and the courts, which are the ultimate guarantor of civil liberties, have always paid a great deal of attention to common law traditions. The Constitution, of course, provides a solid support for civil liberties. Formal amendments are difficult, and informal amendment by the Supreme Court is not likely to restrict individual freedoms. Legislation on its own provides less protection since laws can be changed by Congress as party majorities change. However, it is easier to prevent changes to existing legislation than it is to bring about change. Many liberties were defined in the Bill of Rights, but the interpretation of these rights has evolved over the course of history, reflecting changing attitudes of American public opinion. Of course, the Ninth Amendment, which protects unstated liberties that belong to the people, is, by design, very open to the inclusion of new freedoms, which are not especially well defined.

Establishing Civil Liberties

The Founding Fathers were quite concerned about individual freedoms. Many of the issues in the colonies involved what the colonists saw as infringement on individual liberties by the king, Parliament, and English or colonial officials. They wanted to be sure that the new national government would not abuse individual rights in the same fashion. The argument at the Constitutional Convention and during the ratification debates about the Bill of Rights was in essence an argument about the best way to defend these freedoms. Ultimately, the inclusion of the Bill of Rights as part of the Constitution and the creation of a federal system, where one of the implicit roles for the states was to protect individual freedoms, were the methods chosen to defend individual liberties.

The task of determining the balance between the liberties and needs of the individual and the needs of the state has largely fallen to the judicial branch. The justices of the Supreme Court are not free agents, of course. They have been influenced by the whole system of checks and balances and, to some extent, by public opinion. Sometimes the Supreme Court has followed public opinion, and sometimes it has led public opinion. Initially the Constitution, including the Bill of Rights, protected the civil liberties of individuals against infringement from the federal government. The limitations did not apply to the state governments at the time of the ratification of the Constitution or the individual amendments in the Bill of Rights (although the Fourteenth Amendment led to significant changes in this view).

The most basic civil liberties that are protected in the Bill of Rights are found in the first amendment. This amendment guarantees freedom of speech, freedom of press, freedom of assembly and petition, and freedom of religion. It also prohibits the establishment of a particular national church. Civil liberties noted in other amendments provide a variety of protections for individuals who face trials for criminal charges. A variety of conflicts have centered on these individual liberties and the interpretation of their applications. The federal judiciary has had to consider the issues and render judgments on the extent of the protection that it offered for individuals.

Freedom of the Press

The Founding Fathers were very concerned about freedom of the press. The First Amendment clearly was intended to protect publishers from harassment by the government for printing materials that presented facts or views unfavorable to the government or its leaders. Colonial newspapers had been quite active in providing political commentary on the actions of British officials. At the time the Constitution was written, pamphlets were frequently used as a form of presenting political arguments to broad audiences. Books were less frequently used in this regard, but the freedom to publish was clearly intended to cover them, as well. Interestingly enough, while the first amendment makes no mention of any exception for freedom of the press, **libel** (knowingly printing falsehoods about individuals) is not considered to be protected by the Constitution or the Bill of Rights. Even though no exception for libel is mentioned anywhere in the Constitution, common law practice in the courts normally made an exception for libel, and the Founding Fathers assumed its exclusion from freedom of the press protections. It is also worth noting that there is no constitutional right that permits a journalist to refuse to divulge sources of information. The national courts and many state court systems often honor this claim when it appears to be reasonable, but there is no specific constitutional guarantee.

Normally the courts have supported the free press by not permitting censorship during times of peace. At least some forms of censorship have been accepted by the courts during wartime, especially if the publishing of information would harm military efforts. The courts have generally not accepted the idea of **prior restraint** with the press during peacetime. Prior restraint prohibits the government from banning expression of ideas prior to their publication. This was deemed essential to create a free society by allowing the press the ability to publish stories without fear of retribution. While newspapers may face consequences for what is published, such as libel suits, the newspaper cannot be prevented from publishing material in advance. This issue was dealt with by the Supreme Court in the case of the **Pentagon Papers**, when the Nixon administration attempted to prevent their publication. In *New York Times Co. v. United States* (1971), the newspaper won the right to continue to publish the papers on the U.S. Vietnam policy, even though they were embarrassing to the government. The government could present no convincing arguments that national security was jeopardized by their publication. Although the First Amendment refers to "press," a more modern term would be the "media." The courts have accepted that the liberty associated with freedom of press covers new outlets including radio, television, and to some extent, the Internet. These types of outlets are considered a natural extension of the press in a constitutional context.

TEST TIP

As tempting as it may be to talk about the test with your friends, don't do it! Posting information on a social media website or blog about a certain AP exam test item that gave you trouble may seem harmless, but doing so will result in the cancelation of your score if it's found by the AP Program.

In the landmark case of *Near v. Minnesota*, (1931) the Supreme Court struck down a Minnesota state law that permitted public officials to seek an injunction to stop publication of any "malicious, scandalous and defamatory newspaper, magazine, or other periodical." The law in this case was being applied against an anti-Semitic, racist publications. This decision was quite important because it extended the protection inherent with freedom of the press to defend the media, especially unpopular publications, from interference from state governments, as well as the national government. The Bill of Rights did not initially provide protection against state denial of civil liberties, a limitation that the Supreme Court explicitly accepted in *Barron v. Baltimore* (1833). With this decision, the Court incorporated the First Amendment freedom of the press into the **due process clause** of the **Fourteenth Amendment,** which meant that state governments now faced the same restrictions as the national government with regard to limiting the press.

Freedom of Speech

Freedom of speech has been protected by the Supreme Court with great regularity. The Court has considered speech to be a "near absolute" right. The Court has been particularly protective of the right of individuals to freely use political speech and expression. The Court has talked about a marketplace of ideas in which good ideas will drive out bad ideas. Clearly, opponents of those in power must be able to criticize without fear of imprisonment, or a democracy itself is in jeopardy. The judiciary has overturned some limitation on financial contributions to candidates because of free speech concerns. Efforts to limit personal spending on behalf of a candidate have not been accepted since such limitations would infringe upon the ability to make political views heard—it would muffle political expression for at least some individuals. The Court has accepted limitations on free speech when such speech would cause a "**clear and present danger**" of a negative outcome. The classic example given was yelling "fire" in a crowded theater when there was no fire. If panic ensues, causing injury and death, the individual could be prosecuted for his actions without violating rights to free speech.

Other freedoms related to speech are also covered under the First Amendment in the view of the Supreme Court. Laws making the burning of the American flag a criminal offense have been overturned by the Supreme Court as a violation of freedom of speech. Flag burning has been considered a form of symbolic speech in which the act demonstrates the protestors' dissatisfaction with current government policies. This action is thus political expression or political speech and therefore immune from prosecution. The protection of the rights of protestors to demonstrate their opposition is the type of political speech that the Supreme Court has been careful to support.

The courts have upheld some limitations on political speech during wartime. In 1919, *Schenk v. United States* upheld the 1917 Espionage Act. The Espionage Act along with the Sedition Act of 1918 limited the freedom of expression (press and speech); it stated that treason, insurrection, forcible resistance to federal laws, and encouraging disloyalty in the armed services were not protected by the first amendment. Schenk was convicted of trying to persuade men from serving in the armed forces. The Court has often accepted limitations on the rights of citizens and news organizations during wartime as long as they presented a clear and present danger. More recent cases, such as *Dennis v. United States* (1950), upheld arrest of Communist party leaders for advocating violent change to the government of the United States. Eventually, individuals in the United States have been freer to support such views and even more unpopular political views without fear of prosecution, but such wide-ranging protection has been recent.

Other types of speech are not protected. **Slander**, which is knowingly lying about an individual or organization, is not protected, even though the Constitution and the Bill of Rights make no exception for slander. As is the case with libel, the limitation was understood to be present at the time. When the target of negative speech or written commentary is a public figure—including politicians and office holders, the courts have normally used a higher standard before accepting limitations. The courts have basically said that public figures must accept a certain amount of negative commentary, some of which is not likely to be entirely factual, as a consequence of being in the public spotlight.

The courts have accepted governmental limitations much more frequently in relationship to commercial speech, which would also include advertisements conveyed via the press or the media. Laws requiring truth in advertising or banning false advertising have been upheld. In essence, the courts have been less concerned with unfettered freedom of expression as a means of selling goods or services. The exception, of course, is that the courts are much more protective about advertising that is designed to sell a candidate to the voting public. There is not even a prohibition on "false" advertising in this regard.

Federal courts have also had to deal with conflicts between obscenity and freedom of speech, freedom of press, or freedom of expression. When limitations on works that were considered obscene were challenged in court, it proved to be a difficult standard to create. There were earlier efforts to establish a standard of what is obscenity, but the current standard established by the Supreme Court is that an average person, applying contemporary community standards, must find that the material, as a whole, appeals to the prurient interest; that the material must depict or describe, in a patently offensive way, sexual conduct specifically defined by applicable law; and that the material, taken as a whole, must lack serious literary, artistic, political, or scientific value. While this standard is clear in some respects, it does require constant interpretation in terms of what qualifies as "contemporary community standards" or "serious literary, artistic, political, or scientific value." Of course, community standards will also vary somewhat from location to location. The community standards of San Francisco, California and Spartanburg, South Carolina could be quite different.

Freedom of Assembly

Freedom of assembly is in many respects a logical extension of freedom of speech. Demonstrations are a way in which many individuals join together to provide a more compelling form of political expression. A guarantee of a right to assemble and to petition the government for a redress of grievances seemed important when the Bill of Rights was passed because the English government had restricted such rights. While the federal courts have protected the right to assemble and protest, they have also accepted reasonable limitations on the process of assembling and demonstrating. Parade permits can be required, and reasonable limitations on where the protest can occur have been deemed acceptable. In the past, petitions were often presented in person to members of the government. Today, petitions are much more likely to be transmitted in a form that would be covered by freedom of speech or press. In many ways, freedom of speech, assembly, and press have been linked since the passage of the First Amendment because the key reason for protecting these civil liberties is to provide opportunities for the citizens of the country to make their views know without retribution from the governing authorities.

DIDYOUKNOW?

Demonstrators in England were literally read the Riot Act. The Riot Act warned the demonstrators that their actions were considered illegal and, unless they dispersed, force could be used. The Founding Fathers guaranteed the right of peaceful assembly in the First Amendment as a response to this English practice.

Freedom of Religion

The First Amendment mentions religion twice. The first mention in regard to religion is to strictly prohibit the national government from establishing any religion (the **establishment clause**). The Founding Fathers were very conscious of the fact that public taxes were used to support the Church of England, and they were determined to avoid any effort to establish a national church for the new country. Many of the colonies were established by religious dissidents, so fear of a national church was imbedded in the political culture of colonial society. Since the Bill of Rights did not limit the states initially, it was possible for individual states to provide preferential treatment to particular churches or religions, and a number of them did so.

A succession of court cases has limited the implicit support any government can provide to a particular religion. The prohibition on government support for churches eventually extended to states, which has generated a number of controversies. Governments have not been able to support any church or broad religious denomination by prayer in school, religious displays on public grounds, or displays of only one type of religious document in a public building—there has to be a wall of separation between church and state. These limitations on what had been normal practice in the past have led to public hostility in many cases. It is difficult for a school or government agency to undertake any activity with religious connotations that does not favor one church or religion (Protestantism or Christianity in general) over other religions or atheists. The courts eventually assumed that support for religion in a general sense could constitute establishment of religion that would come at the expense of some members of society. A reading from the New Testament, for example, could be taken by younger children to indicate that the government or school believes that Christianity is better than Judaism or some non-Christian religions. The implication of government preference in the choice of readings or official endorsement could also indicate that Protestantism is preferred over Catholicism since it is the Protestant version of the New Testament that was generally used rather than the Catholic version. The Ten Commandments that some would like posted in public buildings, including schools or courthouses, is invariably the Protestant version rather than the slightly different Catholic version or the Jewish version.

Not all religious activity has been overturned by court decisions. The court has accepted "In God We Trust" as a motto on coin and currency as a relatively innocuous statement. Religious practices (prayers or invocations) have not been prohibited in college settings, in part because the courts believe that college students are less impressionable than those in elementary school or high school.

Other forms of government activity have been prohibited since they could be considered support for a church or religion. State or local governments have not been able to provide direct support to parochial schools since that would be helping to establish religion. *Lemon v. Kurtzman* (1970) overturned subsidies for parochial schools in Rhode Island and Pennsylvania. In *Committee for Public Education and Religious Liberty v. Nyquist* (1972), the Supreme Court prohibited New York from subsidizing parochial schools that served low income students. In this latter case, the state supported parochial schools that provided education for students in special need. The potential support for religion was considered to override the positive benefit that such subsidies might have. Court decisions have permitted support to be given directly to students in the form of provision of transportation or books that are available to all students. In *Everson v. Board of Education of Ewing Township* (1946), for example, the Supreme Court permitted public transportation that was available to both public school and parochial school students. In this bit of legal hair-splitting, the courts were able to distinguish between assistance for students as opposed to support for schools. The free transportation provided was for students, although indirectly it did benefit parochial schools. The issue of such indirect government support is sure to resurface with the issue of school vouchers and other forms of school choice. School vouchers will clearly be used to support religiously based schools as well as private schools. If the voucher system can be seen as support for students, it is likely to be constitutional. If it is determined to be more directly as support for religious schools (as well as other private schools), it may be overturned.

The First Amendment also provides for freedom to practice religion. The national government, and now the state governments, are not able to interfere with the free practice of religion in most cases. The court ruled in *Reynolds v. United States* in 1879 that religious exercises are generally protected, but the protection does not prevent the government from passing neutral laws that can incidentally affect religious practices; in this case, the neutral law was one that prohibited polygamy. Neither the courts nor public opinion would accept the idea that child sacrifice would be an appropriate religious practice that would be protected under the First Amendment. With the same logic, the courts have usually ruled that parents cannot withhold essential medical treatment on the basis of religious principles from children who are too young to make their own decisions. Courts have favored religious practices in other cases. Religious clubs or organizations, for example, have to be treated like any other club in schools. If other clubs can meet in classrooms after normal school hours or utilize school facilities for their activities, then religious groups (or atheist groups for that matter) have to have the same access.

Rights of the Accused

The Constitution protects the rights of those accused of crimes. Bills of attainder and ex post facto laws are prohibited, and the Constitution guarantees the right to habeas corpus. Additional rights for those accused of crimes are found in the Fourth, Fifth, Sixth, and Eighth Amendments. Some of these rights are absolute rights. A person cannot be forced to testify against him- or herself (Fifth Amendment); there is a guarantee to a fair and speedy trial (Sixth Amendment); and there is a right of double jeopardy that prevents a person from being tried a second time for a crime after being acquitted in an earlier trial (Fifth Amendment). Other rights are less absolute. Searches may be conducted with a warrant if **probable cause** is present (Fourth Amendment), and individuals may be questioned if they are informed of their rights (Fifth Amendment). These last two rights are not prohibitions on government activity; they permit the government to undertake searches or to question suspects as long as the proper procedures are followed.

TEST TIP

Although there is no minimum number of words for the essay responses, your answers need to be detailed enough to fully answer the question. Consider writing a standard five-paragraph essay—one introductory paragraph giving your thesis, three paragraphs of supporting information and examples, and one concluding paragraph summarizing your ideas and restating your thesis—to make sure that you provide enough information in your response.

Rights of defendants in criminal trials have been extended over time. In *Gideon v. Wainwright* (1963), the absence of a lawyer in a modern court system was in effect a denial of the right to a fair trial. As a consequence, defendants have to be provided with a lawyer if they cannot afford one. In *Miranda v. Arizona* (1966), the Supreme Court decided that people in custody have to be informed of their legal rights, including the right to remain silent and the right to see a lawyer. However, basic liberties have little meaning if individuals are unaware of them. There have been questions as to what constitutes "in custody" or "official questioning" as sometimes police have learned valuable information from talking to someone that they consider a possible witness rather than a suspect. In *Dickerson v. United States* (1999), the Supreme Court strengthened Miranda rights when it held that Congress and other legislative bodies may not overturn Miranda rights because such constitutional rights are immune to legislative changes. Searches, while clearly possible under the Fourth Amendment, have fallen under stricter regulation over time. As early as *Weeks v. United States* (1913), material from illegal searches could not be introduced as evidence that could be used to convict an individual (the **exclusionary rule**). In *Mapp v. Ohio* (1960), all material from any illegal search was excluded from being used as evidence in a court of law at either the national level or the state level. The restrictions were modified somewhat in 1983 in *United States v. Leon* when evidence from good faith searches (searches where there were technical issues that made the warrants wrong but were executed by police officers who believed them to be valid) to be introduced in court. In *New Jersey v. T.L.O.* (1983), school officials on school grounds, at least through the level of high school, were held to have broader rights in conducting searches (and students had less protection from such searches). In the case of schools, there is an implied consent to some searches by presence on the school grounds, and schools are seen in some sense as serving as local agents of parents.

Some of the protections extended to defendants have been considered controversial since they make convictions harder to achieve, even for people who seem to be guilty of the crimes that they are accused of. The federal courts over time have chosen to err on the side of protecting the rights of innocent defendants who might be wrongly convicted, even if that means letting some other people escape the punishment they might deserve. In addition, it would be a violation of the basic idea of civil liberties if government officials were allowed to ignore individual rights in order to convict them of offenses, even ones they committed.

There is one other issue for defendants charged with major crimes that has been raised in the judiciary. It has been argued that capital punishment is unconstitutional, in part because the Eighth Amendment prohibits cruel and unusual punishment. Of course, punishment is by definition cruel. The cruel and unusual punishments that were known to the Founding Fathers were things such as branding, cutting off the hand of a pickpocket (which was still on the books in England, even if seldom applied), drawing and quartering, and execution by torture. As a consequence, the courts have viewed challenges to capital punishment on the basis of whether it is cruel *and* unusual.

The courts have consistently ruled that in principle capital punishment is not prohibited by the Constitution. The way in which capital punishment is administered must be humane, which has outlawed some ways of inflicting the death penalty. The federal courts have required that capital punishment cannot be inflicted in arbitrary fashions or in ways that show bias. This issue is more one of the fair administration of justice (and thus a civil rights issue) rather than a civil liberty issue. Opponents of capital punishment often use moral arguments, which may be quite valid, but they are not yet part of the Constitution. As a practical matter, there are cases where people on death row have been cleared of crimes they supposedly committed, so it is quite possible that an innocent person has been executed at some point.

The Right to Privacy

The right to privacy has been a controversial issue in some of its applications. It has been suggested that the Fourth Amendment with its limit on searches and the Fifth Amendment with its limit on self-incrimination imply a right to privacy. The Ninth Amendment, of course, with its statement of existing rights not enumerated elsewhere, provides a clear possibility for the protection of privacy as a civil liberty. It is clear that the Founding Fathers wanted to avoid government intrusions into private activities. In *Griswold v. Connecticut* (1964), the Supreme Court used right to privacy to prevent states from prohibiting organizations from providing contraceptive information to married couples. The decisions of married couples about the number of children to have was seen as an intensely private decision that should not be reviewed by local police, and the decision effectively made it virtually impossible for states to try to limit the use of contraceptive devices.

Prior to 1973, abortion was an issue left to the states. Some states permitted abortions without many preconditions while many others did not allow abortion except when medical necessity was an issue. The right to privacy was an important part of the decision in *Roe v. Wade* in 1973 to legalize abortions during the first trimester of a pregnancy without any need for special circumstances. Abortion in the second trimester was permissible if the health of the mother was endangered. States had more flexibility in dealing with whether or not abortions would be possible in the last trimester. In *Webster v. Reproductive Health Services* (1988), the Court permitted Missouri to make receiving abortions in public hospitals more difficult while still upholding the basic principles in *Roe v. Wade*. In 1992, the Court allowed states to enact additional restrictions without eliminating the right to an abortion in *Planned Parenthood of Southeastern Pennsylvania v. Casey.* These restrictions were designed to make abortions more difficult to arrange, and to some extent the restrictions have had that effect. Other decisions have accepted state limitations on abortions, but no case to date has reversed the basic principle of *Roe v. Wade*. In 1976, Congress passed the Hyde Amendment, which barred the use of federal funds to pay for abortions. Federal payments were at least a possibility under Medicaid until this change in the law. The Hyde Amendment has passed judicial scrutiny since not all protected liberties require funding by the federal government. The Bill of Rights defends against government action but does not always compel the government to undertake positive action. In 2003, the Partial-Birth Abortion Ban Act was enacted. This law banned this particular method of abortion between the 15-week and the 26-week of the second trimester. The law was introduced to limit a particular form of medical procedure based on the potential viability of a fetus outside of the womb; this method could conceivably kill a viable fetus. The law banned only a type of abortion procedure in the second trimester, not all abortions within the second trimester. Supporters of the bill saw it as another step in reversing *Roe v. Wade*. Opponents viewed it in the same fashion and mounted legal challenges to this law, but such challenges have not been successful. The battle over the availability of abortions has been continuous since the passage of *Roe v. Wade* and has involved major political conflicts that reflect the lack of consensus in the public over the issue. It is highly unlikely that consensus will be reached anytime in the immediate future; thus, the amount of protection provided for those desiring abortions or limitations on the availability of abortions is still uncertain.

The Right to Bear Arms

It has been argued that the Second Amendment is a guarantee of the right of individuals to bear arms. The Supreme Court has always held that this amendment was a guarantee to the states, as contracting parties to the Constitution, of their right to maintain a state militia (i.e., "The Right of the States to a well-regulated militia" portion that starts the amendment). Some of the rights mentioned in the Constitution and the amendments are designed as guarantees to the states. It has frequently been argued that this amendment is a guarantee of the civil liberties of individuals, but the courts have never accepted this argument when it has been raised; the courts routinely reject cases that argue that controls on gun ownership violate the Second Amendment. It has been left to those who seek to have the fewest limitations possible on gun ownership to rely on Congress or state legislatures to pass the appropriate laws or to prevent limitations on gun ownership.

The Fourteenth Amendment

The Fourteenth Amendment led to significant changes in how the Constitution has been interpreted because it changed the document itself. This amendment provided a national definition of citizenship for the first time in the United States, and it then prohibited the states from infringing on the rights of any citizen. The most obvious intent of this amendment in conjunction with the Thirteenth Amendment (ending slavery) and Fifteenth Amendment (protecting the right of freed slaves to vote) was to provide protection of basic liberties for freed slaves—mostly from state governments in the South. Over time the federal courts honored these provisions of the amendment and prohibited states from limiting civil liberties of all citizens. Various court decisions over time selectively incorporated various rights under the Bill of Rights, and in doing so limited state governments in addition to the national government. With the passage of time, virtually every civil liberty is protected against abuse by both levels of government. Although the intent of the Founding Fathers had been to only limit the national government, the Fourteenth Amendment has, of course, taken precedence since it modified the original document. There have been those who have been opposed to this incorporation, in part because they have seen it as the national government usurping power from the states and weakening them, and, in part, because they opposed the specific decisions of the Supreme Court in this regard. Since the selective incorporation took so much time to occur, opponents of limits on state activities have been able to argue that the Fourteenth Amendment has been misinterpreted. They have also argued that the intent of the state legislators who ratified the amendment has been ignored because they never intended the amendment to let national courts place limitations on state actions.

TEST TIP

The due process clause of the Fourteenth Amendment routinely appears on the AP exam. Students should fully invest the time to understand the importance, ramifications, and the current concerns with this amendment.

Fourteenth Amendment

Citizenship Clause

This section ensured that freed slaves would be considered U.S. citizens. It also overturned *Dred Scott v. Sanford* that had declared that African Americans were not and could not become citizens of the United States.

Equal Protection Clause

This clause was important in that it was later used to protect individual citizens from limitations on basic liberties by the state and local governments.

Selective Incorporation

The Fourteenth Amendment was enacted in 1868, and the due process clause prohibits both state and local governments from depriving persons of life, liberty, or property without certain steps being taken to ensure fairness. It was the first time that some or all of the Amendments could restrict state government's rights and actions on the citizens it governed. *Gitlow v. New York* (1925) was the first time that the Supreme Court offered an opinion that personal rights are protected by the federal constitution and overrode the assertion that the states could act independently of the federal constitution in ignoring civil liberties.

Civil Rights

Issues involving civil rights revolve around discrimination against a group or an individual. The courts have only accepted the different treatment of groups when there is a reasonable basis for doing so, as would be the case with appropriate strength requirements for certain jobs (which would implicitly discriminate against the less strong). The classic civil rights struggles in the United States involved equal rights for black Americans and equal treatment for women. Other groups have claimed that they are victims of discrimination, as well, including Hispanics, Americans with disabilities, and gay and lesbian citizens. All these groups have sought to end discriminatory practices and to achieve equality with other citizens in the country.

DIDYOU**KNOW?**

Roger Taney was Chief Justice of the Supreme Court when the Dred Scott decision was handed down denying citizenship to slaves and former slaves. Taney, however, freed his own slaves and provided pensions to those who were too old to work.

The Struggle of Black Americans for Equality

Former slaves and free blacks had the same civil liberties in theory as whites, but it took a great many years for that equality to become reality. After the Civil War, the Thirteenth, Fourteenth, and Fifteenth Amendments were passed to provide more equality for former slaves. In fact, black Americans were frequently treated as second-class citizens throughout the country. In 1896, the Supreme Court allowed for legal segregation of the races when it ruled in *Plessy v. Ferguson* that separate facilities were allowable and constitutional as long as the facilities were equal in quality. In point of fact, separate facilities did become the norm, but the facilities for black Americans were seldom equal and were often greatly inferior.

In 1909, the National Association for the Advancement of Colored People was established with the stated goal of securing equal rights for all people. One of the major objectives of the **NAACP** was to have the *Plessy* decision overturned and have the doctrine of **separate but equal** reversed. The NAACP followed an incremental strategy to change the doctrine with a variety of court challenges to practices in the

DIDYOU**KNOW?**

Homer Plessy, who challenged the requirement that blacks and whites be segregated, was only one-eighth black. However, under Louisiana law he had to restrict himself to the non-white section of a train.

states. For example, in *Sweatt v. Painter* (1950), a challenge was mounted in Texas. Texas law prohibited integrated legal facilities, so a separate law school was created for black students. The Supreme Court ruled that the separate facility for black students could not equal the quality and opportunities that came with the whites-only law school at the University of Texas with its faculty, library, traditions, and associations; consequently, the Court ordered that Sweatt should be admitted to the existing law school. This case and others helped to set the stage for a major challenge to the whole idea of legally required segregation in educational systems.

Brown v. Board of Education of Topeka, Kansas (1954) provided the key direct challenge to the separate but equal doctrine. The *Brown* case was actually five cases that were supported and funded by the NAACP. The five cases raised important issues about segregated educational facilities. The basic ruling of the Supreme Court was that separate facilities, even when they were equal in quality, created a stigma and branded black children as inferior. The Court then overturned *Plessy v. Ferguson* because separate but equal was an impossible condition. This finding was particularly relevant for the Topeka school district because it was the one case of the five where the facilities were actually equal in quality. As a consequence, the Supreme Court ruled that mandatory segregation in schools was a violation of the equal protection clause of the Fourteenth Amendment. In a follow up to the original decision of *Brown v. Board of Education* (1955), the Supreme Court directed local school districts to develop plans for desegregation with all deliberate.

Governments and schools in the southern states did everything possible to avoid desegregation. Some districts proceeded extremely slowly with changes. In other instances, the local public schools were basically shut down, and private schools educated whites while black children were left to fend for themselves. In other cases, school districts provided for open enrollment in schools, but blacks and whites knew which schools to choose, and black students were discouraged from even trying to attend the "white" schools. It took a series of court cases to effectively end **de jure** (legally required) **desegregation** in schools. Although the *Brown* cases ended mandatory segregation, many schools, especially in the north, suffered from **de facto segregation** because of segregated housing patterns. Students attended local schools, but neighborhood segregation meant that many schools for all practical purposes were segregated. Given the earlier *Brown* decision on the negative impacts of segregation, courts had the options of requiring an end to de facto segregation. In 1971, in *Swann v. Charlotte-Mecklenburg Board of Education*, the Court's decision required busing of students to effectively integrate schools. Bussing has frequently been used as the blueprint for successive cases as a means of bring about integration. Local courts have even required bussing across school district lines to prevent the de facto re-segregation of schools.

Even though the *Brown* case and subsequent court decisions began to end segregation in school systems in the north and the south, equality had not been achieved in other areas. Many black American leaders saw the best way to achieve sympathy and to gain public support was to place civil rights issues at the forefront of the political agenda. In order to do this, a young minister named Martin Luther King, Jr. became one of the leaders of a campaign of civil disobedience designed to raise awareness of the plight of black Americans. There were sit-ins at segregated lunch counters. Black and white freedom riders from the north began to challenge all aspects of segregation. One key early confrontation involved a boycott of the **Montgomery Bus Company** in Alabama after Rosa Parks, 42-year-old black woman, refused to relinquish her seat to a white man. The boycott hurt the bus company since white riders were a minority among bus riders in the city. The boycott then ended the practice of requiring blacks to sit at the back of the buses and to defer to white riders. Peaceful protests such as this one were given wide coverage through the media, and many Americans of all races began to sympathize with the plight of the black Americans. At times local law officers used excessive violence in dealing with civil disobedience and protest demonstrations. These violent official responses received widespread media coverage, which further hurt the cause of desegregation. Racists groups such as the Ku Klux Klan attempted to use violence to defeat equal rights for blacks, and some involved in the civil rights movement began to use violent measures to quickly bring about change. This violence may have provided the more moderate civil rights groups with better opportunities to negotiate for peaceful change.

President Kennedy watched as the racial tension began to grow. It was difficult to bring about legislative change since southern Democrats controlled key congressional committees and a filibuster was likely with any civil rights laws presented on the Senate floor. The assassination of President Kennedy was a key turning point in the struggle for civil rights. President Johnson, a Texas Democrat, was able to mobilize support for action on civil rights issues as support for the slain president's legacy of increasing equality. He was able to achieve passage of multiple civil rights bills that dramatically aided in the integration of the nation. The three most important pieces of legislation were the **1964 Civil Rights Act**, the **1965 Voting Rights Act**, and the **Civil Rights Act of 1968**. The 1964 act was the most sweeping civil rights legislation since Reconstruction, and it prohibits discrimination of all kinds based on race, color, religion, or national origin. The law also provides the federal government with the powers to enforce desegregation and to end discrimination. The 1968 Act prohibits discrimination in the sale, rental, and financing of housing, which would end some of the housing segregation long present in the country. The 1965 Voting Rights Act provided opportunities for federal agencies to ensure that black Americans were able to vote. Some states had been very effective in preventing blacks from voting with arbitrary voting statutes, thereby depriving them of any opportunity to change the system. Many of the protests and demonstrations in the southern states had involved efforts to register blacks to vote. The Voting Rights Act placed a number of states and their local governments under extra scrutiny from the courts and federal agencies. Any actions that effectively limited the right of blacks to vote also had to be racially neutral in terms of how it was.

Presidents before and after President Johnson supported the civil rights movement. President Truman used an executive order to desegregate the armed forces. No action by Congress was required in this case since the segregation in the military had resulted from tradition rather than law. While this action was deeply unpopular in the South and some other parts of the country, it could not be reversed and sent a positive message about equality. Presidents Eisenhower and Kennedy used executive orders to further equality, as well, a trend that has consistently been followed by presidents that succeeded them in office. The civil rights movement benefited from changes in public opinion, which increasingly was opposed to segregation, especially the more demeaning forms as practiced in the south. Public support made it easier for presidents to move equality forward. The passage of the Civil Rights Acts and the Voting Rights Act provided a solid base for additional progress. While true equality has not yet been achieved, legal and constitutional equality has come closer to being a reality.

Women's Rights

Women have also had to struggle to achieve equality in the United States. When the Constitution was written, only a handful of women could vote; voting was linked to property ownership and most property was held in the names of fathers or husbands. Within a few years, women were barred from voting in every state. Women began to seek greater equality, and their involvement in the abolitionist movement before the Civil War allowed them to recognize similarities between their position in society and that of slaves. States still were able to determine who had the right to vote. Of course, the catch was that women could not change the voting laws because until they could not vote for candidates who would support reworking the laws.

In the 1880s, momentum for change began in the western states where women were granted the right to vote. In the frontier society of the west, women were more readily recognized as equals in the economy and society. The trend that began in the west soon spread to other states. The woman suffrage movement (right to vote) fought for extension of the vote in all states. It took a constitutional amendment, however, to guarantee women the right to vote in every state (remember, the Constitution left voting requirements to the discretion of the states). The first attempt at such an amendment was in 1878, but it failed. Finally, in 1920, the Nineteenth Amendment prevented the national government and the state governments from limiting the right to vote on the basis of gender. Women had finally gained the right to vote on a par with men.

Involvement in the women's rights movement declined with the successful ratification of the Nineteenth Amendment. With the passage of time, other issues related to gender equality arose. Women found themselves disadvantaged in the work force. In many cases, they were paid less for the same type of work than their male counterparts. In other cases, jobs that were traditionally filled by women (nursing, teaching, retail sales) paid less than jobs with similar skill levels in traditionally male occupations. Companies were willing to take advantage of their ability to pay women less, and labor unions dominated by men made it difficult for women to find better paying positions. Some of the disparities became obvious during World War II when women became much more active participants in the work force because they replaced men who were on military duty. It was thus difficult for many women to accept lower pay for the same work or to return to lower paying jobs in the old system once the war had ended.

After World War II, women's groups began to press for greater actual equality in society. The Civil Rights Acts of the early 1960s designed to ensure equality for black Americans, also provided a basis for ending discriminatory practices on the basis of sex. Court decisions have forced companies and unions to open positions in traditionally male-dominated professions to women as well. Once in such positions in police forces, firefighting, coal mining, etc., existing rules and contracts have mandated equal pay. In effect, the job descriptions were already gender neutral in many cases; it had been common practice that had kept women out of these jobs. It still required legal challenges in some cases to force equal pay. It has proven to be more difficult to end differential pay scales for occupations that are predominantly male and female; progress has been made in this area, but there is still more that needs to be done.

TEST TIP

You have the option to cancel your score on any AP exam, meaning that the score is permanently removed from your score report and thus not provided to any colleges or universities. You may even request that the test never be scored by submitting the cancellation form within about 30 days of the test date. However, consider doing this only if an illness or some other unexpected mishap prevented you from completing your exam. You probably did better than you think!

Abortion rights have also been an issue of concern for women. Some women's groups have sought to have abortion available as an absolute right since it involves a woman's right to control her own body. Some other groups that support women's rights in general disagree in the area of abortion for religious or moral reasons. As noted in the section on the right to privacy, this issue has been a very contentious one with no real solution in sight. It has divided many interest groups in the United States, not only women's organizations.

Another area of concern is the ability of women to receive promotions on a par with men. Because of past discrimination, most high-level positions have been filled by men who then make decisions about future promotions. In some cases, there have been obvious cases of discrimination that have been easier to rectify through court challenges. It has been easier to generate more equality in this area for positions in national government and state government agencies. Employment is more directly responsive to political pressure, legislation, or regulations in these cases. The private sector has not been immune to challenges, but it has sometimes been more difficult to prove a pattern of discrimination in a court of law. Women's organizations have also been sensitive to issues of sexual harassment in the workplace. They have been successful in the passage of a number of law and changes in regulations that provide penalties for harassment as a civil rights issue. While the laws prohibit all types of harassment (male against female, female against male, male against male, female against female), the most frequent forms of harassment have been males harassing female employees. While women who have charged harassment have not won all the cases they have brought, they have been successful in many cases, and the threat of action under state and federal laws has no doubt been effective in reducing the level of such harassment. The laws and court cases have also made many company executives and personnel directors aware of broader issues of equality.

Most women's organizations devoted to the idea of equality supported the Equal Rights Amendment that was proposed in the 1960s. This amendment would have required the equal treatment of women in all areas of activity. For a period it appeared to be assured of ratification, but a number of more conservative groups raised concerns about the effects of equality. One major fear was that such an amendment would require women to register for the draft and that women would be forced to serve in military and in combat roles. That issue is less important today with volunteer armed forces and women increasingly serving in harm's way. The amendment eventually fell short of ratification, but courts have progressively used civil rights laws to provide the equal protection and treatment that the amendment was designed to give.

Other Groups

Other groups have sought to use civil rights legislation for a reversal of past discrimination. One such group is Hispanic Americans. In the years following black Americans fight for civil rights, Hispanics were able to utilize civil rights laws to seek redress in cases of discrimination. In more recent years, the Courts have been sensitive to some issues in particular, such as bilingual ballots for elections so that Hispanics can better understand the choices. Many governmental agencies today provide options on telephone and Internet menus for instructions or information in Spanish.

Legislation will not end all potential discrimination, but the increasing size of the Hispanic population of the United States guarantees consideration of their concerns. The efforts have, however, generated a backlash that has been most obvious in efforts to have English proclaimed as the official language of the United States. For all practical purposes, of course, English is the official language, but institutionalizing that position in law could make it much more difficult for bilingualism to be present—which, of course, is the intent of at least some of the supporters of the movement to make English the official language.

Americans with disabilities have used the equal rights and equal protection provisions of the Constitution and legislation to effect changes in treatment and the availability of services. In this area, Americans with disabilities differ a bit different from other groups in seeking accommodation because accommodation requires attention to the needs of individuals with specific disabilities. The quickest changes have come with access to government facilities since government offices need to be accessible to all citizens and residents. Legislation has frequently required retrofitting of buildings to be handicap accessible when possible and that new buildings be designed to be handicap accessible. The standard in all buildings, both private and public, now tends to emphasize handicap accessibility. There will, however, remain individuals who experience access problems in one form or another or who face discrimination in employment that will have to be dealt with through the courts, legislation, or regulations.

Gay and lesbian organizations have also tried to gain equal rights in many areas, but their success in this regard has been more limited. Some state and local ordinances prohibit discrimination on the basis of sexual orientation, but not all of them. Some states have permitted civil unions to provide some legal rights to partners of the same sex, and a few even recognize same-sex marriage. In contrast, many states have actively attempted to make such partnerships more difficult. In general, courts and government agencies have made overt discrimination difficult, but have not eliminated it. Anti-gay public opinion has meant that many people do not openly announce their sexual preference for fear of discrimination. Courts cases have been mixed in some regards. In *Romer v. Evans* (1995), the Supreme Court overturned an amendment to the Colorado constitution that prohibited state agencies (executive, legislative, or judicial) from attempting to prevent discrimination against gays and lesbians. While the amendment to the state constitution passed in a public vote, it is hard to envision a statement that is more antithetical to the idea of equal rights because it constitutionally prevented any part of state government from dealing with discriminatory practices. In 1999 in *Boy Scouts of America v. Dale*, the Supreme Court held that the scouts as a private organization had a protected right of association and could prevent homosexuals from serving as scoutmasters. In this case, there was a conflict between two civil liberties. The private nature of the Boy Scouts was a clear factor, since private groups normally have some ability to control their membership. The "Don't Ask, Don't Tell" policy in the military was a partial victory for gays and lesbians. It permitted them to serve without fear of active questioning, but it also permitted their dismissal from the military if their homosexuality was discovered. Full victory came with the end of this policy in 2011, so that gays and lesbians can openly serve in the military without fear of dismissal. The increased role of women in military service (with the obvious increases in the possibility of heterosexual contacts) may have paved the way for the more open policy for gays and lesbians. It is clear that debates about equal rights for this portion of the American population will be present in the future and will be quite contentious.

Policy Changes

The debate over equality for all groups has led to some significant changes in the way in which the issue has been approached. Two particular approaches have involved **affirmative action** programs and **Title IX of the Education Amendments of 1972**. These programs were initially designed to further equality for black Americans and for women, but they have come into play for other groups as well.

Affirmative action was established on September 1965 by Executive Order 11246. This order required government contractors to "take affirmative action" toward prospective minority employees in all aspects of hiring and employment. In 1967, President Johnson added women to the list of minority employees. This order has had profound effects on the ability of minorities to reach higher levels of employment. Affirmative action programs eventually became normal for any area of activity that involved government funding, including most schools from kindergarten to university level. Affirmative action categories have been expanded to include Hispanics, native Americans and Aleut Islanders, Asian Americans, and Vietnam-era veterans, in addition to blacks and women.

In order to provide affirmative action for groups that formerly faced discrimination, many organizations established quota systems whereby it was virtually guaranteed that a certain number of individuals in affirmative action categories would be hired or admitted. In 1978, minority quotas and affirmative action in general were challenged in *Bakke v. the Board of Regents of the University of California.* Bakke, who met the minimum requirements for entry into medical school at the University of California at Davis was not admitted; however, minority candidates who had fallen below the minimum requirements were admitted as part of a quota. The Supreme Court ruled in this case that strict quota systems were illegal. The Court also ruled, however, that admission into university programs could take diversity into account. This somewhat ambiguous standard is still in place. Some affirmative action programs will be supported while others may not. Although affirmative action programs and requirements have helped provide a way for minorities and women to advance in the economy, there is still a glass ceiling that exists that limits advancement and that has generally affected women more than men, regardless of race. The relative number of men in leadership positions in all areas is still higher than it should be by numbers in the work force, but this situation should reverse itself as the number of women receiving advanced college degrees increases and the numbers for their male counterparts begin to decrease.

Title IX of the Education Amendments of 1972 was initially written to end discrimination based on race, color, or national origin. Enforcement of this act was important to help revitalize the women's movement. The greatest impact of Title IX was on female high school and college athletics, but it has also been used to ensure that sex discrimination of all types in educational activities has ended. Under Title IX, universities must provide an equal number of programs and opportunities for men and women, although some attention can be paid to the revenues generated by sports programs. This allowed women the right to have more equal representation in athletics as well as within areas of academia and non-sport activities and clubs. The law applies to any university receiving federal assistance, which covers many of them. Other universities have been required to meet the requirements of Title IX because many of their students are supported by federal grants or other government programs. Title IX has thus provided significant leverage for women's groups seeking to enhance equality in higher education.

Civil liberties and civil rights have been contentious issues for many groups. One can see a progression as different groups have been successful in achieving at least some liberties that should be available to all. Equality has increased in the United States over time, albeit slowly. The federal courts have often been involved in such issues, and it has taken constitutional amendments to redress some of the inequalities that previously existed. With the ratification of amendments it has been possible for legislative action and action by various presidents to occur more easily. The courts, however, have remained a key institution for those seeking equal rights.

Time for a quiz
- Review strategies in Chapter 2
- Take Quiz 6 at the REA Study Center
  (www.rea.com/studycenter)

Take Mini-Test 2
on Chapters 6–8
Go to the REA Study Center
(www.rea.com/studycenter)

Practice Exam

Also available at the REA Study Center *(www.rea.com/studycenter)*

This practice exam is available at the REA Study Center. Although AP exams are administered in paper-and-pencil format, we recommend that you take the online version of the practice exam for the benefits of:

- Instant scoring

- Enforced time conditions

- Detailed score report of your strengths and weaknesses

Practice Exam
Section I

(Answer sheets appear in the back of the book.)

TIME: 45 minutes

60 questions

Directions: Each question or incomplete statement below is followed by five answers or completions. Select the one that is best in each case.

1. Of the following, the *best* example of a participatory democracy is

   (A) the Democratic national convention.

   (B) the U.S. House of Representatives.

   (C) a Cuban village.

   (D) Sweden or Norway.

   (E) a New England town meeting.

2. The phrase "a lawyer's brief justifying a revolution" has been used to describe the

   (A) Declaration of Independence.

   (B) the colonial charters.

   (C) the U.S. Constitution.

   (D) the Bill of Rights.

   (E) the Articles of Confederation.

3. In an early test of the powers of the Articles of Confederation, the Continental Congress failed to deal with an uprising in western Massachusetts known as

   (A) the Whig uprising.

   (B) the Springfield conspiracy.

   (C) the Whisky Rebellion.

   (D) Shays's Rebellion.

   (E) the Massachusetts conspiracy.

4. An amendment can be proposed by

   (A) either a two-thirds vote of both houses of Congress or a national convention called by Congress at the request of two-thirds of the states

   (B) a two-thirds vote by the Senate only

   (C) a two-thirds vote of both houses of Congress

   (D) a national convention called by Congress at the request of two-thirds of the states

   (E) citizens who sign a petition

5. James Madison's main argument in favor of ratification of the Constitution, stated in *Federalist* #10 and #51, was in defense of

   (A) large legislatures with small districts and frequent turnover.

   (B) small democracies governed by direct democracy.

   (C) large republics.

   (D) a bill of rights.

   (E) centralized judiciaries.

6. A conference committee on a military equipment upgrade bill would be composed mainly of

   (A) senior members only from both the House and the Senate.

   (B) committee chairs only from both the House and the Senate.

   (C) the Speaker of the House, the President pro tempore, and other party leaders from both houses of Congress.

   (D) a mixture of interested members of Congress, the President, and key lobbying interests.

   (E) members from the Armed Services committees in both the House and the Senate, with the majority party in each house holding more seats on the conference committee.

7. The primary election system of selecting presidential candidates has had which of the following effects?

   (A) It has increased the importance of state party organizations.

   (B) It has loosened the hold of party leaders over the nomination process.

   (C) It has reduced the role of citizens in the candidate selection process.

   (D) It has lowered the cost of running for office.

   (E) It has led to a decline in the importance of party voter registration drives.

8. All of the following factors add to public disillusionment with members of Congress in terms of their effectiveness and integrity EXCEPT

   (A) pork-barrel politics.

   (B) logrolling.

   (C) frequent use of the franking privilege.

   (D) the influence of lobbyists and PACs.

   (E) case work.

9. Which of the following is true of a presidential veto of a piece of legislation?

   (A) It is rarely overridden by Congress.

   (B) About 25 percent of all bills are vetoed.

   (C) A president can veto any legislation passed with the exception of "revenue raising" bills.

   (D) The veto process is automatically reviewed by the Supreme Court.

   (E) The president's party in Congress must concur with any presidential veto.

10. Which statement below concerning religion is accurate?

    (A) In the United States, people have freedom of religious action but not of religious choice.

    (B) In the United States, people have freedom of religious choice but not religious action.

    (C) Except during extracurricular club periods, no prayer is currently permitted in public high schools.

    (D) The federal or local governments never encourage the building of churches and other places of worship.

    (E) There is no place for religion at all in American politics.

11. Which of the following is considered to be constitutionally protected symbolic speech?

    (A) Hiding obscenities within the lyrics of a rock song

    (B) A police officer's right to wear an earring on the job

    (C) Wearing any legally purchased concert T-shirt to a public high school the following day

    (D) Burning the American flag

    (E) Going barefoot into a shopping mall or restaurant

12. All of the following help explain why such a high percentage of incumbents are reelected to Congress EXCEPT

    (A) their campaigns receive a greater share of federal matching funds.

    (B) their staffs can help constituents deal with the government.

    (C) they can win constituent support by providing pork-barrel projects for the district they represent.

    (D) the franking privilege and media opportunities provide greater name recognition for incumbents.

    (E) PACs are more likely to support incumbents than challengers.

13. Plea bargaining has become commonplace in the American legal system for all of the following reasons EXCEPT

    (A) the public widely supports the practice.

    (B) prosecutors see it as a way to make their caseloads workable.

    (C) many prisons are currently over-crowded.

    (D) the police and prosecutors view it as a trade-off toward more meaningful arrests and convictions.

    (E) once arrested, many suspects opt to make a deal to avoid a trial in the hopes of lessening their sentences.

14. In order to prove libel or slander, it is necessary for the plaintiff to prove that a statement was

   (A) intentionally harmful, whether false or not, and malicious.

   (B) malicious, untrue, and negatively affects the plaintiff's ability to earn a living.

   (C) emotionally damaging and untrue.

   (D) obscene as defined by the you-know-it-when-you-see-it test

   (E) symbolic rather than verbal.

15. The usefulness to the president of having cabinet members as political advisers is undermined by the fact that

   (A) the president has little latitude in choosing cabinet members.

   (B) cabinet members have no political support independent of the president.

   (C) cabinet members are usually drawn from Congress and retain loyalties to Congress.

   (D) the loyalties of cabinet members are often divided between loyalty to the president and loyalty to their own executive departments.

   (E) the cabinet operates as a collective unit and individual members have no access to the president.

16. The George W. Bush administration faced charges of combining church and state with which of the following acts?

   (A) The invasions of Afghanistan and Iraq

   (B) Faith-based initiatives

   (C) The Patriot Act

   (D) No Child Left Behind Act

   (E) Its opposition to stem-cell research

17. The most effective weapon used by the Federal Reserve in its attempt to control inflation is to

   (A) print a new design of currency.

   (B) lower the prime interest rate.

   (C) raise the prime interest rate.

   (D) raise the tariff rate.

   (E) lower the tariff rate.

18. What would be the most likely reason for a president to enter into an executive agreement with a foreign country rather than sign a treaty?

   (A) An executive agreement avoids political wrangling with the Senate since it does not need to be ratified.

   (B) An agreement has more legal validity than a treaty.

   (C) A president can easily back down from an executive agreement with no recourse for the foreign country.

   (D) The 1973 Supreme Court ruling in *Miller vs. California* gave the Senate more scrutiny in the Senate ratification process.

   (E) An executive agreement requires prior Senate approval, making resulting negotiations easier for the president.

19. All of the following are general characteristics of Democratic voters EXCEPT

   (A) blue collar employment.

   (B) that they tend to be Roman Catholic.

   (C) suburban residence.

   (D) a desire for larger government.

   (E) that they're more likely female than male.

20. Which political office has been the most consistent stepping stone for a successful candidate seeking the presidency since 1970?

    (A) United States senator

    (B) State governor

    (C) Vice president

    (D) Secretary of State

    (E) Big-city mayor

21. The Twenty-second Amendment, ratified in 1952,

    (A) limits a president to two full terms, or ten total years of service at maximum.

    (B) defines the order of presidential succession in case of death, disability, or resignation.

    (C) sets the presidential inauguration date at March 4 of the year following the election.

    (D) sets the presidential inauguration date at January 20 of the year following the election.

    (E) makes the Electoral College a formal amendment to the Constitution.

22. When a popular president influences voters to support candidates for other offices from the president's party, the result is called

    (A) straight-ticket voting.

    (B) the coat-tail effect.

    (C) logrolling.

    (D) a mandate.

    (E) a landslide.

23. "Mark-up sessions," in which revisions and additions are made to proposed legislation in Congress, usually occur in which setting?

    (A) The majority leader's office

    (B) In party caucuses

    (C) On the floor of the legislative chamber

    (D) In joint conference committees

    (E) In committees or subcommittees

24. Which of the following is true of the Electoral College?

    (A) It encourages the emergence of third parties.

    (B) It encourages candidates to concentrate their efforts in competitive, populous states.

    (C) It ensures that the votes of all citizens count equally in selecting the president.

    (D) It requires that a candidate win a minimum of 26 states to obtain a majority in the college.

    (E) It tends to make presidential election results appear closer than they really are.

Question 25 refers to the quote below.

"Justice Souter agreed with the decision but cited a separate point of law than that of the other members of the Court in a 9–0 decision favoring a state's right to ban private gambling."

25. The opinion described is

    (A) a concurring opinion.

    (B) a dissenting opinion.

    (C) a majority opinion.

    (D) a defamatory decision.

    (E) an abstaining opinion.

26. Which of the following constitutional amendments prevents "cruel and unusual punishment" and suggests that the amount of bail charged must fit the circumstances of the particular crime involved?

    (A) The Fifth Amendment

    (B) The Sixth Amendment

    (C) The Seventh Amendment

    (D) The Eighth Amendment

    (E) The Ninth Amendment

27. A filibuster

    I. can be used in either the House or the Senate.

    II. is a stall tactic designed to prevent the likely passage/defeat of a bill on the Senate floor.

    III. is commonly blocked by the cloture rule.

    (A) I, II, and III

    (B) II and III only

    (C) III only

    (D) I and II only

    (E) II only

28. Of the following, which *best* predicts the likelihood that citizens will vote?

    (A) Their race

    (B) Their educational level

    (C) Their religion

    (D) Their gender

    (E) Their region of residence

29. When speaking of "balancing a ticket" in the context of a presidential election, which of the following is meant?

    (A) A presidential and vice presidential nominee will be of different racial backgrounds.

    (B) A presidential and vice presidential nominee will be from opposite genders.

    (C) A presidential and vice presidential nominee will be of different regional and ideological backgrounds.

    (D) A presidential and vice presidential nominee will be of different educational levels or social classes.

    (E) A presidential nominee will be younger and vice presidential nominee will be older.

30. Catholic Church officials in the United States had the most trouble supporting 2004 Democratic presidential candidate John Kerry—a practicing Roman Catholic—over his support of

    (A) the death penalty.

    (B) abortion.

    (C) the separation of church and state.

    (D) the war in Iraq.

    (E) equal rights for women.

31. On which of the following issues is a child most likely to share the same position as his or her parents?

    (A) foreign policy

    (B) constitutional interpretation

    (C) party identification

    (D) racial equality

    (E) women's rights

32. White Protestants are the group least likely to display which of the following?

    (A) mistrust of government

    (B) liberal attitudes

    (C) desire for smaller government

    (D) conservative attitudes

    (E) favoritism toward states' rights

33. Which of the following students is most likely to be politically conservative?

    (A) a student at a small, liberal arts college

    (B) a student at a large state university

    (C) a graduate student in a state university

    (D) a high school student

    (E) a junior college student

34. In polling, a random sample is one that

    (A) is generated by a computer using complex algorithms.

    (B) gives each person an equal chance of being in the sample.

    (C) has no pre-selection criteria.

    (D) perfectly matches the population.

    (E) just happens, with no control by any outside force.

35. Voters in the South have become progressively less attached to

    (A) the Democratic party.

    (B) the Republican party.

    (C) liberal ideology.

    (D) conservative ideology.

    (E) Both B and D.

36. The most dramatic example of the winner-take-all principle in the U.S. electoral system is the

    (A) partisan judicial elections.

    (B) municipal elections in Cambridge, Massachusetts.

    (C) two-party system.

    (D) Electoral College.

    (E) ideal of pluralism.

37. Each of the following was an objective of the Framers EXCEPT

    (A) to oppose concentration of power in a single institution.

    (B) to make Congress accountable to the executive.

    (C) to balance large and small states.

    (D) to have Congress be the dominant institution.

    (E) C and D.

38. The Framers sought to prevent legislative tyranny by

    (A) giving the executive the right to appoint both legislators and Supreme Court justices.

    (B) requiring Congress to defer to the other branches of government.

    (C) severely limiting the powers of Congress.

    (D) dividing power among the legislature, the executive, and the judiciary.

    (E) calling for the direct election of the Senate.

39. Article I, Section 8, of the U.S. Constitution confers on Congress all of the following powers EXCEPT

    (A) the power to regulate commerce.

    (B) the power to interpret laws.

    (C) the power to collect taxes.

    (D) the power to declare war.

    (E) the power to establish courts.

40. The purpose of a filibuster is to

    (A) protect majority rule.

    (B) shift legislative power to the Senate committees.

    (C) ensure that all sides of an issue are heard.

    (D) delay action in a legislative body.

    (E) magnify the impact of specific special interests.

41. If you wished to study a large power base in the Senate, you would most likely focus on the

    (A) party whip.

    (B) president pro tempore.

    (C) majority leader.

    (D) chairperson of the Judiciary Committee.

    (E) chairperson of the Policy Committee.

42. Among the many powers of the House Speaker is that he or she

    (A) schedules legislation.

    (B) keeps party leaders informed about the opinions of their party members.

    (C) appoints members of special and select committees.

    (D) takes the minutes.

    (E) assigns party members to the various committees.

43. Because they are usually the only ones that can report out bills, the most important committees are the

    (A) select committees.

    (B) conference committees.

    (C) standing committees.

    (D) joint committees.

    (E) rejoinder committees.

44. The type of committee most likely to deal with a bill near the end of its legislative process is the

    (A) rejoinder committee.

    (B) select committee.

    (C) standing committee.

    (D) joint committee.

    (E) conference committee.

45. The staff agency that advises Congress on the probable economic effect of different spending programs and the cost of proposed policies is the

    (A) Congressional Research Fund (CRF).

    (B) Office of Technology Assessment (OTA).

    (C) Congressional Budget Office (CBO).

    (D) General Accounting Office (GAO).

    (E) Congressional Research Service (CRS).

46. Which of the following statements about the speed with which bills move through Congress is correct?

    (A) It is slow in most cases.

    (B) It has been increasing as a result of teller votes.

    (C) It has been decreasing as Congress has grown.

    (D) It can vary enormously.

    (E) It has been increasing in the electronic age.

47. Each of the following is a fundamental difference between presidents and prime ministers EXCEPT

    (A) presidents choose their cabinets from inside rather than outside Congress.

    (B) presidents and the legislature often work at cross-purposes.

    (C) presidents are often outsiders without previous legislative or executive experience.

    (D) presidents have no guaranteed majority in the legislature.

    (E) presidents do not necessarily remain in power if their party controls Congress.

48. The powers that the president shares with the Senate include

    (A) making treaties.

    (B) granting pardons for federal offenses.

    (C) receiving ambassadors.

    (D) wielding legislative power.

    (E) commissioning officers of the armed forces.

49. The principal function of the White House Office is to

    (A) supervise military intelligence agencies.

    (B) prepare the national budget for the president.

    (C) supervise the national security agencies, such as the CIA and FBI.

    (D) oversee the political and policy interests of the president.

    (E) administer federal departments as the president's representative.

50. The Senate is required to confirm all of the following presidential nominations EXCEPT

    (A) the heads of cabinet departments.

    (B) the heads of Executive Office agencies.

    (C) members of the White House Office.

    (D) federal judges.

    (E) Both B and D

51. Presidents need to rely on their powers of persuasion because of their

    (A) limited staff.

    (B) limited staff and sketchy constitutional powers.

    (C) sketchy constitutional powers and lack of ensured legislative majorities.

    (D) opponents within the party.

    (E) lack of ensured legislative majorities and opponents within the party.

52. Veto power and executive privilege give a president both a way of blocking action and a

    (A) means of forcing Congress to bargain.

    (B) route of appeal to the people.

    (C) means of affecting the party platform.

    (D) trump card to play with the media.

    (E) means of overriding the influence of special interests.

53. When President Reagan was governor of California, he could veto portions of a bill that were irrelevant to the subject of the bill. He was exercising what is called

    (A) a line-item veto.

    (B) constitutional discretion.

    (C) states' rights.

    (D) gubernatorial averaging.

    (E) a pocket veto.

54. The presidential claims for executive privilege are based on the separation of powers and on

    (A) the need for candid advice from aides.

    (B) the U.S. Constitution.

    (C) *Marbury v. Madison*.

    (D) international law.

    (E) the need for cooperation with Congress.

55. *United States v. Nixon* held that

    (A) there is real but limited presidential immunity from judicial process.

    (B) there is no unqualified presidential privilege of immunity from judicial process.

    (C) presidential immunity does not apply to matters which are civil in nature.

    (D) there is absolute presidential immunity from judicial process.

    (E) there is no executive privilege.

56. In *McCulloch v. Maryland*, the Supreme Court held that

    (A) the federal government could pass any laws necessary and proper to the attainment of constitutional ends.

    (B) the federal government had the power to regulate commerce that occurred among states.

    (C) the judicial branch has the power to determine the legitimate governing power in the states.

    (D) states could tax a federal bank.

    (E) state militia were subservient to the federal armed services.

57. What does the U.S. Constitution have to say about the size of the Supreme Court?

    (A) It specifically sets the number of justices at six, later amended to nine.

    (B) It does not indicate how large the Court should be.

    (C) It suggests but does not mandate a Court of nine justices.

    (D) It specifically places the matter in the hands of the House of Representatives.

    (E) It specifically sets the number of justices at nine.

58. A case on appeal reaches the Supreme Court via a writ of

    (A) mandamus.

    (B) habeas corpus.

    (C) certiorari.

    (D) injunction.

    (E) appeal.

59. Under the doctrine of sovereign immunity, a citizen cannot

    (A) appeal a case that was decided more than one year earlier.

    (B) appeal a case that has already been ruled on by the Supreme Court.

    (C) sue the government without its consent.

    (D) bring the same suit to courts in two different states.

    (E) bring two suits against one individual for the same crime.

60. The case that ended mandatory segregation and declared that separate facilities were inherently unequal was

    (A) *Brown v. Board of Education of Topeka, Kansas.*

    (B) *Mapp v. Ohio.*

    (C) *Sanders v. Board of Education of Birmingham, Alabama.*

    (D) *Bakke v. California.*

    (E) *Plessy v. Ferguson.*

Section II
Free-Response Questions

TIME: 100 minutes

4 Questions

Directions: You have 100 minutes to answer all four of the following questions. Unless the directions indicate otherwise, respond to all parts of all four questions. Spend approximately 25 minutes on each question. In your response, use substantive examples where appropriate. Make certain to number each of your answers as the question is numbered below.

Question 1

Federal Budget Outlays (in billions of dollars)

	1970	**1989 (est.)**	**% Increase 1970–1989**
Fixed Costs	120.3	865.1	719.12
Variable Costs	83.8	306.3	365.51

For the purpose of this question, fixed costs are those over which the president has relatively little control. These are costs that can be adjusted only by an act of the U.S. Congress. Variable costs are those that can be changed by presidential decision. Fixed costs include entitlement programs, interest on the deficit, and other programs approved by Congress. Variable costs include defense spending and other executive branch programs.

(a) From the information in the table above, how much responsibility does the presidency bear for the growth in federal spending?

(b) Since politics in the real world is more complicated than a simple table, what might have to happen before federal spending is reduced?

Question 2

The legislative process can be described as time consuming and difficult even when one party controls the White House and both chambers of Congress. In order for a bill to become a law, there are many steps and obstacles in the process.

(a) Discuss four of the stages in the legislative process at which a bill can be delayed or killed.

(b) List and discuss the types and roles of the committees in Congress.

(c) What role do interest groups play in the bill-passing process?

Question 3

The Office of the U.S. President is the single most powerful government position in our country. Answer each part of the questions below. Be sure to give specific examples when you can.

(a) What are the qualifications to be president?

(b) What constitutional powers does the president have that give the office such power and what other powers does the president have that can make him or her a great leader?

(c) Are there limits to presidential power, and if so, what are they?

Question 4

Argue that the influence of politics and the government on the media is greater than the reverse. Does one type of media (internet, broadcast or newspaper) have an advantage in its relationship to the political process? Examine the advantages of each in forming a conclusion.

Answer Key

1. (E)	16. (B)	31. (C)	46. (D)
2. (A)	17. (C)	32. (B)	47. (A)
3. (D)	18. (A)	33. (D)	48. (A)
4. (C)	19. (C)	34. (B)	49. (D)
5. (C)	20. (B)	35. (A)	50. (C)
6. (E)	21. (A)	36. (D)	51. (C)
7. (B)	22. (B)	37. (B)	52. (A)
8. (E)	23. (E)	38. (D)	53. (A)
9. (A)	24. (B)	39. (B)	54. (A)
10. (B)	25. (A)	40. (D)	55. (B)
11. (D)	26. (D)	41. (C)	56. (A)
12. (A)	27. (E)	42. (C)	57. (B)
13. (A)	28. (B)	43. (C)	58. (C)
14. (B)	29. (C)	44. (E)	59. (C)
15. (D)	30. (B)	45. (C)	60. (A)

Detailed Explanations of Answers

Section I

1. **(E)**

    Because New England town meetings are intended to include the entire community in the decision-making process, they are the best example of participatory democracy.

2. **(A)**

    The Declaration of Independence systemically lays out the main arguments for the colonists' break with Great Britain. It basically describes the legal justifications for replacing British rule and fighting the Revolutionary War.

3. **(D)**

    Shays's Rebellion had a powerful effect on public opinion and showed the need for change in the Articles of Confederation because of fear that state governments were about to collapse from internal dissension.

4. **(C)**

    The most common method of amending the Constitution is to have a joint resolution proposed by both houses of Congress, passed with a two-thirds vote and then ratified by three-fourths of the states.

5. **(C)**

    In *Federalist No. 10* Madison wrote that he believed that if a faction is less than a majority, then it will rely on majority rule to control it. If a faction is in the majority, then it will rely on the type of political system to control it. The cure to the problem of factions is a large republic.

6. **(E)**

Conference committees meet only after both houses of Congress pass a different bill on the same issue. The conference committee is a bipartisan effort to reach a single compromise bill; it would be composed mainly of members from the committee of origin, who would have the greatest stake in its final passage.

7. **(B)**

Primaries have taken power from the major parties and given it to the states and to those relatively few voters who actually participate in primaries. Previously, the parties used the famous "smoke-filled room" scenario to broker deals and decide which candidate would be most electable and "manageable" and would carry out the party's platform. With the advent of the primaries, surprise candidates have emerged, à la Jimmy Carter in 1976 and Bill Clinton in 1992.

8. **(E)**

"Casework" describes the tasks and favors that a member of Congress provides for constituents. This could include anything from a letter of recommendation for entrance to West Point, to a copy of the Freedom of Information Act requested for a college paper, and so on. This would obviously aid the member of Congress at re-election time and would lead to less public disillusionment.

9. **(A)**

Presidential vetoes, or even the threat of their use, are rare in themselves. A president obviously does not want to antagonize Congress needlessly, as positive executive-legislative relations will help the administration get its agenda passed into law. However, it is even rarer that a presidential veto would be overridden by Congress because that would require a two-thirds vote in each house.

10. **(B)**

In the United States, people have freedom of religious choice but not religious action. They may worship whomever they choose or nothing at all. However, religious action is not legally protected. For instance, a Jamaican Rastafarian cannot smoke marijuana legally by claiming it is a religious ritual. Nor can a Mormon legally commit bigamy claiming a traditional church belief in the practice.

11. **(D)**

Burning the American flag has been constitutionally protected in such Supreme Court cases as *Texas vs. Johnson*, 1989.

12. **(A)**

Federal matching funds are available equally to the major party presidential candidates, not congressional candidates. Fundraising does favor congressional incumbents because of committee clout (C), franking (D), established PAC relationships (E) and generally higher name recognition.

13. **(A)**

Although law enforcement, defense attorneys, and prosecutors all see plea bargaining as a necessity, given clogged courts and prisons and the need for information to aid ongoing police investigations (answers B through E), the public sees plea bargaining as a negative, a sort of "easy way out" for accused felons.

14. **(B)**

Proving libel (written defamation) or slander (oral defamation) is extremely difficult under the First Amendment and the United States court system. The deck is stacked in favor of the person making the statement in terms of legal protection. Generally, to be awarded monetary damages in a libel or slander case, a defendant must prove that the uttered or written expression made was false, that the accused knew this, and that it cost the defendant a reasonable opportunity to earn a living (or a portion thereof) in his/her chosen profession. Obviously, a slander/libel case is extremely difficult to prove and, thus, to win.

15. **(D)**

Cabinet members are torn between competing agendas; they advise and serve the president but also administer a large bureaucratic department of various programs and personnel. Presidents have great latitude in choosing cabinet members (A), but must also pick someone that the Senate will confirm. This has historically not been a problem. Cabinet members have support of interest groups and of the U.S. Senate, which confirms them (B). Cabinet members sometimes come from within Congress, but must resign their seat if they are to serve in the cabinet (C). The cabinet rarely meets collectively, and some members are more important than others to a given president, but individual contact would be much more likely than a collective meeting of all cabinet members (E).

16. **(B)**

The so-called faith-based initiatives allowed federal funds to be used by church organizations in various social and volunteer service programs. The invasions of Iraq and Afghanistan (A) and the Patriot Act (C) were components of the "war on terrorism." The No Child Left Behind Act (D) deals with public schools and special education (D), and while the opposition of stem-cell research (E) by George W. Bush does have religious overtones, (B) is a stronger, more direct answer.

17. **(C)**

Raising the prime interest rate would be a way to stem spending (via loans) and thus would curb inflation. (B) would lead to the opposite: increasing inflation. (A) is irrelevant and Congress, not the Federal Reserve, would control the levels of tariffs (D) and (E).

18. **(A)**

Executive agreements are simply between heads of government and hold the same force of law as treaties (B) and (C). They hold one large advantage for a U.S. President: unlike the case with treaties, the Senate does not need to ratify them. Executive agreements do not require previous Senate approval (E). The *Miller* case dealt with obscenity and is irrelevant to this issue (D).

19. **(C)**

Suburban residence is much more commonly a GOP voting trait. The "gender gap," resulting from females being significantly more likely than males to be liberal, prevents (E) from being the correct answer.

20. **(B)**

Governorships have been the most common launch pad to the presidency since 1970. Jimmy Carter, Ronald Reagan, Bill Clinton, and George W. Bush all ascended to the presidency having been governors prior to their successful White House bids. Nixon (1972) and George H.W. Bush (1988) had been vice presidents prior to their election as president.

21. **(A)**

The Twenty-second Amendment limits a president to two elected terms. Ten years total could be served if a president finishes a predecessor's term, serving two years or less time. (B) describes the Twenty-fifth Amendment; (C) was repealed by the Twentieth Amendment (D); and the electoral college itself was always formally part of the Constitution (E).

22. **(B)**

The coat-tail effect is the carry-over from a popular candidate to lower party members appearing further down the ticket. Straight-ticket voting is merely pulling a lever for the Republican or Democratic Party to vote strictly for that party's candidates (A). Logrolling is a trade-off of votes between members of Congress on a bill that is essential to one member but not to the other (C). A mandate is a go-ahead voters give candidates to enact their programs (D) and it results from a landslide victory (E), which is generally considered to be a popular vote of 60 percent or greater.

23. **(E)**

The amendment of bills, which happens in a mark-up session, generally occurs in subcommittee or less likely, in full committee. Committees serve as a screen for bills, and most generally kill them at a rate of 90 percent.

24. **(B)**

The Electoral College is based on the number of total representatives a state has in Congress. Since House seats are based upon population, it would make sense for candidates to concentrate in populous, competitive states. It makes no sense to spend a lot of time in a populous state if it is already won or lost, however. The "winner-take-all" aspect discourages votes from going to third parties, which are seen largely as "wasted votes" (A). The votes of citizens from the least populous states are proportionally exaggerated in importance via the Electoral College (C). A candidate is required to win 270 Electoral College votes, which is a majority of the total available without regard to how many states that candidate wins (D). Currently, this could be done by winning as few as eleven states if they were the most populous eleven states in the country. The Electoral College tends to exaggerate the margin of victory as compared to the popular vote because of the "winner-take-all" aspect (E).

25. **(A)**

A concurring opinion agrees with the majority decision yet cites a different constitutional precedent for doing so. A majority opinion (C) is written by a justice representing the main body of thought used by the justices in ruling on a case. A dissenting opinion (B) is written by a justice who opposes the majority's ruling in a case. Neither choice (D) nor (E) represents a realistic Supreme Court opinion.

26. **(D)**

The Eighth Amendment of the Bill of Rights deals with defining proper legal punishment, including the fair allowance of bail for the accused.

27. (E)

A filibuster is a stalling tactic used by a minority group of Senators to thwart the presumed path of a bill. Senators seize the floor via marathon talking—often about unrelated events—to keep a bill from being voted on in a third reading. While this is occurring, supporters of the filibuster who are not holding the Senate floor attempt to persuade their colleagues to support their measure. At the very least, Senators involved in a filibuster can tell their constituents, "I went to extreme measures and fought the good fight—they just wouldn't listen to reason."

A filibuster may not be used in the House of Representatives, where debate must be germane, or on-subject (A) and (D). The Senate prides itself on much freer rules of debate and thus, is loathe to censor even a filibuster. Although a cloture motion can bring a bill to a vote, ending a filibuster, it is rarely invoked (A) and (B). Cloture requires the vote of 60 Senators.

28. (B)

Educational level most correlates to likelihood to vote; the more education one has, the more likely one is to exercise suffrage. This factor overrides gender, race, income, and area of residence in correlation to likeliness to vote.

29. (C)

When speaking of "balancing a ticket" in the context of a presidential election, what is generally meant is a balance between the geographical region of the candidates and their ideology. Age (E) is less of a factor. The candidates on a ticket generally come from the same educational background and social class (D). Race (A) has not been a factor in balancing the presidential ticket thus far and gender (B) has been a consideration in only one presidential election.

30. (B)

Catholic Church officials in the United States had the most trouble supporting 2004 Democratic presidential candidate John Kerry—a practicing Roman Catholic—over his support of a woman's right to choose an abortion. On the other issues, including opposition to the death penalty (A), Kerry lines up with mainstream Catholic positions. Some church officials in the U.S. went so far as to suggest refusing Kerry communion for his stance on abortion.

31. (C)

Even though there are many factors that contribute to determining influences on individuals and voting patterns, studies have shown the family to be the most dependable indicator.

32. (B)

Mistrust of government, desire for a smaller government and favoritism toward states' rights are all traditional conservative positions. White Protestants are more likely or tend to support those conservative positions.

33. (D)

Studies have shown that the lower the level of education, the more likely individuals are to be conservative and by contrast, higher level of education generally leads to more liberal attitudes.

34. (B)

In a random sample poll, any given person, or any given voter or adult, has an equal chance of being interviewed. Most national surveys draw a sample of between a thousand and fifteen hundred people as part of a process called stratified or multistage area sampling.

35. (A)

Voters in the South were referred to as the "solid South" for decades in their support of the Democratic Party, but in recent years have consistently voted more Republican, especially after the Civil Rights movement.

36. (D)

In 48 of the 50 states, all of the Electoral College votes go to the winner of the general election in the states.

37. (B)

The main focus of the Framers was to create three co-equal branches of government with a system of checks and balances to keep the branches separate and relatively equal.

38. **(D)**

    The Framers felt that the best way to preserve liberty was with a system of separation of powers dividing governmental power among the branches.

39. **(B)**

    Article I, Section 8 of the Constitution lists the delegated powers of the legislative branch and regulating commerce, collecting taxes, declaring war and establishing courts are all mentioned as legislative powers.

40. **(D)**

    The filibuster is a rule in the Senate that is intended to aid the minority when they feel their views are not being heard. Recently it has become a delaying tactic to stop the Senate or the majority in the Senate from advancing controversial issues.

41. **(C)**

    Leadership roles in the Senate are strongly guided and controlled by the two parties. Therefore, more power is held by the party leadership than with the formal offices in the Senate like the President *Pro Tempore*.

42. **(C)**

    As the single most powerful individual in the House, the Speaker has many powers. One key power is the ability to appoint other House members to special and select committees that ultimately decide the fate of many House actions. For example, the Speaker appoints members of the conference committee when ironing out differences between House and Senate versions of the same bill.

43. **(C)**

    There are four main types of committees in the House and Senate. Standing committees are the only ones that remain for every session of Congress, giving its members the opportunity to establish power and influence by serving on the same committee for years.

44. **(E)**

    Almost all legislation has to go through both the House and the Senate. It is rare that the House version and the Senate version come out of their respective chambers exactly the same. Only one final version of the bill can be presented to the president for his signature, and the conference committee combines the two versions into one before sending it on to the president.

45. **(C)**

   The Congressional Budget Office was established in 1974 to advise Congress on the likely economic effects of different spending programs and provide information on the cost of proposed policies. It is nonpartisan.

46. **(D)**

   Some bills zip through Congress while others make their way slowly and painfully. Congress is like a crowd, moving either sluggishly or with great speed.

47. **(A)**

   Most presidents select their cabinet from key individuals who helped them get elected, key advisers during their campaign, key business and industry leaders, etc. However in a parliamentary system, the prime minister picks the cabinet from within his/her party to maintain a power base within that party that focuses on the legislative process.

48. **(A)**

   Article II, Section 2 of the Constitution gives the president the power to negotiate treaties "by and with the advice and consent of the Senate, provided two-thirds of the Senators present concur."

49. **(D)**

   The president's closest assistants have offices in the White House, usually in the West Wing. They have different titles, but generally the men and women who hold these offices oversee the political and policy interests of the president.

50. **(C)**

   The White House Office can be looked upon as the president's personal advisers, those that see and help him or her in the everyday operation of the White House. Most of the president's other appointees, including Cabinet members, heads of the executive agencies, and federal judges have to be approved by the Senate.

51. **(C)**

   The Constitution is vague about the president's enumerated, or specific, powers, especially when compared with the delegated powers of the Congress. As a result, the president must rely on his or her power of persuasion to accomplish many goals. The power of the "office of the president" is greater than any specific power mentioned in the Constitution.

52. **(A)**

   As the power of the presidency has grown over the years, the president, with his power to persuade, can send a message to Congress and to the American people about what he will accept or not accept. If a president states that he or she will "veto" a bill without a specific provision, then Congress must act to deal with the president's position since it is so difficult to override a veto. This in effect gives the president the power to block legislation without being a member of the legislative branch.

53. **(A)**

   Most state governors can veto a particular part of a bill and approve the rest, giving them a line-item veto. The theory is that in the hands of the president this would give him/her the ability to stop unwarranted spending without vetoing the other provisions of the bill. Congress passed the Line-Item Veto Act in 1996 giving the president the line-item veto, but it was found unconstitutional by the Supreme Court in the case *Clinton v. City of New York* in 1998.

54. **(A)**

   The concept of executive privilege is not discussed in the Constitution, but tradition has allowed the president under the doctrine of separation of powers and the privilege of confidentiality to keep private conversations between himself and his principal advisers. This concept was modified in 1973 in the *U.S. v. Nixon* case when the Supreme Court ruled that there is a sound basis for the claim of executive privilege, but there is no "absolute unqualified presidential privilege of immunity from judicial process under all circumstances."

55. **(B)**

   See description for question 54.

56. **(A)**

   In 1819, the court, in a unanimous decision, answered two questions in ways that expanded the powers of Congress and confirmed the supremacy of the federal government. First, Congress has the power to decide what is "necessary and proper" for the regulation of commerce and second, that a state cannot tax a federal bank since the power of the federal government is superior to that of the states.

57. (B)

Article III of the Constitution states, "the Judicial Power of the United States, shall be vested in one Supreme Court, and in such inferior courts as the Congress may from time to time ordain and establish." It makes no mention of the size of the court or the qualifications of the justices. The size of the Court is set by Congress.

58. (C)

A case can reach the Court by a writ of certiorari when the Court grants or orders a case to be sent to the justices. The Court operates under the Rule of Four: if four justices agree that a case should be heard, then the Court will take jurisdiction over the case. However, 96 percent of all cases appealed to the Court are denied.

59. (C)

The doctrine of sovereign immunity states that in order for an individual to sue the federal government, the government itself must give consent to be sued.

60. (A)

By this decision, the Supreme Court ruled unanimously to end segregation in public schools. Chief Justice Earl Warren wrote that "separate educational facilities are inherently unequal. [Students are]... deprived of the equal protection of the laws guaranteed by the Fourteenth Amendment."

Detailed Explanations of Answers

Section II

Free Response Answers

Question 1–Sample Response that Would Achieve a Top Score

While the president has control over a significant portion of the federal budget, the growth in federal spending cannot be attributed solely to the president. In fact, most of the growth in federal spending is a result of either acts of Congress or of other items over which the president has little or no control. In fact, over the past thirty years or so, while both kinds of spending have grown considerably, the portion of the budget over which the president has relatively less control has grown twice as fast. In order for this growth to be curtailed (if one assumes that federal spending is too high), some change in how budgets and spending are approved would most likely have to occur.

It is too simplistic to say that Congress should just limit spending. If the answer were as easy as that, it seems likely that the federal budget would not have grown so much in the first place. Over the years, various presidents have suggested means by which they could gain more control over the budget and supposedly cut wasteful spending and programs.

One popular suggestion has been a "line item veto," a method by which the president could veto, or reject, parts of a bill—in this case, the federal budget—rather than being forced to choose to either accept or reject the bill in full. This would give the president the ability to cut programs that the president does not think would benefit the nation as a whole. Some argued, however, that this change would violate the Constitution and the doctrine of separation of powers.

Congressional opponents of the line-item veto brought their case to the U.S. Supreme Court in the belief that the shift in power brought about by the veto authority would change "the legal and practical effect" of their votes. Thus, the lawmaking procedure set forth in the Constitution would, in effect, have the rug pulled out from under it. But the high court struck down the Line Item Veto Act, one reason being that it gave too much power to the president thus upsetting the government's system of checks and balances.

But back on the legislative front, there is growing reason to be cautiously sanguine about the prospects for bringing federal spending under control. In July1997, with both Republicans and Democrats practically falling over each other to claim victory and credit, the House overwhelmingly approved landmark legislation to balance the federal budget by 2002. The Senate was expected to follow suit. This kind of bipartisan effort, the result of very difficult negotiations, is encouraging in and of itself. But at the same time, one needs to take note of the credit claiming of lawmakers. To vote against a package that combines long-promised tax cuts with a balanced budget is political suicide. The most worrisome aspect is its so-called back-loading, whereby tax breaks are planned to bring about the greatest revenue losses after 2002. Add to that the fact that legislators avoided dealing with the issues of medical and pension cost containment, and you are again falling into deficit spending.

Ultimately, if politicians or citizens want to decrease public spending, there will have to be a change in the way federal budgets are developed, either through a formal change in law, or in the informal way Congress and the president draw up a budget agreement.

Question 2

Response Outline

(a) A bill can be delayed

1. at the time of referral if it is a complex bill; both parties will try and have the bill assigned to the committee that will best represent the views of the party or to a committee with sympathetic members to the bill's topic.

2. at the time of subcommittee consideration.

3. in a committee mark-up, when the bill is checked for final additions and errors and critics of the bill can use various delaying tactics to keep the bill in committee.

4. in the House, where the Rules Committee can attach a rule that benefits the majority party or hurts the minority party.

5. when the bill is considered in the other chamber, the same delaying tactics can be used, adding amendments, stalling debate, as well as filibusters and holds, which are procedures unique to the Senate.

6. when the bill finally passes both houses, the conference committee, though it can't kill a bill, can use most of the same delaying tactics.

7. the president can use his power of veto or the threat of veto to strongly influence the debate and eventually the content of the final bill.

(b) Committees

1. Standing Committees: Permanent committees established under the standing rules of the Senate and House specialize in the consideration of particular subject areas. There are currently sixteen standing committees in the Senate and twenty in the House.

2. Special and Select Committees: A select or special committee of the United States Congress is a congressional committee appointed to perform a special function that is beyond the authority or capacity of a standing committee.

3. Joint Committee: Committees including membership from both houses of Congress. Joint committees are usually established with narrow jurisdictions and normally lack authority to report legislation. Chairmanship usually alternates between the House and Senate members from session to session of Congress.

(c) Interest groups generally provide the following types of support in the legislative process:

1. provide information.

2. help gather other legislators in support of, or in opposition to, the bill.

3. influence by letters from constituents.

Question 3

Response Outline

(a) Qualifications

1. 35 yrs. old

2. resident for 14 years

3. natural-born citizen

(b) Constitutional Powers

1. Executive

- appointment power: judges, cabinet officials, ambassadors, etc.

- impoundment—the power of the president to not spend funds approved by Congress

- create and regulate the executive agencies; for example, CIA, FCC, FEMA, NASA

- executive departments, appointment of the leaders of the various cabinet-level departments such as Treasury, State, Defense, Homeland Security, etc.

- Executive order, the power to issue an executive without the consent of Congress that has the effect of law, for example President Truman integrating the military after WWII.

2. Legislative

- veto or threat of veto

- impoundment

3. Judicial

- appointment: the president has tremendous influence in the appointment of not only Supreme Court justices, but also hundreds of federal judges around the country.

- pardons and reprieves

4. Military-Diplomatic

- treaties: constitutional power to negotiate treaties

- appointment: most ambassadors and other high ranking State Department officials

- As Commander-in-Chief, the president has the power to commit U.S. forces quickly and easily without the consent of Congress for less than sixty days.

- Executive agreement: when it appears the president will have trouble getting a treaty through Congress, he can always sign an executive agreement between the U.S. and the leaders of other countries.

5. Non-constitutional powers: the president has a number of powers based primarily on the strength, tradition, and importance of the office

- persuasion

- executive privilege

- leadership

- economic influence

(c) Limits on Power

1. veto override

2. War Powers Act: limits the president by requiring congressional approval for troops overseas in a combat situation for more than sixty days

3. Electoral limits for reelection: cannot campaign everywhere, has to moderate or change his policies to improve chances for reelection or election

(d) Money

- Legal limits: is still somewhat limited to raising money and spending money during the election process, particularly if he or she accepts public financing

- Congressional limits based on majority-minority party—if the government is divided by party control, the president has to moderate or change policies to win approval in a divided government.

Question 4

Response Outline

(a) Reporters must compromise their own views to keep access to a source. Thus, government sources can influence the conclusions of many news reports.

(b) Politicians grant or withhold interviews and scoops depending on a reporter's prior publications.

(c) The government regulates the broadcast media to serve the public interest. This ensures that all sides of an issue are covered and not only the opinion of the radio or television station.

(d) The advantages of the broadcast media over newspapers are: television is the most trusted form of media; television is the primary source of news for most Americans; television reaches more people.

(e) The disadvantages of the broadcast media compared to newspapers are: educated people rely more heavily on newspapers and they are more likely to participate in the political process; the broadcast media are more closely regulated by the government; people use selective attention and mental tune-out to filter the broadcast media.

Answer Sheet

Section I

1. Ⓐ Ⓑ Ⓒ Ⓓ Ⓔ
2. Ⓐ Ⓑ Ⓒ Ⓓ Ⓔ
3. Ⓐ Ⓑ Ⓒ Ⓓ Ⓔ
4. Ⓐ Ⓑ Ⓒ Ⓓ Ⓔ
5. Ⓐ Ⓑ Ⓒ Ⓓ Ⓔ
6. Ⓐ Ⓑ Ⓒ Ⓓ Ⓔ
7. Ⓐ Ⓑ Ⓒ Ⓓ Ⓔ
8. Ⓐ Ⓑ Ⓒ Ⓓ Ⓔ
9. Ⓐ Ⓑ Ⓒ Ⓓ Ⓔ
10. Ⓐ Ⓑ Ⓒ Ⓓ Ⓔ
11. Ⓐ Ⓑ Ⓒ Ⓓ Ⓔ
12. Ⓐ Ⓑ Ⓒ Ⓓ Ⓔ
13. Ⓐ Ⓑ Ⓒ Ⓓ Ⓔ
14. Ⓐ Ⓑ Ⓒ Ⓓ Ⓔ
15. Ⓐ Ⓑ Ⓒ Ⓓ Ⓔ
16. Ⓐ Ⓑ Ⓒ Ⓓ Ⓔ
17. Ⓐ Ⓑ Ⓒ Ⓓ Ⓔ
18. Ⓐ Ⓑ Ⓒ Ⓓ Ⓔ
19. Ⓐ Ⓑ Ⓒ Ⓓ Ⓔ
20. Ⓐ Ⓑ Ⓒ Ⓓ Ⓔ

21. Ⓐ Ⓑ Ⓒ Ⓓ Ⓔ
22. Ⓐ Ⓑ Ⓒ Ⓓ Ⓔ
23. Ⓐ Ⓑ Ⓒ Ⓓ Ⓔ
24. Ⓐ Ⓑ Ⓒ Ⓓ Ⓔ
25. Ⓐ Ⓑ Ⓒ Ⓓ Ⓔ
26. Ⓐ Ⓑ Ⓒ Ⓓ Ⓔ
27. Ⓐ Ⓑ Ⓒ Ⓓ Ⓔ
28. Ⓐ Ⓑ Ⓒ Ⓓ Ⓔ
29. Ⓐ Ⓑ Ⓒ Ⓓ Ⓔ
30. Ⓐ Ⓑ Ⓒ Ⓓ Ⓔ
31. Ⓐ Ⓑ Ⓒ Ⓓ Ⓔ
32. Ⓐ Ⓑ Ⓒ Ⓓ Ⓔ
33. Ⓐ Ⓑ Ⓒ Ⓓ Ⓔ
34. Ⓐ Ⓑ Ⓒ Ⓓ Ⓔ
35. Ⓐ Ⓑ Ⓒ Ⓓ Ⓔ
36. Ⓐ Ⓑ Ⓒ Ⓓ Ⓔ
37. Ⓐ Ⓑ Ⓒ Ⓓ Ⓔ
38. Ⓐ Ⓑ Ⓒ Ⓓ Ⓔ
39. Ⓐ Ⓑ Ⓒ Ⓓ Ⓔ
40. Ⓐ Ⓑ Ⓒ Ⓓ Ⓔ

41. Ⓐ Ⓑ Ⓒ Ⓓ Ⓔ
42. Ⓐ Ⓑ Ⓒ Ⓓ Ⓔ
43. Ⓐ Ⓑ Ⓒ Ⓓ Ⓔ
44. Ⓐ Ⓑ Ⓒ Ⓓ Ⓔ
45. Ⓐ Ⓑ Ⓒ Ⓓ Ⓔ
46. Ⓐ Ⓑ Ⓒ Ⓓ Ⓔ
47. Ⓐ Ⓑ Ⓒ Ⓓ Ⓔ
48. Ⓐ Ⓑ Ⓒ Ⓓ Ⓔ
49. Ⓐ Ⓑ Ⓒ Ⓓ Ⓔ
50. Ⓐ Ⓑ Ⓒ Ⓓ Ⓔ
51. Ⓐ Ⓑ Ⓒ Ⓓ Ⓔ
52. Ⓐ Ⓑ Ⓒ Ⓓ Ⓔ
53. Ⓐ Ⓑ Ⓒ Ⓓ Ⓔ
54. Ⓐ Ⓑ Ⓒ Ⓓ Ⓔ
55. Ⓐ Ⓑ Ⓒ Ⓓ Ⓔ
56. Ⓐ Ⓑ Ⓒ Ⓓ Ⓔ
57. Ⓐ Ⓑ Ⓒ Ⓓ Ⓔ
58. Ⓐ Ⓑ Ⓒ Ⓓ Ⓔ
59. Ⓐ Ⓑ Ⓒ Ⓓ Ⓔ
60. Ⓐ Ⓑ Ⓒ Ⓓ Ⓔ

FREE-RESPONSE ANSWER SHEET

For the free-response section, write your answers on sheets of blank paper.

Glossary

ABC programs also termed the alphabet agencies, describes the programs implemented by Franklin Delano Roosevelt during the Great Depression to give relief to the unemployed as well as boost industry and improve labor conditions.

absentee ballot a ballot marked and mailed in advance, allowing registered voters to vote without being present in their district on election day.

activist a person, often outside of government, actively engaged in political activities or working toward a specific cause.

administration the people and organizations that make up the executive branch of government.

administrative law the rules and regulations that regulate administrative agencies.

affirmative action an effort designed to overcome past discriminatory actions by providing employment or educational opportunities to members of a group that were previously denied access because of racial or other discriminatory barriers.

alien one who is not a citizen of the state or country in which he/she lives.

ambassador a resident representative appointed by the head of a nation to represent that nation in matters of diplomacy in a foreign country.

amendment a modification to the constitution or a law.

amicus curiae literally, "friend of the court"; voluntary legal advice or arguments in a case from a person or entity that is not a party to the litigation.

amnesty a general pardon, granted by a government, especially for political offenses.

Anti-Federalist people opposed to the creation of a strong national government out of fear that individual and states' rights would be destroyed.

appeasement the act of making concessions to a political or military rival.

appellate courts courts that have the authority to review the findings of lower courts.

appellate jurisdiction the power to review the decisions of lower courts.

appropriation funds granted by Congress to be utilized for a specific purpose.

Articles of Confederation first U.S. constitution creating a union of states; ratified 1781. The national government it established did not have the authority to act directly upon the people; an antecedent to the U.S. Constitution of 1787.

Australian ballot a uniform ballot printed by the government and distributed at the polls to be marked in secret.

bail sum of money exchanged for the release of an arrested individual as a guarantee of his/her appearance at trial.

Baker vs. Carr a decision in which the Supreme Court held that congressional district reapportionment may not be used to dilute representation of minorities.

Bakke vs. California a decision in which the Supreme Court declared strict numerical quotas as unconstitutional affirmative action mechanisms.

ballot device by which a voter registers a choice in an election.

bicameralism having a two-house legislature.

bill proposed law presented to a legislative body.

bill of attainder legislative act that inflicts punishment on an individual or group for the purpose of suppressing that person or group.

Bill of Rights the first ten amendments to the U.S. Constitution.

bipartisan politics that emphasize cooperation between the two major parties.

blanket primary a nominating election in which voters may switch from one party's primary to another on an office-by-office basis.

block grants federal money provided to a state or local government for a general purpose, such as reducing crime or improving education, with relatively few requirements on how the states can spend the money.

blue states Label given to the states that tend to support Democratic candidates and have more liberal views, including California and New York.

boycott a method of protest in which the public is urged not to purchase or consume certain goods and services or deal with certain people and/or companies.

Brown vs. Board of Education of Topeka this Supreme Court decision declared the doctrine of "separate but equal" unconstitutional.

bureaucracy large or complex group of individuals and agencies with the purpose of managing government and implementing policy; the term is typically used to refer to the departments and agencies of the federal government and related institutions.

bureaucrat an appointed government official who insists on rigid adherence to rules.

Bush doctrine notion of preemptive strikes against potential enemies.

cabinet the heads of the various departments in the Executive branch who aid in the decision-making process.

Camp X-Ray detention camp at the U.S. naval base in Guantánamo Bay, Cuba, where many detainees with terrorist ties have been held since shortly after the Sept. 11, 2001, terrorist attacks.

capital money or property invested in businesses by one or more individuals.

capital punishment the execution of an individual by the state as punishment for heinous offenses.

capitalism an economic system in which the means of production are held by an individual or corporation for the benefit of that individual or entity.

categorical grants type of grant or funding given by the federal government to a state for specific purposes.

caucus a closed meeting of Democratic Party leaders to agree on a legislative program.

censure official expression of blame or disapproval.

census official population count.

CEO (Chief Executive Officer) top officer of a corporation.

checks and balances constitutionally distributed power where the powers overlap so that no branch of government may dominate the other.

chief administrator term for the president as head of the administration of the federal government.

chief citizen term for the president as the representative of the people, working primarily for the public interest.

chief diplomat term for the president as the architect of foreign policy and spokesperson representing the United States in diplomatic affairs.

chief executive term for the president as vested with the executive powers of the United States.

chief legislator term for the president as architect of public policy and the one responsible for setting the Congressional agenda.

chief of party term for the president as the leader of his/her political party.

chief of state term for the president as the head of the government of the United States.

citizen one who owes allegiance to a government and is entitled to its protections.

civics branch of political science dealing with citizens and their activities.

civil law the legal code that regulates the conduct between private parties.

civil liberties guarantees of the safety of persons, opinions, and property from the arbitrary acts of government.

civil rights positive acts of government to make constitutional guarantees a reality for all.

Civil Rights Act of 1964 legislative act that removed racial barriers in all places vested with a public interest.

civil servant name given to a federal government employee hired and promoted based on merit.

class action suit a lawsuit filed on behalf of a group of people with the same legal claim against a party or individual.

closed primary form of direct primary in which only declared party members may vote.

cloture congressional procedure for ending debate and calling for an immediate vote on a pending matter.

coalition a union of people or groups of diverse interests; a form of alliance of parties for the purpose of forming a government or initiating action.

coattail effect favorable influence that a popular candidate has on the voters' selection of other candidates in his/her party.

collective security a system in which participating nations agree to take joint action to meet any threat to or attack against another member; basic purpose of the United Nations and a major goal of U.S. foreign policy.

commander in chief term for the president as commander of the nation's armed services.

commerce power excusive power of Congress to regulate interstate and foreign trade.

common law a body of judge-made law created as court cases are decided.

concurrent jurisdiction power shared by federal and state courts to hear certain cases.

concurrent powers powers held by both the national and state governments.

concurrent resolution measure passed by both houses of a legislature that does not have the force of law and does not require the president's approval; often used to express the legislature's opinion or for internal rules and housekeeping measures.

concurring opinion the opinion of a Supreme Court justice who agrees with the majority ruling but for different reasons.

confederation a system of government created when nation-states agree by compact to create a centralized government with delegated powers, but in which the nation-states do not give up individual autonomy.

conference a meeting between committees of the two branches of the legislature to reconcile differences in pending bills.

conference committee temporary joint committee created to reconcile any differences between the two houses' versions of a bill.

conglomerate a corporation that has many businesses in unrelated fields.

congressional oversight review by legislative committees of the policies and programs of the executive branch.

Connecticut Compromise agreement during the Constitutional Convention that Congress should be composed of a Senate in which the states would be represented equally and a House in which representation would be based on state population.

conservative a person who is apt to oppose change, to be more religious, to prefer smaller government and the Republican Party; also believes that people themselves, not government, should solve their own problems.

Conservative Coalition a grouping of conservative Republicans and Southern Democrats that would vote together on some legislation in the 1950s and 1960s.

constituents all people represented by a legislator or other elected office holder.

constitution the rules that determine the scope and function of government, as well as how the government is to be run.

constitutional formal limitations on how political power is granted, dispersed, or used within the framework of a constitution.

constitutional court federal court with constitutionally based powers and whose judges serve for life; the Supreme Court, the courts of appeals, and the district courts are the most significant in the U.S. system.

constitutional body of law composed of the four components (formally written U.S. Constitution, informal amendments, the most important acts of Congress, current Supreme Court case precedents).

court packing the act of placing members of the same political party on the bench so that opinion of the court will be consistent with the political party's (seen most dramatically with Franklin Delano Roosevelt).

criminal law the legal code dealing with the actions of all people.

crossover vote a vote in which a member of one party votes in the primary of the opposition party.

dark horse candidate one who receives unexpected support as a political candidate.

de facto segregation segregation that results from nongovernmental action; i.e., administered by the public.

de jure segregation legally established segregation.

Declaration of Independence the formal declaration of the United States' secession from England.

defendant the party in a civil action or criminal action charged with the offense.

deficit yearly shortfall between revenue and spending.

delegated powers those powers granted to the national government by the Constitution.

demagogue a person who gains power through emotional appeals to the people.

democracy a system of government in which supreme authority rests with the people.

Democrat any member of the Democratic Party, one of two major parties in the U.S.; party's lineage traces to Jefferson's Democratic Republican Party (1792).

denaturalization court revocation of naturalized citizenship through due process of law.

Department of Homeland Security newest cabinet department, created in the wake of the 9/11 terror attacks, coordinating the efforts of the FBI, CIA, and other such agencies to create a more coordinated approach to internal security.

deregulation the act of reducing or eliminating economic controls.

desegregation the removal of racial barriers either by legislation or judicial action.

deterrence the U.S. defense policy that uses the threat of military attack to discourage hostile enemy action.

diffuse support support for the political system as a whole, as opposed to a specific candidate's policies.

diplomatic immunity practice in international law under which ambassadors and other diplomatic officials have special privileges and are not subject to the laws of the state to which they are assigned.

direct democracy a democratic system of government in which the people participate directly in government decision-making.

direct primary a nominating election in which all party members may vote to choose the party's candidate for the general election.

direct tax a tax that must be paid by the person on whom it is levied.

discharge petition a procedure to bring a bill to the floor of the legislative body when a committee has initially refused to report on it.

discrimination the unfair treatment of an individual based on group membership alone (i.e., race or gender).

dissenting opinion disagreement with the majority opinion of the Supreme Court by another Supreme Court justice.

domestic policy programs, laws, and regulations focusing on the internal affairs of the nation.

double jeopardy the act of being tried for the same crime twice by the same level of government.

Dred Scott vs. Sandford the Supreme Court case that upheld the right of a slave owner to reclaim his property after the slave had fled into a free state.

due process clause Constitutional guarantee that government will not deprive any person of life, liberty, or property by any unfair, arbitrary, or unreasonable action; the government must act in accordance with specified rules.

duty governmental tax, usually on imports.

economic protest parties political parties formed during periods of economic discontent.

elastic clause the Constitutional clause that allows Congress to pass laws as necessary and proper to carry out its authorized powers.

electioneering the process of actively supporting a candidate or political party.

elector a member of the Electoral College.

Electoral College group of people chosen in each state every four years who make a formal selection of the U.S. President.

electorate all of the people entitled to vote in a given election.

elite theory the view that a small group of the rich and powerful dominates the decision-making processes of government.

eminent domain the power of a government to seize private property for *public* use, usually with compensation to the owner.

enabling act a congressional act that allows the people of a United States territory to prepare a constitution as a step toward admission as a state.

English Bill of Rights a document created by Parliament in 1689 to prevent abuse of power by English monarchs; serves as the foundation for much of current American government and politics.

equal pay for equal work a measure by which men and women are paid equally, given similar job descriptions and similar performance evaluations.

equal time doctrine the Federal Communications Commission requirement that equal radio and television airtime must be made available to all candidates running for public office.

equity of redemption judicial solution used when suits for money damages do not provide just compensation.

Establishment Clause part of the First Amendment that prohibits either the establishment of a religion or the sanctioning of an existing religion by the government.

ex post facto laws laws created to make past actions punishable that were permissible when they occurred.

excise tax a tax on a specific consumer item such as alcoholic beverages.

exclusionary rule the principle that evidence gained by illegal or unreasonable means cannot be used at the court trial of the person from whom it was seized.

exclusive jurisdiction the power of the federal courts alone to hear and rule on certain cases.

exclusive powers most of the delegated powers; those held by the national government alone in the federal system.

executive agreement informal agreements made by the executive with a foreign government.

executive order rules and/or regulations issued by the chief executive and his/her subordinates based upon either constitutional or statutory authority and having the full force of law.

executive privilege the president's right to withhold information or refuse to testify before Congress and/or the courts.

Expatriation act by which one renounces citizenship.

expressed powers powers constitutionally given to one of the branches of the national government.

federal budget the document that details how much money the government collects and spends each year.

federal system governmental system in which power is constitutionally divided between a national government and its component members.

Federalist person who supported the ratification of the Constitution before 1787.

fighting words words that inflict injury upon persons.

filibuster means by which a senator who gains the floor has the right to go on talking until the senator relinquishes the floor to another.

fiscal policy policy that affects the economy by making changes in government spending, borrowing, and tax rates.

fiscal year the 12-month period for which an organization plans its budget.

floor leaders members of the House and Senate chosen to carry out party decisions and steer legislative action in an effort to meet party goals.

focus groups about ten to fifteen people and a moderator who have an opportunity to discuss their opinions about issues and candidates in depth.

foreign aid a government's financial or military assistance to other nations.

foreign policy treaties, agreements, and programs focusing on the relations between the United States and other nations.

formal amendment a modification to the Constitution brought about through one of four methods set forth in the Constitution.

Framers the group who met in 1787 and collaborated to draft the Constitution of the United States.

franchise the right to engage in the electing of public office holders.

franking free postal service for letters sent by members of Congress to their constituents.

Free Exercise Clause part of the First Amendment that guarantees all people the right to practice religion in their own way.

Full Faith and Credit Clause the Constitutional clause stating that acts or documents considered legal in one state must be accepted as valid by all other states.

general election regularly scheduled election during which voters choose public officeholders.

gerrymandering redrawing of congressional districts in order to secure as many representative party votes as possible.

Gideon vs. Wainwright case decided by the U.S. Supreme Court in 1963 that established the right to legal representation for all defendants in criminal cases.

glass ceiling a reference to the perceived limits that a woman can reach compared her to male counterparts, especially in corporate America.

GOP the Republican Party.

government the institutions, people, and processes by which a nation-state or political unit is ruled and its public policy created/administered.

grand jury body of twelve to twenty-three persons convened by a court to decide whether or not there is sufficient evidence to justify bringing an accused person to trial.

grass roots of the common people; used to describe opinion and pressure on public policy and movements that originate with average voters.

gridlock a conflict between the legislative and executive branches that often results in inaction.

home rule a city or local government's power to self-govern.

hyperpluralist theory the idea that there are so many organized interest groups that it becomes virtually impossible for government to undertake any action.

ideological party political party based on a particular set of beliefs, with a comprehensive view of social, economic, and political matters.

immunity granted exemption from prosecution.

impeachment the process used to remove certain officials, including the president, from office. Similar to a trial, impeachment does not necessarily mean that an official will be removed from office; he or she must be found guilty of an impeachable offense.

implied powers powers that have been reasonably inferred for the carrying out of expressed powers.

in forma pauperis decision that indigents bringing cases to the Supreme Court do not have to pay regular fees or meet all standard requirements.

impoundment a president refuses to spend money appropriated by Congress for a particular project.

income tax a tax on annual income.

incumbent a candidate currently holding a given office.

independent voter who does not identify or regularly support any particular political party.

independent agency agency created by Congress outside of the regular cabinet departments.

indictment accusation by a grand jury; a formal finding by that body that there is sufficient evidence against a named person to warrant his/her criminal trial.

informal amendment an accepted (meaning understood and applied), but unwritten, change to the Constitution.

inherent powers powers exclusively controlled by the national government such as foreign affairs.

initiative and referendum a procedure by which voters pass or reject laws directly. In this way, laws are approved directly by voters, not through representatives.

injunction court order that requires or forbids some specific action.

interest group group of persons who share some common interest and attempt to influence elected members of the government.

Jim Crow laws laws designed to promote racial segregation.

joint committee legislative committee composed of members of both houses.

joint resolution legislative measure that must be passed by both houses and approved by the chief executive to become effective; similar to a bill, with the same force of law, but often used for temporary or somewhat unusual situations.

judicial activism using the power of the bench to broaden the interpretation of the Constitution.

judicial restraint using the power of the bench to limit the interpretation of the Constitution.

judicial review assumed power of the courts to declare an action of the president or Congress unconstitutional.

Judiciary Act of 1789 congressional act that set the scope and limits for the federal judiciary system.

jurisdiction power of a court to try and decide a case.

jus sanguinis a social policy by which citizenship is acquired through one's parents.

jus soli the principle that citizenship is established through place of birth.

Kennedy, John F. elected in 1960 as youngest President of the United States; established the Peace Corps in 1961; issued challenge to NASA to land a man on the moon; assassinated in 1963.

keynote address an opening speech of a national nominating convention that sets the tone of the upcoming campaign.

King, Jr., Martin Luther civil rights leader who fought for the rights of minorities by the use of peaceful civil disobedience.

lame duck a defeated office holder after that person has lost re-election but is still in office until the newly elected official is sworn in.

legislative veto the power of Congress to void an action of the executive branch.

libel published defamation of another person.

liberal a person who believes that government can and should help solve social problems, is more prone to prefer change, political experimentation and the Democratic Party, and to champion the rights of the individual over the needs of the state.

liberal/loose constructionist one who believes that the provisions of the Constitution, and in particular those granting powers specifically to government, are to be interpreted in broad terms.

limited government basic principle of the American system of government in which government is limited in what it may do and each individual has certain rights that government may not take away.

line-item veto the objection by the president to a single item in a piece of legislation; this authority, signed into law by President Clinton in 1996, was successfully challenged as unconstitutional and declared so by the U.S. Supreme Court.

litigation a lawsuit.

litmus test requiring a judicial appointment to have the "correct" view on an issue in order to be nominated or approved.

lobbying activities aimed at influencing public officials and the policies they enact.

logrolling mutual aid among politicians to achieve goals in each one's interests.

Magna Carta the Great Charter that established the principle that the power of the monarchy was not absolute in England.

Malcolm X radical Muslim leader who wanted a total separation of the races.

major parties the dominant political parties in government.

majority leader the legislative leader of the party holding the majority of seats in the House or the Senate.

majority opinion written statement by a majority of the judges of a court in support of a decision made by that court.

malapportionment distribution of representatives among congressional districts in unequal proportion to the population.

mandate a rule issued by the federal government that must be followed by the states; an instruction or command.

Mapp vs. Ohio a decision by the Supreme Court which recognized that evidence seized without a search warrant cannot be used.

Marbury vs. Madison the U.S. Supreme Court, in this landmark decision of 1803, established the concept of judicial review.

mass media means of communication that reaches large audiences; includes television, newspapers, radio, magazines, and the internet.

maverick a person who holds no party allegiance and has unorthodox political views.

McCarthyism the act of seeking out subversives without cause or need (seen during the 1950s when Senator Joseph McCarthy stoked fear of Communism).

McCulloch vs. Maryland Supreme Court decision that set the stage for a broad interpretation of the Constitution and which prevented the states from taxing federal property.

media bias the real or perceived tilt by reporters and producers in the mass media toward a conservative or liberal viewpoint in news reporting. AP students should be attentive to the distinction between news and opinion columns.

military-industrial complex the assumption that there is an alliance between the military and industrial leaders.

minor party one of the less widely supported political parties in a governmental system.

minority leader the legislative leader and spokesperson for the party holding the minority seats in the House or Senate.

Miranda vs. Arizona 1966 case in which the U.S. Supreme Court decided that all persons who are detained or arrested must be informed of their rights.

misdemeanor offense that is less than a felony with punishment ranging from a fine to a short jail term.

moderate a person opposed to extreme views; one whose political attitudes are between those of a conservative and a liberal.

monetary policy economic policy that controls the money supply, primarily through the Federal Reserve System.

muckraker an investigative journalist who seeks to expose scandals and problems in the political system.

multilateral a foreign policy approach in which multiple countries work in unison.

national supremacy clause constitutional doctrine that the actions or decisions of the national government take priority over that of the state or local governments.

nation-state a political unit with a defined territory organized under a government and having the authority to create and enforce laws.

naturalization process by which persons acquire citizenship.

Necessary and Proper Clause See *Elastic Clause*.

New Deal legislation championed by Franklin Delano Roosevelt during the Great Depression that provided a safety net (e.g., Social Security) for all members of society.

New Jersey Plan single-house legislature with equal representation for all states.

9/11 a series of coordinated terror attacks carried out on the United States on September 11, 2001.

Nixon, Richard M. the only President of the United States to resign after being confronted with impeachment (because of his alleged actions in the Watergate scandal).

nomination process of selecting or naming candidates for office.

nonproliferation treaty an agreement not to distribute nuclear arms to countries that do not have them.

obscenity any work that, taken as a whole, appeals to a prurient interest in sex.

oligarchy government by the few based on wealth or power.

ombudsman person or office that hears formal complaints against the government.

open primary form of direct primary in which any qualified voter may participate without regard to his/her party allegiance.

original intent a doctrine of Constitutional interpretation that says Supreme Court Justices should base their interpretations of the Constitution on its authors' intentions.

original jurisdiction the authority of a court to hear a case being brought up for the first time.

PAC (political action committee) a group set up by labor unions, corporations, or other special interest groups to support candidates via campaign contributions in hopes of influencing policy in their favor.

pardon release from the punishment or legal consequences of a crime, granted by the President or a state governor.

partisan political opposition drawn along party lines.

party caucus a meeting of party leaders to conduct party business.

party identification person's sense of attachment or loyalty to a political party.

party whip assistants to the congressional floor leaders, responsible for monitoring votes.

Patriot Act legislation passed in the aftermath of 9/11 giving extra powers to intelligence and law enforcement officers in the effort to combat terrorism. Examples include the interception of mail, phone tapping, e-mail surveillance, and so on. The law has proven to be controversial.

patronage dispensing government jobs to persons who belong to the winning political party.

personal property all property held by an individual excluding real estate.

petit (or petty) jury a trial jury of 12 impaneled for civil/criminal cases.

pigeonhole to put aside or ignore a proposed piece of legislation.

plaintiff the party who brings a civil action to court for the purpose of seeking a monetary remedy.

platform written declaration of the principles and policy positions of a political party, usually adopted at a party convention.

plea bargain an agreement between a prosecutor's office and the accused to avoid a trial.

Plessy vs. Ferguson the Supreme Court case which established the rule of "separate but equal" as being constitutional. Later overturned by *Brown v. Board of Education*.

pluralist theory the interaction of many different interest groups determine policy outcomes.

plurality in any given election, at least one more vote than that received by any other candidate.

pocket veto type of executive veto used by the president after the legislature has adjourned; applied when the president does not formally sign or reject a bill within the time allotted to do so.

police power power to regulate people or property in order to promote health, welfare, and safety.

political action committee See *PAC*.

political efficacy influence or effectiveness in politics and the workings of government.

political party organized group seeking to control government by winning elections and holding public office.

political question constitutional question that judges refuse to answer because to do so would encroach upon the authority of Congress or the President.

political socialization complex process by which individuals acquire their political attitudes and views.

politics the methods involved in managing government and maintaining power.

poll tax the requirement of a person to pay for the right to vote.

popular sovereignty basic principle of American government in which the people are the only source of any and all power, forcing the government to act in accordance with the people's will.

pork barrel a government project that benefits a specific location or lawmaker's home district and constituents.

precedent judicial use of prior cases as the test for deciding similar cases.

precinct local voting district.

President of the Senate presiding officer of a state or national senate.

President *pro tempore* the member of the U.S. Senate, or of the upper house of a state legislature, chosen to preside in the absence of the President of the Senate.

presidential succession manner in which a vacancy in the presidency is to be filled.

primary election at which a party's voters choose some or all of a party organization's delegates and/or express preference among various contenders for the party's nomination.

prior restraint censorship enacted before the speech, publication, etc., is released to the general public.

probable cause reasonable grounds for believing a crime to have been committed.

procedural due process constitutional requirement that a government proceed by proper means.

progressive tax a tax that requires higher-income citizens to pay more than lower-income citizens.

prohibited powers the powers that are denied to the federal government, the state government, or both.

pro-choice supports a woman's right to choose regarding abortion.

pro-life opposed to abortion.

propaganda a persuasion technique aimed at influencing public opinion to create a particular belief.

proportional representation a system in which candidates are elected in proportion to the popular vote they receive.

public assistance aid programs funded by state and federal tax money; typically, eligibility requirements must be met to qualify.

public debt the sum of money borrowed by the government over the years that has not yet been repaid in addition to all interest accrued on the loan.

public-interest group a group that works for the common good, not for the benefit of specific individuals or interests.

public opinion the beliefs, preferences, and attitudes of the people about an issue that involves the government or society at large.

public policy principled government action in accordance with public needs and institutional or governmental customs.

quorum fewest number of members who must be present for a legislative body to conduct regular business.

radical a person with extremely liberal political views who favors rapid and widespread change to the current political and/or social order.

ratification formal approval of a constitution, amendment to a document such as the constitution, or a treaty.

reactionary a person with extremely conservative political views who favors the changes necessary to return to an earlier and more traditional government or society.

Reagan, Ronald W. two-term President during the 1980s whose economic policies followed supply-side theory.

reapportionment redistribution of political representation based on population changes; typically takes places after a census.

recall the process by which voters can remove an elected public official from office.

red states Label given to the states that tend to support Republican candidates and have more conservative views, including Texas and Florida.

referendum the process whereby a legislative proposal is voted upon by popular vote.

regressive tax a tax that is more burdensome for low-income people than for those with higher incomes.

remand to turn over authority of a case.

representative democracy a democratic system of government in which decisions are made by officials who are periodically selected by and accountable to voters.

reprieve an official postponement of the execution of a sentence.

republic form of government that derives its powers directly or indirectly from the people and those who govern are accountable to the governed.

Republican any member of the Republican Party, one of the U.S.'s two major political parties; the GOP came into being 1854–1856, unifying anti-slavery forces.

reserved powers powers retained by the states.

resolution measure relating to the internal business of one house in a legislature or expressing that chamber's opinion with the force of law.

revenue sharing government financing in which money collected in federal income tax dollars is distributed to state and local governments.

reverse discrimination giving preference to females and/or nonwhites discriminates against members of the majority group; often used as a counter-argument to affirmative action measures.

revolution complete change of the form of government and its leaders.

rider an addition or amendment to a bill that has nothing to do with the bill's true subject.

Roe vs. Wade case in which the Supreme Court established a woman's right to an abortion.

Roosevelt, Franklin Delano president of the United States during the Depression and World War II; most noted for his enactment of New Deal programs such as the Social Security Act.

rule of four in order for a case to be heard by the Supreme Court, four justices must agree to hear the case.

runoff primary a second primary involving the two top candidates in the first contest; held where election law requires a majority vote for nomination but no clear majority appeared the first time.

safe seat electoral office, usually in the legislature, for which the party or incumbent is strong enough that reelection is almost taken for granted.

search warrant court order authorizing the search of a subject's person or property.

sedition conduct or language inciting rebellion against the authority of the state.

select committee legislative committee created temporarily and for a specific purpose.

senatorial courtesy the practice in which a presidential nomination is submitted for initial approval to the senators from the nominee's state.

seniority rule unwritten rule in both the House and the Senate that the top posts in each chamber will be held by ranking members.

separation of powers basic principle of American government that holds that the executive, legislative, and judicial powers are divided among three independent and equally important branches.

session the meeting of a legislative or judicial body for a specific period of time for the purpose of transacting business.

Shays's Rebellion uprising in western Massachusetts against state policies that led political leaders to seek a stronger national government than was present under the Articles of Confederation.

single-issue parties political parties that concentrate on a single public policy issue.

single-member district An electoral district in which only the one candidate with the most votes is elected to office.

slander verbal defamation of a person's character.

social insurance programs programs created to help the elderly, the ill, and unemployed citizens; typically these programs are funded by personal contributions and available to those who have paid into them.

soft money money, not regulated by federal law, used by political parties for general expenses.

sovereignty having absolute power within a territory to self-govern.

Speaker of the House presiding officer of the House of Representatives, chosen by and from the House majority party.

spin an attempt by a candidate or his or her staff to frame a message a certain way, generally ignoring the potential negatives to a particular policy.

splinter parties political parties that have split away from one of the major parties.

split-ticket voting voting for candidates of more than one party in the same election.

Square Deal program of President Theodore Roosevelt designed to reduce the power of monopolies and preserve natural resources.

standing committee permanent committee in the legislative body to which bills are referred.

stare decisis a rule of precedent in which an established rule of law is considered binding on all judges whenever a similar case is presented.

state a body of people in a defined territory, organized under a government power and having the authority to enforce the law without the consent of a higher power.

statism the rights of the state over those of the citizens.

statutory law law enacted by a legislative body.

stay the temporary delay of punishment, usually in a capital offense case.

straight-ticket voting voting for the candidates of only one party in an election.

straw vote/poll an unofficial vote or poll indicating the trend of opinion about a candidate or issue.

strict constructionist one who advocates a narrow interpretation of the Constitution, specifically in reference to the degree of government power.

subcommittee division of existing committee, formed to address specific issues.

substantive due process constitutional requirement that government actions and laws be reasonable.

suffrage the right to vote.

suspect classification racial or national origin classifications created by law and subject to careful judicial scrutiny.

symbolic speech nonverbal communication of a political idea.

tariff any tax levied on imported goods.

Tea Party a movement that appeared around 2010 that is opposed to higher taxes and government activity and is influential within the Republican Party.

term specified length of time served by officials in their elected office.

term limit restriction placed on the number of terms one public official may serve in a particular office.

Three-Fifths Compromise an agreement at the Constitutional Convention that slaves should be counted as three-fifths of a person for purposes of determining a given state's population.

ticket-splitting when a citizen votes for some Democrats and some Republicans on election day.

trial court any court of original jurisdiction that empowers a jury to decide the guilt or liability or innocence of an individual.

Treaty formal agreement made between two sovereign states.

two-party system political system in which the candidates of only two major parties have a reasonable chance of winning elections; the political system of the United States.

unicameral legislature single-house legislature.

unilateral a foreign policy approach in which the U.S. acts as it sees fit without consideration for the views of traditional allies or of the UN Security Council.

unitary system a system of government in which power is concentrated in the central government.

United States vs. Nixon the Supreme Court ruled that material vested with a public interest could not be withheld from evidence under the rule of executive privilege.

veto chief executive's power to reject a bill passed by the legislature.

Virginia Plan a plan proposed during the constitutional convention for a strong central government with a bicameral legislature.

War Powers Act requires Congress to approve stationing American troops overseas for more than 90 days.

ward local unit of party organization.

Watergate the illegal entry and phone monitoring in 1972 of Democratic headquarters in the Watergate complex in Washington by members of the Republican Party.

welfare aid given by the government or private agencies to the needy or disabled.

West Virginia Board of Education vs. Barnette case in which the Supreme Court decided that compulsory flag salute in schools is unconstitutional.

winner-take-all system a system whereby the presidential candidate who wins the preference vote in a primary automatically wins the support of all the delegates chosen in the primary.

WMD weapons of mass destruction.

writ of appeal formal request to have a court review the findings of a lower court.

writ of certiorari a formal appeal used to bring a case up to the Supreme Court.

writ of habeas corpus court order requiring jailers to explain to a judge why they are holding a prisoner in custody.

writ of mandamus court order directing an official to perform a nondiscretionary or ministerial act as required by law.

Index

NOTES

NOTES

NOTES

NOTES